Christ

in the

Voting Booth

Christ

in the

Voting Booth

Thomas A. Droleskey, Ph.D.

 Hope of Saint Monica, Inc.

CHRIST IN THE VOTING BOOTH

Thomas A. Droleskey, Ph.D.

Published by: Hope of Saint Monica, Inc.
                  P.O. Box 308
                  Newtonsville, Ohio 45158-0308
                  U.S.A.

        Phone: 513-575-5942
        Toll-free phone: 888-260-6283

        Fax: 513-575-5947
        Toll-free fax: 888-260-7371

Copyright © 1998, Thomas A. Droleskey, Ph.D.

ISBN: 1-891431-01-3
Library of Congress Catalog Card Number: 98-71722

Front cover designed by Mrs. Peg Heimlich.

Table of Contents

Preface

This manuscript was prepared to address issues of concern to Catholic citizens of the United States. Catholics have been cowed by the self-appointed guardians of the prevailing culture into believing that they are an illegitimate force in civil political discourse. We have forgotten that we have been elected first by Christ to be His ambassadors in the midst of an unbelieving world.

A debate is raging right now between groups in camps labeled as "Theocons" and "Neocons." That is, Father Richard John Neuhaus, the publisher of *First Things*, sponsored a symposium in his magazine recently questioning the legitimacy of the American regime because of its support of one unbridled evil after another. This enraged many "neoconservatives," who contended that the constitutional system just needs the right people in public office to direct it according to the designs of the Founding Fathers.

This debate, however, misses the point. Admitting, naturally, that the remote reason for disorder within human souls and their societies is Original Sin, the *proximate* reason for the disorder around us at present is the Protestant Revolt against the authority of Peter and his successors to govern men and their societies on matters of faith and morals. Yes, there needs to be a frank recognition of the authority of the Vicar of Christ in all nations of the world. Christ the King needs to be recognized and honored in the hearts of all men—and their societies.

As the state of Catholic catechesis and apologetics in the United States is not good in this last decade of the second millennium of Christianity, part of this book contains an *apologia pro ecclesia* to indicate that the Mystical Body of Christ is *not* a democracy. The irony is inescapable: the democratic ethos has infected the way the Church is viewed by her own members; this infection, in turn, leads to demands being made upon the Vicar of Christ by "interest groups" to change that which is unchanging, the teaching of Christ. The resultant confusion within the Church worldwide, and particularly here in the United States, makes it all the more difficult for faithful Catholics to be taken seriously by non-believers. Why should anyone take us seriously when there is so much dissension within the Body of Christ? This is nothing less than diabolical.

The state of confusion within the Church has permitted our ancient Adversary the opening he needed to poison our culture with the bobbles of pride, ambition, careerism, materialism, hedonism, irreverence, sacrilege, legal positivism, moral and theological relativism—and rampant utilitarianism sanctioned by the ethos of egalitarian majoritarianism. We are facing a world that is arguably in worse shape today than when the Apostles went out to the pagan lands nearly two thousand years ago. We are facing a world suffering from the consequences of unrepented sin.

Since there is so much confusion within our country at present, since electoral politics has become an end in and of itself without regard for the fundamental principles of true justice, it would be good for every Catholic to consider the words of Jesus Himself:

> If the world hates you, realize that it hated me first. If you belonged to the world, the world would love its own; but because you do not belong to the world, and I have chosen you out of the world, the world hates you. Remember the word I spoke to you, "No slave is greater than his master." If they persecuted me, they will also persecute you. If they kept my word, they will also keep yours. And they will do all these things to you on account of my name, because they do not know the one who sent me (Jn. 15:18–21).

> Blessed are they who are persecuted for the sake of righteousness, for theirs is the kingdom of heaven. Blessed are you when they insult you and persecute you and utter every kind of evil against you [falsely] because of me. Rejoice and be glad, for your reward will be great in heaven. Thus they persecuted the prophets before you (Mt. 5:10–12).

> You will be hated by all because of my name, but whoever

endures to the end will be saved. When they persecute you in one town, flee to another. . . . And do not be afraid of those who kill the body but cannot kill the soul; rather, be afraid of the one who can destroy both body and soul in Gehenna. . . . Everyone who acknowledges me before others I will acknowledge before my heavenly Father. But whoever denies me before others, I will deny before my heavenly Father (Mt. 10:22–23, 28, 32–33).

Whoever wishes to come after me must deny himself, take up his cross, and follow me. For whoever wishes to save his life will lose it, but whoever loses his life for my sake and that of the gospel will save it. What profit is there for one to gain the whole world and forfeit his life? (Mk. 8:34–36).

As the Holy Father commented in Detroit in 1987:

Yes, America, all this belongs to you. But *your greatest beauty and your richest treasure is found in the human person*: in each man, woman and child, in every immigrant, in every native-born son and daughter.

For this reason, America, your deepest identity and truest character as a nation are revealed in the position you take toward the human person. *The ultimate test of your greatness is the way you treat every human being, but especially the weakest and most defenseless ones.*

The best traditions of your land presume respect for those who cannot defend themselves. If you want equal justice for all, and true freedom and lasting peace, then, America, defend life! All the great causes that are yours today will have meaning only *to the extent that you guarantee the right to life and protect the human person*. . .all this will succeed only if respect for life and its protection by the law is granted to every human being from *conception until natural death*.

Every human person, no matter how vulnerable or helpless, no matter how young or how old, no matter how healthy, handicapped or sick, no matter how useful or productive for society—is a being of inestimable worth created in the image and likeness of God. This is the dignity of America, the reason she exists, the condition for her survival—yes, the ultimate test of her greatness: to respect every human person, especially the weakest and most defenseless ones, those as yet unborn.

Pope Pius XI noted in 1922:

God and the Lord Jesus Christ have been removed from the conduct of public affairs; authority is now derived not from God but from men; and it has come about—in addition to the fact that the laws lack the true and sound sanctions and the supreme principles of justice which even pagan philosophers like Cicero recognized must be sought in the eternal law of God—that the very foundations of authority have been swept away by removing the primary reason by which some have the right to rule, others the duty of obedience (*Urbi Arcano*, December 23, 1922).

He further noted in *Quas Primas* three years later:

With God and Jesus Christ excluded from political life, with authority derived not from God but from man . . . the result is that human society is tottering to its fall, because it has no longer a secure and solid foundation.

When once men recognize, both in private and in public life, that Christ is King, society will at last receive the great blessings of real liberty, well-ordered discipline, peace, and harmony.

This book is dedicated to advancing the social reign of Christ the King and Mary our Queen.

Introduction

The turn introduced by the Renaissance was probably inevitable historically; the Middle Ages had come to a natural end by exhaustion, having become an intolerable despotic repression of man's physical nature in favor of the spiritual one. But then we recoiled from the spirit and embraced all that is material, excessively and incommensurately. The humanistic way of thinking, which had proclaimed itself our guide, did not admit the existence of intrinsic evil in man, nor did it see any task higher than the attainment of happiness on earth. It started modern Western civilization on the dangerous trend of worshiping man and his material needs. Everything beyond physical well-being and the accumulation of material goods, all other human requirements of a subtler and higher nature, were left outside the area of attention of state and social systems, as if human life did not have any higher meaning. Thus gaps were left open for evil, and its drafts blow freely today. Mere freedom per se does not in the least solve all the problems of human life and even adds a number of new ones.

And yet in early democracies, as in American democracy at the time of its birth, all individual human rights were granted on the ground that man is God's creature. That is, freedom was given to the individual conditionally, in the assumption of his constant religious responsibility. Two hundred or even fifty years ago, it would have seemed quite impossible, in America, that an individual be granted boundless freedom with no purpose, simply for the satisfaction of his whims. Subsequently, however, all such limitations were eroded everywhere in the West; a total emancipation occurred from the moral heritage of Christian centuries with their great reserves of mercy and sacrifice. State systems were becoming ever more materialistic. The West has finally achieved the rights of man, and even to excess, but man's sense of responsibility to God and society has grown dimmer and dimmer. In the past decades, the legalistic selfishness of the Western approach to the world has reached its peak and the world has found itself in a harsh spiritual crisis and a political impasse. All the celebrated technological achievements of progress, including the conquest of outer space, do not redeem the twentieth century's moral poverty, which no one could have imagined as late as the Nineteenth Century (Aleksandr Solzhenitsyn, *A World Split Apart*).

Aleksandr Solzhenitsyn's analysis of Western society was not received well by his audience at Harvard University on June 6, 1978. It was not received well by Western society, either. The Russian exile and Nobel Laureate dared to express ideas that contradicted the accepted norms of political and cultural life in the United States and Western Europe. That one speech was enough justification for the Western media to ignore Solzhenitsyn for well over a decade, breaking its self-imposed censorship only after the tumultuous events in Eastern Europe and the Soviet Union in 1989 and 1991.

Solzhenitsyn's principal thesis in analyzing Western society has been this: that the process of secularization—which started during the Renaissance, quickened during the Age of the Enlightenment, and was solidified during the French Revolution—has resulted in massive social and political disarray. Moral relativism has replaced a once nearly universally held belief in moral absolutes. Elected officials in Western democracies, aided by the media and influential academicians, have convinced themselves and their societies that the fulfillment of majoritarian sentiments is the essence of popular sovereignty.

The net result of the cultural triumph of utilitarianism in the United States and Western Europe has been the miseducation of the masses concerning the roots of Western civilization—and the relationship of religion in general, and Christianity in particular, to societal order and self-governance. Concepts such as democracy, human rights, majority rule, the relationship of Church and State, and objective morality are all distorted beyond recognition to appeal to the passions and sentiments of the contemporary era.

The purpose of this book is to provide a ready reference for Catholics about the relationship of their faith to their life in the societal order. It was not too long ago that the average Catholic understood that the Church to which he or she belonged, created by Jesus Christ upon the Rock of Peter, the Pope, is *counter-cul-*

tural by her very nature. The Church, the Mystical Body of Christ, is the visible Sign of Contradiction in the world in imitation of her Divine Bridegroom, Christ Himself. For just as Christ hung on Calvary as a Sign of Contradiction—crucified for not being the *political messiah* desired by the people of His time, so must His Church, guided infallibly by the Holy Spirit in the person of the Vicar of Christ, remain true to His unchanging teaching in spite of the world's opposition.

Those days are over. Two generations of young Catholics have grown up having virtually no exposure to the content of their faith. Even once well-educated Catholics have forgotten that the Church is the bulwark of Western civilization and culture; the "world" has been embraced enthusiastically, with the net result being considerable confusion on the part of the average Catholic about the purpose of their faith and its relationship to civil government.

The plain fact of the matter is that many Catholics in public life have convinced their co-religionists that their faith has no application in a pluralistic society. It is perfectly acceptable, from the perspective of these public officials, to *hold* Catholic beliefs on a private basis; it is quite another, they assert, to "impose" such beliefs on the body politic.

Lost in the polemics of a "pluralistic society" in opposition to an "autocratic" Church is an understanding of human history. Criticism of public officials by religious figures for failing to stand up for objective truth is *not* a new phenomenon. The major and minor prophets of Old Testament times, such as Isaiah, Jeremiah, Ezekiel, Amoz, and Hosea, were very harsh in their condemnation of the leaders of God's Chosen People for their materialism, self-indulgence, and unbridled commitment to personal political expediency. Those prophets were willing to suffer beatings, exile, imprisonments, and rejection by society in order to remain faithful to the unchanging Word of God. But how many people in contemporary Western society have any understanding of this as a frame of reference for discussing current controversies about such issues as abortion, homosexual behavior, the proliferation of Acquired Immune Deficiency Syndrome (AIDS), the breakdown of the family, the profanation of all things sacred, the acceptance of sexual promiscuity, the societal commitment to career advancement at all costs, the uncritical acceptance of democracy as being nothing more than the fulfillment of majoritarian sentiments as gauged by public opinion polls?

Western civilization has reached, as Solzhenitsyn accurately diagnosed in 1978, a turning point. Does it forge ahead into the Third Millennium of Christianity on its unchecked commitment to personal, political, economic, and cultural utilitarianism? Or does it renew itself in its Christian roots by turning away from the path it has chosen for most of this last century of Christianity's Second Millennium?

The answers to those questions will come partly as a result of choices that citizens make when they exercise their electoral franchise in the selection of public officials. It is those officials, rightly or wrongly, who are viewed by their respective societies as the collective "conscience" of their nations. Unless Catholic voters are educated about the roots of Western civilization, unless they understand the very public dimension required by their faith ("Even so let your light shine before men, in order that they may see your good works and give glory to your Father in heaven," Mt. 5:16), unless they are willing to run the risks that are required of them to be counter-cultural signs of contradiction, individuals will be elected who will continue—in all sincerity—to look for answers to societal problems in ways that are fallacious, and harmful to the common good.

A failure to understand who God is is at the root of the failure to understand the relevance of the Catholic faith to public order. An understanding that God is the Creator, the Redeemer, and the Sanctifier of the universe, leads individual human beings to understand that they have been created to know, to love, and to serve Him. The lack of such an understanding leads prideful human beings, always trusting infallibly in their own reasonableness and intellectual acumen, into becoming, in Solzhenitsyn's words, irreligious automatons who attempt to re-invent the wheel over and over again. It is as though the pot, as Scripture tells us, is telling the potter how it is to be shaped.

The essence of God is simplicity. His Truth is relatively simple: He made us, He redeemed us, and He wants us to cooperate with the grace He sends us to live with Him for all eternity in Heaven. The Father wants all human beings in all parts of the world to be members of the one, true Church: the Roman Catholic Church. He wants all human beings to feed worthily upon the Body, Blood, Soul, and Divinity of the Second Person of the

Blessed Trinity made man. In essence, He wants each person to image Jesus Christ to an unbelieving world by cooperating with the working of the Holy Spirit in his or her life. He wants all people to know that there is a purpose to human life; there is a purpose to suffering, disease, misfortune, poverty, rejection, and death.

As will be explained more fully in the next chapter, human beings reject simple truths because of fallen human nature. Creatures who did not create themselves want to determine the terms upon which they will use the gift of free will that God has gratuitously bestowed upon them. They want to listen to denials of objective truth in order to rationalize their own wants, ambitions, and desires.

This is nothing new. Saint Paul wrote to Saint Timothy:

> But know this, that in the last days dangerous times will come. Men will be lovers of self, covetous, haughty, blasphemers, disobedient to parents, ungrateful, criminal, heartless, faithless, slanderers, incontinent, merciless, unkind, treacherous, stubborn, puffed up with pride, loving pleasure more than God, having a semblance indeed of piety, but disowning its power. Avoid these. . . . Preach the word, be urgent in season, out of season; reprove, entreat, rebuke with all patience and teaching. For there will come a time when they will not endure the sound doctrine; but having itching ears, will heap up to themselves teachers according to their own lusts, and they will turn away their hearing from the truth and turn rather to fables. But do thou be watchful in all things, bear with tribulation patiently, work as a preacher of the gospel, fulfill thy ministry (2 Tim. 3:1–5; 4:2–5).

Our contemporary era is certainly one where people are "puffed up with pride"—and have not endured sound doctrine. The Vicar of Christ, Pope John Paul II, is criticized regularly for not "relaxing" the "rules" of the Church. Such attitudes betray a lack of understanding about God, His Church, and human nature.

Therefore, this book is an effort to present Catholics with an understanding of the relationship of their faith to social and political order, with special emphasis upon the framework of the American constitutional regime. We live at a time which some commentators are calling the "post–Christian" era. There is an urgent need for that same apostolic zeal, which motivated Christ's

Chosen Twelve, to become an attribute of all baptized and confirmed members of the Catholic Church. A failure on our part to present Christ's unchanging truths to our society out of fear of rejection—or out of a confusion caused by an uncritical acceptance of the way of the world—will produce tragic consequences for all of us.

There is no guarantee that our fellow citizens will agree with us. But that does not lessen our obligation to *try* to be Christ's leaven in a world turned flat by unbelief and pride. A return to basics is essential. It is hoped that this book makes a contribution to the awakening of Catholics with regard to their responsibilities as citizens, as they take Christ into the voting booth, as they attempt to establish His social Kingship here in the United States.

CHAPTER ONE

Politics and Government from the Perspective of the Natural Law

Even the pagan Greek philosophers of antiquity, who did not have access to (or belief in) Divine Revelation, understood that the human being was flawed, imperfect. Reason alone, unaided by Revelation, led the likes of Socrates, Plato, and Aristotle to conclude that the human being was responsible for all of the social problems of the world. Plato, for example, wrote that there was a direct connection between private morality and public order. Human beings who violated the precepts of the natural law brought disorder into their own lives, hence into the life of the societies in which they lived. This understanding of the connection between human moral behavior and social order was rejected by the Sophists, who believed that "man was the measure of all things"; human moral choices are irrelevant to social order.

The debate between moral absolutists, represented in Athens by Socrates, Plato, and Aristotle, and the moral relativists, symbolized so powerfully by Protagoras, is essentially the same one taking place in the United States today. Those who contend that there are absolute moral norms which do not depend upon human acceptance for their binding force are dismissed by the prevailing culture as authoritarian, bigoted, narrow-minded, homophobic, exclusivist, racist, and sexist. Socrates, who was put to death because of his defense of the existence of objective truths, was treated to similar rhetorical treatment from the Sophists.

The Sophists were culturally and politically dominant in the Fifth Century before Christ. They are dominant in the United States in the last decade of the Twentieth Century. That is why a discussion of government and politics is clouded by misconcep-

1

tions about democracy, majority rule, morality, and the legitimate relationship between Church and State. Those who reject the heritage of the Greco-Roman natural law tradition and the religious heritage of Judaism and Catholicism have convinced a large percentage of people that contingent beings, whose bodies are destined for the corruption of the grave, can determine right and wrong without regard for any "mythical" transcendent standards.

HUMAN NATURE

The basic thrust of the Greek philosophers cited above, along with Cicero from Rome of the First Century before Christ, was that human nature is essentially unchanging. Human beings have the same problems now, for example, that they had then, that they had 4,000 years ago. Each man wants to know why he was created, to know the purpose of human existence, to be loved, and to offer himself in love. Each man must struggle between good and evil, between selfishness and selflessness, between chastity and lust, between temperance and self-indulgence. Some succeed, some fail, most of the time. Most people over the course of history have taken halting steps in one direction or the other, depending on the circumstances of their lives. There are those who will go so far as to sacrifice their own lives to assist others, while there are others who wantonly seek to destroy other human beings. The human story is unchanging from epoch to epoch.

The Greeks knew, from reason alone, that the essence of human nature was unchanging because each man is composed of a body and a soul. The body, the soma, is a visible reality. But it is subject to unchanging laws, to truths, over which no man has control. The physical world itself undergoes changes according to laws which exert their binding force upon men without their willing it. We know today about the law of gravity; this is a physical truth. No public opinion poll can undo the truth of the law of gravity. Or of the law of aging. People can dye their hair, undergo plastic surgery or wear hairpieces in a vain attempt to disguise their age. Their bodies, however, are a certain age. No amount of human denial is going to prevent the aging process from leading us to death's door. These are truths. Those who deny that there are truths engage in absurd argumentation; the palpable reality is that the physical world, of which the body is part, is subject to laws, to truths.

TRUTH

Truth, as Socrates taught Plato, is not a matter of individual interpretation. Truth exists. Truth exists. It is. Human beings either admit its existence and adhere to it—or they deny it and suffer the consequences. The people of our own age, much like the Sophists, contend that what is true for one person might not be true for another. That is, morality is dependent upon personal perspective. This defies basic logic. If one statement is true, no contradictory statement can be true.

A truth about the human being perceived by the Greek philosophers was that each man had a soul which animated his body. The body belongs to—and is subject to—the laws of the physical world. But the human being is not defined by the body, by what can be called the "accidents" of genetics. Every human being has the same unchanging essence which defines his very humanity, a soul. That is one of the truths proclaimed by Socrates and Plato. The accidents, the environmental circumstances, of human history change. The essence of human nature remains the same, however, because each human is defined by an immortal soul. We may be living in different environmental circumstances in the 1990s than the Greeks did 2,500 years ago, but we have essentially the same problems.

SOULS

The Sophists then, as the prevailing culture today, denied such a concept; the soul could not be seen. A physician told a college professor, in a debate on abortion which took place in the 1980s, that he had opened up many bodies without ever seeing a soul. The professor asked him if he had ever done any brain surgery; the doctor said he had. The professor then queried, "Have you ever seen an idea?" Ideas are invisible, but they are nevertheless real.

What the Greeks understood, again, without any recourse to Divine Revelation, was that each man lived in a world beyond the merely physical—what could be called the metaphysical, spiritual world. Every human being has a whole series of dreams, hopes, anxieties, ideas, and beliefs which are distinctly invisible but nevertheless real. And there is a connection between the *psyche*, the

3

soul, and the *soma*, the body. A person who is in a state of euphoria often exudes an exterior glow to others, a tangible manifestation of their internal disposition. Those who are worried, on the other hand, might display their anxiety in how they carry themselves. Many physical illnesses are caused by emotional distress. Even some physicians who do not believe in God understand that some patients can will themselves to get better, while others do not have a will to live.

The human soul, the Greeks observed, is rational, capable of knowing right from wrong, reality from unreality, of explaining, to a certain degree, why things are the way they are, of creativity. No other being on earth has a rational soul. That rational soul is capable of perceiving the unchanging physical truths of the world which govern the body; it is also capable of perceiving moral laws which govern the soul, which are also unchanging. A rational person can observe that human behavior is as unchanging from age to age as the coming and going of the four climatological seasons. There must be unchanging norms to govern human moral behavior, norms which are knowable through what is called the conscience.

CONSCIENCE

Conscience is the moral imagination. Although it is imperfect (and can be misinformed, malformed, killed), the human conscience can determine right and wrong on the basis of nature itself. Morality, ultimately, is determined by the nature of individual acts. Certain acts, such as the intentional killing of an innocent human being, is always and in all circumstances wrong. Every person has an intuitive knowledge of morality, no matter how attenuated, which leads us to feel guilt when we do that which, of its nature, is wrong. Not all people feel guilt, granted; and a healthy guilt which accompanies an evil act might fade upon repeated acts of evil. It is of our very nature, however, to know that there is a natural moral law which binds human consciences at all times in all circumstances.

A child, for example, is the natural consequence of human sexual love between a man and a woman. The male and the female are anatomically complementary to each other. Fecundity is the natural consequence of their conjugal union during the fertile years. Falling down a flight of stairs might be an accident. Pregnancy, however, is no accident; it is what is intended by the very nature of human conjugal love. That is why Hippocrates could come to the conclusion that for anyone to invade the sanctuary of the womb in order to destroy, dismember, or burn that which belongs there by nature is a grave offense against nature itself. The natural law condemns abortion, which is why those who support it in our own era are so full of anger, desiring to eliminate all voices speaking up in defense of the unborn. Even though they are unaware of it, they are rebelling against their own human nature, supporting a fundamental injustice against life, denying a fundamental biological fact.

THE NATURAL LAW

The natural law can be defined as those unchanging principles which govern human moral behavior, and which are knowable by reason. Cicero, the great Roman orator, defined it thus:

> True law is right reason in agreement with Nature, it is of universal application, unchanging and everlasting; it summons to duty by its commands, and averts from wrong-doing by its prohibitions. And it does not lay its command or prohibitions upon good men in vain, although neither have any effect on the wicked. It is a sin to try to alter this law, nor is it allowable to attempt to repeal a part of it, and it is impossible to abolish it entirely. We cannot be freed from its obligations by Senate or People, and we need not look outside ourselves for an expounder or interpreter of it. And there will not be different laws at Rome and at Athens, or different laws now and in the future, but one eternal and unchangeable law will be valid for all nations and for all times, and there will be one master and one rule, that is God, over us all, for He is the author of this law, its promulgator and enforcing judge.

The natural law is a reality which does not depend upon human acceptance for its binding force, for its validity. Just as it would be an absurdity for any human legislature or judicial body to deny one of the physical laws of the universe, it would be equally absurd for any such body to declare the dictates of the natural law to be "outdated"—or not to exist at all. Even the Founding Fathers of this nation, who rejected the office of the

Successor of Saint Peter as the ultimate interpreter of the natural law, understood that the mere weight of numbers in a democratic republic could never make legitimate that which was otherwise illegitimate. In other words, democratic might does not equal moral right. In fact, Cicero was incorrect when believing that human beings could interpret the natural law on their own without guidance; as one who lived before the doctrine of Original Sin was expounded by the Church fathers, Cicero did not understand that flawed human nature makes an individual's interpretation of the natural law unreliable at times.

MORALITY AND ORDER

The Sophists opposed the existence of the natural law, subjecting Socrates to a trial on charges of corrupting the youth of his day. In like manner, the relativists of our day gratuitously deny the existence of the natural law, treating with contempt anyone who posits its existence as a fundamental truth of all personal and social order. A Sophist, whether of the Fifth Century before Christ or of our day in the last decade of the Twentieth Century, believes that man is the measure of all things, that the pursuit of personal material and physical pleasure justifies the use of whatever means necessary to achieve ephemeral pleasure. Sophists derive their "moral authority" from the fact that their defense of moral relativism is supported by great numbers of people. As Saint Paul wrote in his Letter to the Romans, when condemning the immorality of the city which became the seat of the Catholic faith, "Not only do people do these things. They want others to applaud them for doing so."

Socrates' student, Plato, carried on the work of his mentor, using simple logic to demonstrate that there is a direct connection between private morality and public order. A person who defies the precepts of the natural law, Plato argued, introduces disorder into his soul. Such a person is at war with himself, as his nature is made for the good. And a person at war with himself becomes an instrument of disorder in his relations with others, starting in his own family. The selfishness begotten by this disorder sows the seed of confusion and disarray in all of society.

JUSTICE

There can be no justice in any particular society if its citizens are pursuing injustice in their own private lives. Justice is ultimately the fruit of well-ordered souls; there is no "governmental" solution to the injustices human beings wreak upon each other. Human beings must resolve to enlighten their intellects and strengthen their wills to know the good, to choose the good, to do the good.

A person who defies the natural law by committing what even Plato called sin (although it is rather obvious he did not understand that word in its Christian context) suffers the consequence of his actions even if he is unaware that he is doing anything that is objectively wrong. A diabetic may not realize that he is hurting his body by defying a doctor's carefully devised diet; he nevertheless suffers the consequences of such a defiance, even though he might not be subjectively aware of what he is doing. The same thing is true on the moral level; one who does that which is morally wrong suffers all manner of internal confusion and anxiety, which worsens the more one does that which is wrong, even though he does not recognize it is his own freely chosen actions which are the root of his problems.

POLITICS

Recognizing that the human being is the source of all personal and social problems is essential to understanding how the Greeks and Romans, no less the American Founding Fathers, viewed politics and government. Aristotle, for example, knew that politics is a natural outgrowth of human nature, particularly of the tendency of human beings to seek self at the expense of others. Politics is nothing mysterious or remote; it is the essence of man's relationship to man in the secular order. All human beings are engaged, broadly speaking, in political relationships.

Politics can be defined as the study of the competition for the allocation of scarce resources. That is, human beings are naturally inclined to compete with each other for the goods and resources of this world. As will be demonstrated more fully in the next chapter, original and actual sin incline men to gratify self. Even from reason alone, unaided by the light of Divine Revelation, it is possible to understand that the human being is by nature competitive. Brothers and sisters, for example, frequently develop sibling rivalries long before they are consciously aware of competing with each other.

COMPETITION AS THE ESSENCE OF POLITICS

Because human beings are rational, however, they only compete for that which is valuable; that which is valuable is, by definition, scarce. A determination of what is valuable (and what, therefore, will be the object of man's competition with his fellow man) varies from person to person, from culture to culture, from time to time, from place to place. (We are not talking about moral values; we are talking about those things that a particular person deems valuable enough to compete for.) The diversity which exists among human beings in the accidentals of human existence is such that people have different interests, likes, and dislikes.

For example, some people may enter a drawing to get tickets to a baseball World Series (assuming there is no players' strike), while others might compete with fellow parishioners for tickets to a Papal Mass. Still others may compete for trading card or comic book collections, while others may compete in prestigious auctions for objects of fine art. The list is endless. The point is, however, that all people everywhere compete. It is part of human nature.

The value of a commodity being competed for depends not only on the subjective considerations of the people involved but also on the law of supply and demand. A simple piece of chalk has no value, as its supply outstrips its demand. That changes if there are more professors on a college campus demanding chalk than the supply which exists at that time; the very thing that lacked value, chalk, can suddenly become very valuable. This is exactly what has happened with respect to crude petroleum in the past two centuries; a commodity which had virtually no value in 1796, largely because there was little use for it, is now the basis of the world's economy, and a good deal of the reason that the Persian Gulf War was fought in 1991. And the relative value of a ticket to a New York Mets baseball game at Shea Stadium, which had great value when the team was winning the World's Championship in 1986, declined in the early 1990s when the team went into a competitive tailspin.

SCARCE COMMODITIES—TANGIBLE AND INTANGIBLE

The scarce commodities for which men compete are tangible and intangible. Men compete for tangible goods, things they can see, feel, and hold. Such things as land, food, water, other natural resources (precious metals, minerals, oil), money, and a multiplicity of other material items. But human beings also compete for things that cannot be seen, the intangible goods of the world— love, honor, respect, ideas (philosophical and religious). Indeed, the Cold War between the Soviet Union and the United States, although fraught with many geopolitical considerations, had an ideological component; which set of ideas would prevail in the world? It is not an exaggeration to state that competition for the *intangible* goods of this world can be more intense than that for the tangible goods.

The competition for the intangible goods of the world is seen very clearly when two children believe that their parents only have a finite amount of love to give them. Love, as will be explored more fully in the next chapter, is infinite. Its source is Love Himself, the Triune God. Most little children are unaware of this; they think in finite terms. And they are selfish, they want more attention from their parents than their siblings get. So it is natural for a child to think that the way to get more of his parents' love is to make his brother look bad by comparison, thinking that love will be subtracted from the sibling and given to him.

Yes, politics influences all human relationships. It is everywhere. Politics is found in families, in parishes, in dioceses, in schools, in businesses, in all social settings. One even finds politics, broadly defined, on the Long Island Expressway in New York, where motorists during rush hour are competing for a scarce commodity, a space in a lane of traffic. Politics is even to be found among aboriginal people, who, though living in different cultural situations, have the same human nature as all other people. There are chiefs and braves, leaders and followers. Politics is eternal and universal; it is part of the human condition.

POLITICAL COMMUNITIES

Societally speaking, the study of politics involves how a particular community (local, state, or national) divides its resources.

How much will citizens be taxed? What ideas are going to drive public policy? Will ideas founded in the Divine and natural laws, which respect the reality of the family as the basis of the well-ordered society, be used to develop policy in accord with the principle of subsidiarity? Or will the modern-day equivalent of Sophism—moral relativism and legal positivism—"liberate" a particular society from the precepts of the Divine and natural laws? Indeed, the conflict between a belief in (and adherence to) transcendent moral norms and the rejection of such norms is the basis of politics all around the world today. For there are a variety of governmental and non-governmental organizations dedicated to the Sophistic proposition that even the mere assertion that transcendent norms exist is somehow unacceptable in the realm of political discourse.

GOVERNMENT

The competition for the allocation of scarce resources which is politics does not take place in a vacuum. There needs to be some framework to give structure to this competition. Government, therefore, is a natural response to the reality of politics. All human social relationships have forms, no matter how crude, of governance. As order is something that human beings crave as a part of their unchanging nature, it is natural for governments to spring up to provide some semblance of direction, whether weak or strong, to the human competition for the goods and resources of this world.

Governance is natural even to the human body. The head is the governing principle of the body. Pain, for example, is not felt where it occurs. It is triggered in the leg or the back, but it is *felt* in the brain (which is why a paraplegic or an amputee can have "itchy" feet). A stroke or a heart attack can do untold damage to the human brain, thereby disrupting the rest of the body.

FAMILY

Well, the same is true in human relationships. As the family is the building-block of society, it is easy to see a form of government there. (The family is being discussed in this book in the context of the Divine and natural laws—a husband and a wife who welcome children generously as the natural fruit of their conjugal love in Christ.) There is a hierarchy within a family, for children are not the equal in authority to their parents. They are obliged, particularly under the precepts of the Fourth Commandment, to obey their parents in all things that are not sinful. The parents, in turn, have an obligation to care for the spiritual and temporal welfare of their children, to make sure that they are given an education in the truth, the fullness of which is found in Christ and His Holy Church founded upon the Rock of Peter, the Pope, so that they will know the life of peace that comes from being in a state of sanctifying grace.

The American concept of strict equality of persons—a notion born in the Renaissance and Enlightenment, reaching its radical height in the French and Bolshevik Revolutions—would reject all hierarchical relationships (God and His Church over man, parents over children, teachers over students, employers over employees). But this is not in accord with the Divine and natural laws, which are meant to be cultivated within the family unit. For it is there that children learn that all *legitimate* authority comes from God, that the salvation of one's immortal soul depends in part on having the humility to subject one's self to those who are lawfully their superiors in authority. This is precisely what the Second Person of the Blessed Trinity, Jesus Christ, did when subjecting Himself to the authority of His foster-father, Saint Joseph, and His Blessed Mother, and when He delivered Himself into the hands of us sinful men, delivering Himself up to the Roman procurator Pontius Pilate.

ROLE OF GOVERNMENT

Part of the reason that there is so much confusion about the role of government in society today is because children have not been taught to learn or to respect what the meaning of governance is within the context of the human family. A child's place is to do the chores assigned to him by his parents, who in turn are to surround the child with a true love based on an abiding concern for his spiritual and temporal growth. By extension, a child is to learn that a teacher is acting *in loco parentis* in the classroom—and is therefore entitled to the same respect and obedience as are his parents. A student is to be punctual, quiet, obedient, and committed to the earnest fulfillment of all assignments as part of fulfilling the obligations imposed by his state in life.

Government exists on the macro, or societal, level to provide for a balance between the competing values of liberty and order within a given community. The Greeks and Romans understood from reason alone that government is an organized entity designed to provide order in a particular polity (or it can be seen as the framework in which the drama of politics is played out on the human stage). Parents are needed to provide order within a family; teachers are needed to provide order within a classroom; governments are needed to provide order in society.

Governments do not exist as ends in and of themselves. They are a means to a higher end, justice, as the Greeks and Romans taught. Composed of flawed human beings who frequently seek self at the expense of others, governments can never magically resolve all of the problems of the world. They can never make all human beings equal in the accidents of life (wealth, talent, intelligence, athletic ability). They are merely the means by which human beings can be assured of the social conditions which will advance their dignity; the ultimate dignity of each man is the defense of innocent human life. Indeed, justice (giving to each person that which is his due) is premised upon respecting the right to life, without which all other human rights are meaningless.

HUMAN RIGHTS

As means to an end, governments do not "bestow" rights upon anyone. Human rights do not emanate from constitutions, decisions of the Supreme Court, laws passed by Congress, edicts of the President. Human rights inhere in the soul. As all men share the same essential human nature, the possession of human rights is not dependent upon the laws or constitutions of any government. Human beings possess rights in the Divine and natural laws that exist independently of any governmental decrees. However, it has been the case, and continues to be the case, that governments either fail to recognize the existence of basic human rights, and/or seek to eliminate the *exercise* of those rights, seeking its own self-aggrandizement instead.

As governments are not the font of human rights, there is no such thing as a "new" right. No one has the right to do that which objectively wrong. One may have the ability, as will be discussed presently, to perform a given act, but that does not mean that one is morally *free* to commit the act. Governments cannot make an immoral act legitimate. Nor can governments legitimately penalize those who are doing what is objectively correct. Governments must be founded upon an abiding respect for—and adherence to—the Divine and natural laws.

Legitimate human rights are not contingent upon government recognition. Because this is so, governments can only do two things with respect to human rights:

1. They can permit human beings the responsible, restrained exercise of human free will; or

2. They can *illegitimately* seek to restrict and/or eliminate the exercise of that free will.

A just government seeks to find a balance between liberty and order, the most vexing problem faced by individuals—and by the societies in which they live.

LIBERTY V. LICENSE

Human freedom has been exalted as an end in and of itself, particularly in the Twentieth Century. Even the Greek and Roman pagans, however, understood that human freedom was a means to a higher end, right living. Humans, they knew, had the capacity to misuse free will, to do that which was violative of the Divine and natural laws, that which brought disorder upon themselves and their societies. Each human being struggles to find the *via medium* in his life; each person struggles between doing what he knows is right—and doing that which is convenient or expedient, regardless of any transcendent norms.

Human freedom, or liberty, can be defined properly as being the natural condition of man, wherein he can use his free will responsibly in accord with the dictates of right reason and the natural law. As mentioned earlier, one is not morally free to do everything he is physically capable of doing. What many people in our world today take for freedom is actually license, unrestrained physical freedom. The average person believes that "freedom" is a synonym for fulfilling each one of his primal urges. Even the

13

pagan philosophers of antiquity knew such a notion was specious.

ABILITY V. RIGHT

A thief might have the physical potentiality to steal an object from someone. Just because a thief may possess the physical freedom to steal does not mean that he is morally free to do so. One is never morally free to do that which is in violation of the Divine and natural laws. Although one may have the ability to choose evil, one does not possess any "right" in the natural order of things to do so. And no human law or court decree can legitimize evil actions (whether in Nazi Germany, the old Soviet Union, or in the United States today, as happened with particular clarity in the U.S. Supreme Court case of *Roe v. Wade* on January 22, 1973).

Human beings are morally free only to choose the good. They have the capacity to know the good through their intellects; each person must use his will to *choose* the good, understanding that a failure to do so has a variety of consequences in his own life—and in his relations with others. Each person is called to discipline his life to such an extent that he is able to restrain himself from succumbing to a preoccupation with his disordered passions. On the simple level of eating, for example, a man has to use balance, knowing that too much salt might lead to hypertension, heart disease, stroke, and/or kidney failure.

Pope John Paul II wrote at length about freedom—and its relationship to truth—in his encyclical letter *Veritatis Splendor*, issued in 1993:

> Revelation teaches that *the power to decide what is good and what is evil does not belong to man, but to God alone.* The man is certainly free, inasmuch as he can understand God's commands. And he possesses an extremely far-reaching freedom, since he can eat "of every tree of the garden." But his freedom is not unlimited; it must halt before the "tree of the knowledge of good and evil," for it is called to accept the moral law given by God. In fact, human freedom finds its authentic and complete fulfillment precisely in the acceptance of that law. God, who alone is good, knows perfectly what is good for man, and by virtue of his very love proposes this good to man in the commandments.

God's law does not reduce, much less do away with human freedom; rather, it protects and promotes that freedom. In contrast, however, some present-day cultural tendencies have given rise to several currents of ethics which center upon *an alleged conflict between freedom and law*. These doctrines would grant to individuals or social groups the right *to determine what is good or evil*. Human freedom would thus be able to "create values" and would enjoy a primacy over truth, to the point that truth itself would be considered a creation of freedom. Freedom would thus lay claim to *a moral autonomy* which would actually amount to an *absolute sovereignty* (No. 35, *Veritatis Splendor*).

SELF-DISCIPLINE

As will be discussed more fully in the next chapter, fallen human nature makes it difficult for us to arrive at the happy medium. A student might know he has to study for a particular exam; it is one thing to know that, quite another to actually make a free will choice to put aside the distractions that entice him to do anything *but* study. It can even be difficult for a student to *motivate* himself to study, preferring to waste time by watching television. The good student finds it necessary to discipline himself by developing a routine which makes it possible for him to use his freedom wisely.

If a person can understand how difficult it is for him to use his free will correctly (even on the levels of eating and studying, no less cleaning one's room or house, attending to daily chores, being responsible with money) when no other human beings are involved, then it is pretty easy to understand that striking a balance between liberty and order is at the heart of all interpersonal relationships.

MUTUAL TRUST AND RESPECT

Insecurity and possessiveness are two characteristics that are in rather plentiful supply in many families and relationships these days. A man who is dating a woman seriously (and a Catholic understands that the only legitimate purpose of dating is to find a spouse, something that is only open to those who are canonically free to marry) may doubt himself or the woman who is the object of his affections. Not having a love of detachment, nor under-standing the unconditional nature of true Christian love, a man might be tempted to "check up" on his girlfriend to see if she is dating another man. (Some women have been known to do the same thing.) Such "checking up" has been known to take the form of "hang-up" phone calls, in which one party calls the other merely to see if he is at home. Finding a level of mutual trust in a relationship can be a difficult thing.

The same thing is true of parent-child relationships. Many parents are unwilling to let go of their children once they are grown. They believe that they have the right to command their adult children in areas not involving transcendent truths (where to live, what kind of job to take, when to leave home). Some parents are simply unwilling to realize the difference between offering what they consider to be sound advice on practical aspects of liv-ing—respecting their children's ability to disagree with them—and judging their children's love for them on whether they com-ply completely with such advice all the time. While it is the duty of a parent to offer correction, particularly as it relates to matters of faith and morals, adult offspring do have the legitimate right in the natural order of things ordained by God to choose careers and to have lives of their own. Finding a balance demanded by a love based in detachment is very difficult.

(I am not referring here to the legitimate right of parents to raise their children as they are growing up, to train them in the faith, to demand them to fulfill family obligations. Rather, I am referring to the situation in which many parents, unwilling to admit that both they and their children are getting older, refuse to let grown children make choices in the accidentals of human exis-tence that they have complete freedom to make.)

PUNISHMENT

It is because human beings find it difficult to use their free wills rightly, whether individually or in relation to others, that a society must find a means to discipline those who do that which is violative of the Divine and natural laws. As the natural law is not self-enforcing, those who break its precepts must be forced to pay a penalty for doing that which of its nature is objectively wrong. That is why a just government enacts criminal laws; such laws do not make an action right or wrong, they merely apply a societal penalty on those who do that which is of its nature wrong. For example, the killing of an innocent human being is proscribed by the natural law. All that a just criminal statute passed by a human legislative body (say, the United States Congress or state legislatures) does is apply a particular penalty to those person or persons who have committed an immoral act. It is not just for a legislative body to legitimize actions that are immoral (such as legalizing the killing of innocent children in their mothers' wombs); nor is it an act of justice to penalize people for doing what is right (rescuing children in front of abortuaries), attempting to silence those who criticize abortion. Civil law must be conformed to the natural law. A Catholic understands that a truly just society must conform its laws on the fundamentals of human existence to the mind of Christ Himself.

LEGAL POWER—JUST OR ABUSIVE

Just as liberty can be abused by individuals, so can order or law be used by governments. The United States Supreme Court found that slavery was a constitutional exercise of property rights in the case of *Dred Scott v. Sanford* (1857), going so far in that case as to deny the rights of citizenship to any black person. It also upheld the legitimacy of racial segregation in the case of *Plessy v. Ferguson* (1896). *Griswold v. Connecticut* (1965) and *Roe v. Wade* (1973) found that grave offenses against the Divine and natural laws, contraception and abortion, respectively, are protected by a convoluted interpretation of the language found in the U.S. Constitution. And this is to say nothing of the offenses against the Divine and natural laws committed by Nazi Germany and the Union of Soviet Socialist Republics. The Nazi Fuhrer, Adolph Hitler, was careful to observe all legal precepts; he and his regime broke no German laws. But Nazi war criminals were prosecuted at Nuremberg after World War II because they had violated the natural law.

Governments pursue justice only if they seek a means to balance the tension between liberty and order. Human liberty must be respected, but individuals within a society must be so formed as to understand that no one has the "right" to do whatever it is he wants to do whenever it is he wants to do it. On the other hand, every right carries with it a corresponding responsibility, and a society has the right and duty in the natural law to impose penalties upon those who use their physical freedom without regard for moral right.

Pope John Paul II spoke at length about these concepts at the United Nations on October 5, 1995:

> It is important for us to grasp what might be called the *inner structure* of this worldwide movement [for freedom]. It is precisely its global character which offers us its first and fundamental "key" and confirms that there are indeed universal human rights, rooted in the nature of the person, rights which reflect the objective and inviolable demands of a *universal moral law*. These are not abstract points; rather, these rights tell us something important about the actual life of every individual and of every social group. They also remind us that *we do not live in an irrational or meaningless world*. On the contrary, there is a *moral logic which is built into human life* and which makes possible dialogue between individuals and peoples. If we want a *century of violent coercion* to be succeeded by a *century of persuasion*, we must find a way to discuss the human future intelligibly. The universal moral law written on the human heart is precisely that kind of "grammar" which is needed if the world is to engage this discussion of its future. . . .
>
> Freedom is not simply the absence of tyranny or oppression. Nor is freedom a license to do whatever we like. Freedom has an inner "logic" which distinguishes it and ennobles it: *freedom is ordered to the truth*, and is fulfilled in man's quest for truth and in man's living in the truth. Detached from the truth about the human person, freedom deteriorates into license in the lives of individuals, and, in political life, it becomes the caprice of the most powerful and the arrogance of power. Far from being a limitation upon freedom or a threat to it, reference to the truth about the human person—a truth universally knowable through the moral law written on the hearts of all—is, in fact, the guarantor of freedom's future.

As instructive as the natural law is in understanding politics and government as the consequence of human nature, it is only through the eyes of faith that we can come to a clearer picture of why problems exist in society, and how those problems can be ameliorated. It is only through the eyes of faith that politics and government become fully comprehensible.

CHAPTER TWO

Human Nature as Seen Through the Eyes of Faith

Human beings want to know why they are here. What is the purpose of human life? Why do we have war, poverty, disease, injustice, suffering, death? As Pope John Paul II pointed out in his very first encyclical letter in 1979, *Redemptor Hominis*, the human being is made for love. All people desire to be loved—and to offer themselves in love. And they desire to develop a relationship with something (or someone) to answer the eternal questions of the human heart: hence the proliferation of cults and of interest in the *occult*, the transformation of sports into a quasi-religion, the seductive allure of political ideologies as the means to "save" societies from all manner of social problems, and the trust in material wealth as a "sign" of Divine election.

OUR DEEPEST LONGING

The Prologue to the *Catechism of the Catholic Church* starts with a quotation from Saint John's Gospel, reminding us that we are made to know the "only true God, and Jesus Christ whom you have sent." The reflection continues with a passage from Saint Paul's first letter to Timothy, "God our Savior desires all men to be saved and to come to the knowledge of the truth." Yes, the purpose of human existence is to know the only true God, Who has revealed Himself fully in the Person of His Divine Son Jesus Christ. It is the Divine will that all men will be saved, that they will come to know Truth Incarnate.

The human heart has a great hunger to know what it is true, to believe in some kind of salvation, to find some sort of message

19

to give sense to a disordered world bombarded by a cacophony of voices proclaiming to speak in behalf of human happiness. "As the deer longs for running water," says the Psalmist, "my soul pines for you, my God." In the words of Saint Augustine, "My heart will not rest until it rests in Thee." It is only the Triune God Who gives peace and direction to human hearts.

> God, infinitely perfect and blessed in himself, in a plan of sheer goodness freely created man to make him share in his own blessed life. For this reason, at every time and in every place, God draws close to man. He calls man to seek him, to know him, to love him with all his strength. He calls together all men, scattered and divided by sin, into the unity of his family, the Church. To accomplish this, when the fullness of time had come, God sent his Son as Redeemer and Savior. In his Son and through him, he invites men to become, in the Holy Spirit, his adopted children and thus heirs of his blessed life (*Catechism*, No. 1).

GOD'S LOVE

God is infinitely perfect and blessed in himself. He has always existed. His existence is not contingent upon anything or anyone. He is not the invention of a "community" in search of a supreme intelligence to the universe. He is total perfection, the summit and fountain of all blessedness. He is lacking nothing. Omniscient, omnipresent, omnipotent. The perfection and blessedness of God is not evolving. It is not in the "process of becoming." He is in need of nothing. He always was, is now, will be forever.

Although He is infinitely perfect and blessed, He desired to bestow love on human beings made in His image and likeness in that they have been endowed with a rational soul. They have been created to share in the very inner life of the Trinity. So intense is God's love for His creatures that He wants them to *share* in his blessedness, which is the source of all human happiness here and in eternity.

OUR LOVE FOR OTHERS

God's love for us is not a mere sentiment; it is an act of his

Divine will, which seeks the salvation of all men. This is the love we are to have for our fellow contingent beings. Our love for others is meant to be an act of the will, to will the good of everyone else. And the ultimate good of each person is to live in a state of friendship with God here in this life so as to live forever with Him in Heaven. We are a friend to no one if we do anything, by word or by example, to impede the salvation of his immortal soul.

OUR LOVE FOR GOD

God calls, *invites*, man to seek him, to know him, to love him with all his strength. As Francis Thompson notes, God is the "Hound of Heaven." The Third Person of the Blessed Trinity, the Holy Spirit, will move us with various promptings, in *all* of the circumstances of our lives, to respond to God's invitation to know, love, and serve Him with every breath that we take. And our response is not to be half-hearted; it is to be total. Father John Hardon noted in a spiritual conference in New York in 1979, "We are to love God to the point of sheer exhaustion." That is why so many people, including the rich young man who refused to respond to our Lord's invitation to follow Him because of his attachment to many riches, are afraid to respond. They do not want to make a total commitment to God, to image the Cross of Jesus Christ as a living sign of contradiction. God respects human free will. He will never do violence to human free will. But He will continue to try to prompt our free will response to His love.

Mankind is scattered and divided by sin. Families are frequently torn apart by disputes over inheritances. Grudges are harbored for years on end. The Church herself is divided by the effects of sin; many, including those who hold high ecclesiastical office, feel free to denigrate the unchanging teaching of Jesus Christ as an irrelevancy in today's world. Christendom is divided into a variety of sects which relativize the Gospel into meaningless. But that is not God's will. He wants all men to be united in the one sheepfold of Peter. That is why Our Lord was enfleshed in our Lady's virginal and immaculate womb. By the working of the Holy Spirit in baptism we become the adopted children of God—and heirs of the Trinity's Blessedness.

THE GREAT COMMISSION

The gift we receive is to be offered freely to all others. We received a mandate by virtue of our Baptism and Confirmation to proclaim the Gospel, to make disciples of all nations. We cannot be content with the fact that we have received the Good News, that *we* share in the blessedness provided by sanctifying grace. We need to provide others with the answers to the questions harbored in the hearts of those who have not yet come to know the truth.

For the life of man is incomprehensible to the human heart unless we know—and love—God. This essential message of the *Catechism*'s Prologue is summary of Christian life. Indeed, the entire structure of the *Catechism*, outlined at length in the Prologue, is designed to lead those who read it to respond ever more deeply into a relationship of love with Love Himself.

Human life itself is meant to be rooted and lived in the Name of the Father, and of the Son, and of the Holy Spirit. We are to see all things through the eyes of faith, to see our very definition as human beings in light of Who has Created, Redeemed, and Sanctifies us. God wants us to *see*, to be free of the blindness imposed on us by fallen human nature. The *Catechism*'s Prologue is an invitation for all men everywhere to have darkened intellects enlightened by the light of the grace won for us on Calvary.

THE HOUND OF HEAVEN

As a creature of God endowed with a rational soul, man has an innate desire to be in contact with his Creator. Human reason, unaided by the light of Divine Revelation, can come to an understanding that there has to be a Supreme Being which has given order to the universe. Of itself, however, reason cannot tell us anything about that Being; He must take the initiative to communicate Himself to us. And He does so out of love. No man can come to a full understanding of himself if he does not know the Truth Who is God—and responds to Him with love upon love (cf. No. 27, *Catechism*).

The universality of this desire for God is such that all peoples throughout the world have sought to find some means of expressing their belief in a force above them. Such expressions were primitive, crude; they were based upon a human desire to find

person who seeks God discovers certain ways of coming to know him. These are also called proofs for the existence of God, not in the sense of proofs in the natural sciences, but rather in the sense of "converging and convincing arguments," which allow us to attain certainty about the truth (*Catechism*, No. 31).

Human beings are creatures of God. As such, even persons whose souls have not been reborn into baptismal innocence have a *natural longing* to discover the answer to the questions about human existence, to find a supreme intelligence or ultimate cause for the beauty and the perfection of the world. This can be done by looking at the world itself, "starting from movement, becoming, contingency, and the world's order and beauty." A person can, by reason alone, attain to a knowledge that there must be some ultimate cause for all that the eye can behold.

PROOFS OF GOD

As the Greek philosophers, such as Socrates, Plato, and Aristotle, understood, the physical world is subject to unchanging laws which do not depend upon human acceptance for their validity. While their knowledge of such laws was not as extensive as it would become in the future, the Greek philosophers, unaided by the light of Divine Revelation, knew that the physical world was not created by fallible, contingent beings whose bodies are destined for the corruption of the grave. The seasons of the year come and go without humans willing it (and without their necessarily liking it; even those of us who are believers of the one, true God can accept the winter season from His hand, but we may not like it all that very much).

The Greek philosophers knew, however, that the world was composed of much more than a physical component. Human beings are physical entities. But they also possess immortal souls, which themselves are subject to unchanging laws. Reason alone led the men of ancient Athens to conclude that human nature is universal and eternal. The problems of humanity were the same then as they had been before their time; an honest assessment of human history since that time shows us that it is the same today. People still struggle between good and evil. People are still trying to find answers to life's mysteries.

It is in the human person, as the *Catechism* notes (cf. No. 33), that men can find certain immutable truths. "In all this he discerns signs of his spiritual soul. The soul, the 'seed of eternity we bear in ourselves, irreducible to the merely material,' can have its origin only in God" (*Catechism*, No. 33). A person who is sincerely searching for the meaning of life must come to the inescapable conclusion that there is a God (cf. *Catechism*, No. 34).

A PERSONAL GOD

God desires much more for us, however, than for us to possess a merely intellectual perception of His existence. It is one thing to know that someone exists; it is quite another to know that someone as a person. God wants us to know Him *personally*. "But for man to be able to enter into real intimacy with him, God willed both to reveal himself to man and to give him the grace of being able to welcome this revelation in faith" (*Catechism*, No. 35).

Although man can come to know about God's existence through the light of reason, it is only by the light of faith that we can come to know Him in the intimacy described above. The *Catechism* quotes from Pope Pius XII's *Humani Generis*:

> Though human reason is, strictly speaking, truly capable by its own natural power and light of attaining to a true and certain knowledge of the one personal God, who watches over and controls the world by his providence, and of the natural law written in our hearts by the Creator; yet there are many obstacles which prevent reason from the effective and fruitful use of this inborn faculty. For the truths that concern the relations between God and man wholly transcend the visible order of things, and, if they are translated into human action and influence it, they call for self-surrender and abnegation. The human mind, in its turn, is hampered in the attaining of such truths, not only by the impact of the senses and the imagination, but also by disordered appetites which are the consequences of original sin. So it happens that men in such matters easily persuade themselves that what they would like to be true is false or at least doubtful (*Catechism*, No. 37).

That is why, as the *Catechism* notes (cf. No. 38), we need to be enlightened by God's own revelation. It is not unreasonable, as we shall see in later installments, to trust someone we know. It is possible to know—and to place trust in the Word of—God. This is the necessary precondition to spiritual and moral growth.

The *Catechism*'s defense of man's ability to attain to the knowledge of God by reason is meant to remind us that we have to have some way to speak to those who do not believe about God in a manner that they can understand (cf. *Catechism*, Nos. 39–41). In so doing, however, "we must therefore continually purify our language of everything in it that is limited, image-bound or imperfect, if we are not to confuse our image of God—'the inexpressible, the incomprehensible, the invisible, the ungraspable'— with our human representation. Our human words always fall short of the mystery of God" (*Catechism*, No. 42). We must rely upon Holy Mother Church to guide us to a true understanding of God as He has revealed Himself in Scripture and Tradition.

KNOWING GOD

There are various ways that the human being can come to know *about* God. But that is not the same thing as *knowing* Him. The traditional proofs of the existence of God can affirm His existence, but tells us nothing of His inner essence.

Every human relationship is premised upon the process of revelation. We do not know everything there is to know about a person upon meeting him. We reveal ourselves to others over the course of time. Others come to know us by how we speak and act. And we are apt to reveal *more* of ourselves when we get to know others more fully; we will share with them secrets and stories that we will not relate to casual acquaintances.

Part of the self-revelation in human relationships is the acceptance of the fact that we will not be able to know *everything* about others. Certain aspects of the personalities and lives of our family and friends have a mysterious dimension to them. We can *observe* patterns of behavior, for example, but we may not be able to explain them. How many husbands and wives, married for as much as a half-century, do not fully understand everything their spouses do? But they accept those mysteries as part of an ongoing process of self-revelation.

GOD'S SELF-REVELATION

The concept of gradual self-revelation is important to take into account when considering how God communicated His very self to His creatures in preparation for His own coming in the Flesh at the Annunciation. "Through an utterly free decision, God has revealed himself and given himself to man. This he does by revealing the mystery, his plan of loving goodness, formed from all eternity in Christ, for the benefit of all men" (*Catechism*, No. 50).

God does not want His creatures grasping to find Him by the light of natural reason alone. He wants them to respond to His own self-revelation in Christ (cf. *Catechism*, Nos. 51 and 52).

> The divine plan of Revelation is realized simultaneously "by deeds and words which are intrinsically bound up with each other" and shed light on each other. It involves a specific pedagogy: God communicates himself to man gradually. He prepares him to welcome by stages the supernatural Revelation that is to culminate in the person and mission of the incarnate Word, Jesus Christ (*Catechism*, No. 53).

The *Catechism* quotes Saint Irenaeus of Lyons, who wrote about the "divine pedagogy using the image of God and man becoming accustomed to one another. The Word of God dwelt in man and became the Son of man in order to accustom man to perceive God and to accustom God to dwell in man, according to the Father's pleasure" (*Catechism*, No. 53). In other words, the human nature is not capable of grasping everything at once; it needs time to respond to the Divine invitation contained in God's self-revelation in Christ.

The conclusive revelation of God in the person of Jesus Christ came after centuries of preparation. He "'manifested Himself to our first parents from the very beginning.' He invited them to intimate communion with himself and clothed them with resplendent grace and justice" (*Catechism*, No. 54). Although Adam and Eve would fall from grace, causing the whole of human nature to be wounded forever (a subject to be discussed in later installments), God did not cease revealing Himself, did not stop preparing for the way for man to be reconciled to Him through His Son's Holy Cross. It is God's desire to "give eternal life to all those who seek salvation by patience in well-doing" (cf. *Catechism*, No 55).

EFFECTS OF ORIGINAL SIN

Original sin so wounded human nature, however, that men fell into great decadence. Divisions arose. Licentiousness abounded. Polytheism and idolatry become commonplace. Men gathered themselves in nations, a phenomenon which played a part in the economy of salvation, as God would choose to make covenants with Noah and Abraham to signify that He would make nations of them and their descendants (cf. *Catechism*, Nos. 56–59). It is to Abraham, our father in faith, that God chose to build up the people from whom He would assume His Sacred Humanity to effect our own reconciliation with Him.

Abraham, whose name was elongated from Abram to signify the spiritual progeny to be generated from his line, responded to God's revelation to him in perfect faith. He trusted God so much that He was willing to sacrifice Isaac, his long-awaited son by his wife Sarah. He was willing to go wherever God sent Him, a foreshadowing of the willingness exhibited by the twelve Apostles, who would replace the twelve tribes of Israel, to go out into the whole world to proclaim the Gospel (cf. *Catechism*, Nos. 59–61).

God fully formed Israel as His own people by choosing Moses, to whom He definitively revealed Himself as the only true God, to lead the Hebrew people out of their slavery in Egypt (cf. *Catechism*, No. 62). The first Passover out of Egypt instituted a paschal feast which would be supplanted and replaced by the New and Eternal Passover inaugurated by our Lord at the Last Supper. Just as the Chosen People were freed from their captivity in Egypt, so are we, the people of the New and Eternal Covenant, freed from our captivity by the New Moses, the New Adam, Jesus Christ. They spent forty years wandering in the desert before entering the Promised Land; we spend a lifetime wandering along the rocky road that leads, if we persevere, to the narrow gate of Life Himself.

PREPARATION FOR REVELATION

The people of the Old Covenant were being prepared, without knowing it, for the New Covenant, for the definitive revelation of the Father in the person of Jesus Christ. "In him he has said everything; there will be no other word than this one" (*Catechism*, No. 65).

29

In giving us his Son, his only Word (for he possesses no other), he spoke everything to us at once in this sole Word—and he has no more to say . . . because what he spoke before to the prophets in parts, he has now spoken all at once by giving us the All Who is His Son. Any person questioning God or desiring some vision or revelation would be guilty not only of foolish behavior but also of offending him, by not fixing his eyes upon Christ and by living with the desire for some other novelty (*Catechism*, No. 65).

Those "private revelations" which have been approved by the Church as containing nothing contrary to faith and morals do not "add" anything to the message of our Lord. While the Church continues to grasp the significance and meaning of the faith for nearly two millennia, there is no new revelation. As the *Catechism* relates, "Christian faith cannot accept 'revelations' that claim to surpass or correct the Revelation of which Christ is the fulfillment, as is the case in certain non–Christian religions and also in certain sects which base themselves on such 'revelations'" (*Catechism*, No. 67).

The final revelation will occur when our Lord manifests Himself in glory to the whole world at the end of time. The just will welcome Him with joy; the unjust will flee in fright. Yet people look still for the "secular savior," the person who will solve all of the problems of the world without demanding any personal sacrifice.

FAITH

It is through His Revelation that God invites each man to discover his true identity. This invitation requires a response, one borne of faith (cf. *Catechism*, No. 142). On a purely natural level, faith can be defined as trusting in the word of another without demanding proof. That is, we put faith in the words of those we know. We do not demand proof for every statement we hear. Those we know *reveal* themselves to us over the course of time; we learn from that process of revelation whether or not to trust what they tell us. It is not unreasonable to trust in a person we know. This is the essence of all interpersonal relationships. It is also true of our relationship with God, which is, of course, the penultimate of interpersonal relationships (cf. *Catechism*, No.

154). God is a community of Divine Persons.

Supernatural faith, as the *Catechism* tells us, is the submission of a man's "intellect and his will to God. With his whole being man gives his assent to God the revealer. Sacred Scripture calls this human response to God, the author of revelation, 'the obedience of faith'" (*Catechism*, No. 143). God calls us into a very intimate relationship with Him. He wants us to get to know Him through His Holy Church. He wants us to put trust in His word, revealed definitively through the Word-made-Flesh, Jesus Christ. It is not opposed to reason to trust in the Triune God. Trusting in God, however, requires us to "submit freely to the word that has been heard, because its truth is guaranteed by God, who is Truth itself" (*Catechism*, No. 144). We must obey His word.

Faith exemplars

Our Lady is the archetype of perfect faith. We call Abraham our "father in faith" because he put perfect trust in God's word. He was willing to go wherever God wanted to send him, not knowing where that would be. He trusted that he would be rewarded for his obedience, knowing that God must have had some good purpose in mind when He asked him to offer his long-awaited son Isaac in sacrifice (cf. *Catechism*, No. 145). This is the sort of faith that we are called to have. We are called to put total trust in Almighty God, seeing all the events of our lives with the eyes of faith. We must travel by faith with all of our being, making sure that we are conforming our actions with the Divine will. The Old Testament is replete with examples of men and women who put their total faith in God, who accepted everything from His hand with perfect equanimity (cf. *Catechism*, Nos. 146–147).

It is our Lady, however, who is the exemplar of faith. "By faith Mary welcomes the tidings and promise brought by the angel Gabriel, believing that 'with God nothing will be impossible' and so giving her assent: 'Behold I am the handmaid of the Lord; let it be [done] unto me according your word. . . .' It is for this faith that all generations have called Mary blessed" (*Catechism*, No. 148). Mary's faith was such that she could endure the horror of her Divine Son's Crucifixion, hearing the taunts that the children who were being entrusted to her care at that very moment were shouting at Him. How quick *we* are to think that some

31

tragedy or loss is unique to us, that no person has ever endured the suffering we have experienced. All we need to do is to look at Mary as she stood at the foot of the Cross. No one had to endure what she did. And she trusted in God totally. So must we (cf. *Catechism*, No. 149).

MISPLACED TRUST

There are people in this world who put all of their trust in celebrities, political leaders or political ideologies, athletes, money, career success. They are looking for something to give their lives meaning and purpose. Such trust is bound to be betrayed. Human beings cannot find their identity in creatures and/or created objects. "Christian faith differs from our faith in any human person. It is right and just to entrust oneself wholly to God and to believe absolutely what he says. It would be futile and false to place such faith in a creature" (*Catechism*, No. 150). As Catholics, we put faith in Jesus Christ, Who professed Himself to be the Son of God, God Incarnate. Jesus Christ is Who he says He is or He is a liar. There is no middle ground. "We can believe in Jesus Christ because He is himself God, the Word made flesh: 'No one has ever seen God; the only Son, who is in the bosom of the Father, he has made him known'" (*Catechism*, No. 151).

Only God, however, moves men close to Him. The Holy Spirit prompts the hearts of men to respond in faith to God's call. This is so because "one cannot believe in Jesus Christ without sharing in his Spirit. It is the Holy Spirit who reveals to men who Jesus is. . . . Only God knows God completely; we believe in the Holy Spirit because he is God" (*Catechism*, No. 152). The Holy Spirit leads us to know the Son, Who has made it possible for us to live in His Father's house forever. There is no division in God, Father, Son, and Holy Spirit.

FAITH—A GIFT

Not all people have the supernatural gift of faith. And not all people have the same *level* of faith. Saint Peter, for example, declared our Lord to be God not by his own ability. It was the Father in Heaven Who revealed this to him (cf. *Catechism*, No. 153). *"Faith is a gift of God, a supernatural virtue infused by him.*

Before this grace can be exercised, man must have the grace of God to move and assist him; he must have the interior helps of the Holy Spirit, who moves the heart and converts it to God, who opens eyes of the mind and 'makes it easy for all to accept and believe the truth" (*Catechism*, No. 153). We must pray each day for an increase in the supernatural virtue of faith. "O Lord, I believe. Help me in my unbelief" (paraphrase of Saint Augustine). Help me to believe more each day.

Supernatural faith requires, nevertheless, a response that is truly human. The human intellect and will must cooperate with divine grace, and must submit to the clear authority of God, Who provides us with helps in this regard. The external proofs of faith (the miracles of Our Lord and the saints, the Church's indefectibility) are given to us to help us believe in the authority of the One Who reveals Himself to us, Who asks for our faith. These helps are, as the *Catechism* relates, the *motives of credibility* "which show that the assent of faith is 'by no means a blind impulse of the mind'" (*Catechism*, No. 156). God knows that we are weak vessels of clay. He wants to give us signs to help us believe in His infallible Word.

FAITH AND REASON

That is why faith is certain. "It is more certain than all human knowledge because it is founded on the very word of God who cannot lie." Not even "ten thousand difficulties" can make one doubt (cf. *Catechism*, No. 157). Even so, we want to know more about our faith. Faith seeks understanding. Yes, there are, to be sure, mysteries that will never be fully revealed to us in this life. Part of understanding our faith, however, is accepting these mysteries in the same spirit of abandonment as Abraham and Mary, neither of whom fully understood what was being asked of them. We have an obligation to know our faith as well as we possibly can, starting with a good sacramental and prayer life as the basis of permitting the light of the sacred mysteries to penetrate our darkened intellects, to strengthen our weakened wills (cf. *Catechism*, No. 158).

The Renaissance and the Enlightenment (also known as the "Age of Reason") tried to posit the sophistic thought that faith is opposed to reason, particularly in light of scientific discoveries being made in those epochs. This is even truer today. We know, as people of faith, that there can never be any legitimate conflict between faith and science, as the latter is a tool given us by God to uncover some of the mysteries of the physical world. " 'Since the same God who reveals mysteries and infuses faith has bestowed the light of reason on the human mind, God cannot deny himself, nor can truth ever contradict truth.' Consequently, methodical research in all branches of knowledge, provided it is carried out in a truly scientific manner and does not override moral laws, can never conflict with the faith, because the things of the world and the things of faith derive from the same God" (*Catechism*, No. 159).

FREE RESPONSE IN FAITH

Our response to God must be free. Our Lord invited, never coerced, people to follow Him. "If you want to be my disciple. . . . If you want eternal life. . . . If you want to be perfect. . . ." Love is a free gift. God freely bestows His love upon us. He wants us to respond to Him in faith freely, understanding that we are returning love to Love Himself. For without faith it is impossible to please God, impossible to know what is true, impossible to have eternal life (cf. *Catechism*, Nos. 160–161). And we must persevere to the very end. Faith can grow weak. It can be lost. We must be faithful sons and daughters of Holy Mother Church until the very end, seeing faith as the pathway to the Beatific Vision (cf. *Catechism*, Nos. 161–162).

Although we do not see clearly in this life, our supernatural faith in Jesus Christ and His Holy Church will lead us to the fullness of vision in eternity. We will undergo many trials, as the Adversary wants us to abandon our faith and to convince others to do so, too. That is why we must have recourse to the witnesses of the faith, those who trusted totally in God, those who viewed life unwaveringly through the eyes of true faith. As the *Catechism* quotes the Letter to the Hebrews, " 'Therefore, since we are surrounded by so great a cloud of witnesses, let us also lay aside every weight, and sin which clings to us so closely, and let us run with perseverance the race that is set before us, looking to Jesus the pioneer and perfecter of our faith' " (*Catechism*, No. 165).

CHAPTER THREE

Original Sin as the Source of All Human Problems

There is a terrible disease which is ravaging our land at present. This disease is costing the lives of millions upon millions of people. Yet the sad reality is that very few people even recognize this disease at all.

No, this disease is not AIDS. No matter how terrible AIDS is to those who are afflicted with it, it is only a symptom of the much more prevalent disease afflicting our world: spiritual blindness. People of all walks and ages around the world refuse to recognize the light of Christ shining through His Holy Church created upon the Rock of Peter, the Pope. There are even those who have been incorporated into the Mystical Body of Christ by means of Baptism and Confirmation who have been overcome by the allure of the world, the flesh, and the devil.

Of course, the spiritual blindness so prevalent at this moment in the history of salvation is nothing new. Human beings have always exhibited a pronounced tendency to proclaim themselves to be the masters of the universe—the sole arbiters of right and wrong. Moses himself incurred sin by the anger which flared up within him when he saw how the Chosen People had fashioned a molten calf to worship when they thought he had abandoned them. The gratitude of the people of the Old Covenant was quite short; they who had complained about their slavery to the Egyptians complained loud and long *after* their liberation. They were blinded by the glitter of the world.

The prophet Isaiah wrote of this spiritual blindness:

Hear, O heavens, and listen, O earth, for the Lord speaks: Sons have I raised and reared, but they have disowned me! An ox

35

knows its owner, and an ass, its master's manger; But Israel does not know, my people has not understood (Is. 1:2–3).

Saint John tells us in his Gospel:

He was in the world, and the world came to be through him, but the world did not know him. He came to what was his own, but his own people did not accept him (Jn. 1:10–11).

THE GREAT LIE

Spiritual blindness is a byproduct of original sin. God does not want His beloved creatures to walk in darkness. He wants them to *choose* to live in the light. However, each of us has a darkened intellect and a weakened will as a result of the Fall from grace in the Garden of Eden. Baptism washes away original sin from our souls, but the *vestigial aftereffects* of original sin remain: a lessened capacity to accept objective truths *and* a weakened desire to *live* out what we know to be true. The life of grace which is flooded into our souls at Baptism—and fortified in Confirmation—gives us the *supernatural helps* which are sufficient to resist all temptation *if* we want to do so.

Original sin entered the world because of the pride of our first parents. The Prince of Darkness deceived them into believing that they would have the same power, knowledge, and authority as God *if* they disobeyed God's clear command not to eat of the fruit of the Tree of the Knowledge of Good and Evil. This appealed to their pride. Mere creatures—who had been created out of the clay of the earth—were convinced that they could become gods.

It is the same today. Adam and Eve forgot God. We forget God. Most people in the world do not have a clue as to Who God is. Even many within the Church have never really understood the depths of God's inner life. All of the dissension we see so clearly in the life of the Mystical Body of Christ—dissension which is sown by our ancient adversary to lead people away from the Church—is the result of a lack of clear evangelization and cate-chesis about the identity of God.

WHO IS GOD?

God is pure, uncreated spirit. Possessing an intellect and a will, He is the same yesterday, today, and tomorrow. He had no beginning, and He will have no end. He is a community of persons: Father, Son, and Holy Spirit. The Trinity is a community of Love. The Son is the perfect reflection of the Father's Love—and the Holy Spirit is the breath of the Father and Son's Love for each other. God is all powerful, all knowing, all seeing, all creating, all loving, all just, all merciful. He is complete in and of Himself. There are no parts outside of parts in God.

God desired to share His Love with others. The Father created the invisible world through His Son by the working of the Spirit. He created angels (Archangels, Angels, Cherubim, Seraphim, Virtues, Powers, Thrones, Dominations, Principalities), endowing them with an intellect and a will. But He gave them a *free will*. God could have created automatons. However, He wanted His creatures to *choose* to love Him.

Love is inauthentic if it is forced or coerced. Love must be chosen freely. He *is* Love. Authentic love is nothing less than *willing* what God wills. That is what we mean when we say that God is love; we are not saying that God looks the other way at immorality. Love is not some sentimental feeling or attraction. Authentic love is to will the Good—the Good who is God—to think with the mind of God and to act accordingly.

REBELLION

The chief of the angels, however, envied God. He wanted to have God's power and intelligence. A battle broke out in Heaven—and Lucifer, the Light Bearer, was defeated by Michael the Archangel. The fallen angel Lucifer was thrust down into the fiery furnace of Hell, hating God and all of His handiwork, especially human beings. Therefore, he wants to hurt God's creatures by leading them away from the Truth Who is Christ and His Mystical Body, the Church.

Satan wants people to believe that truth is relative. "Truth. What is that?" Pilate asked our Lord. As Catholics, we believe that Truth is a Person, and that that person—the God–Man Jesus Christ—remains the invisible head of His Holy Church. We believe that He governs through His visible head, the Pope, by the working of the Holy Spirit. If Christ is the Truth, then it stands to reason that Truth does not change. He is the same yesterday, today, and tomorrow. Satan does not want people to accept that *simple* truth, which pacifies souls and enlightens them on the path to personal sanctity. Satan wants people to be angry with God and His Church.

GOD FORGOTTEN

Long before the coming of Christ, however, the secular and religious worlds were in love with relativism, as was mentioned in Chapter One. The fact that human history is replete with civilizations which have crumbled from within because of the misuse of the sexual appetite does nothing to deter modern day sophists from concluding that we live in a "new, enlightened, and liberated" era of human behavior. Ancient Rome was so "enlightened and liberated" that it freed itself from existence.

We do not understand this collectively in our self-absorbed society because we have committed spiritual suicide; our utilitarian materialism has made war on the very religious underpinnings of the whole of Western civilization. We have done in a cultural manner what was attempted through the use of force by the dialectical materialists of Soviet communism: to exclude religion from all aspects of culture. No "serious" person thinks supernaturally. That is considered to be simply old-fashioned and unresponsive to social problems.

As Aleksandr Solzhenitsyn commented recently, "We have forgotten God." That is why human beings violate the sixth and ninth commandments without impunity today. That is why human beings deceive themselves into thinking that *they* are the masters of their own lives. That is why there is so much unhappiness, confusion, disarray and despair in the midst of the greatest affluence known in the annals of human history. We have forgotten God, the Author of nature and the natural law.

IF JESUS IS GOD. . . .

A lot of people today would say that it is a ridiculous idea to assert in the last part of the Twentieth Century, "That takes faith!" But words have consequences. If Jesus Christ is Who He says He is, then individuals have the obligation to follow Him, societies must be founded on His immutable truths, culture must be rooted in a concern for First and Last Things. There must be a fusion between faith and culture.

Today, however, the natural desire of human beings to find contact with the supernatural is perverted. The answers to such eternal questions as the meaning of human existence are to be found, we are told, in self-help books, or in all manner of political ideologies. Forgetting about the fact that God has revealed His very self to us through Scripture and Tradition, people look to put their faith in politics, politicians, political ideologies of the left and right, sports figures and sports teams, entertainment figures, authors, poets, philosophers, boyfriends, girlfriends, husbands, wives, and so forth.

There are plenty of people who *consciously* model their lives around a sports figure or a sports team. There are people who want to dress and act like some famous person. And there are plenty of people who are looking for the political leaders who will painlessly "solve" the problems of the nation without demanding any interior spiritual or moral reform. A newsmagazine asked in late 1995, "Can Colin Powell save America?" (The answer to that is a resounding "no." No person who supports the destruction of innocent human life is a fit holder of the public trust. Such a person cannot be an instrument of the common good.)

God created the human being to know, to love, and to serve Him, to be with Him for all eternity in Heaven. He made our first parents in his Divine image and likeness in that He endowed them with an intellect, a will, and a memory. All He asked of them was that they *choose* to use their free wills to love Him in return.

GOD IS GOOD

God created free beings in order to demonstrate how utterly dependent we are upon Him for everything that is good. Thus, He *permitted* our ancient Adversary, the devil, to tempt our first parents into disobeying Him. Satan appealed to their pride. They succumbed. God does not cause or *will* evil; evil occurs by the free will choice of human beings.

Archbishop Fulton J. Sheen said that the greatest triumph of Satan was not sin. The power of sin and death was destroyed by the Son of God made Man on the Holy Cross. The human being has the means of triumphing over the power of sin and death by cooperating with the graces won on Calvary—and which are administered to humans by the working of the Holy Spirit in the sacramental life of the Church Christ created upon the Rock of Peter, the Pope. Every human being who is baptized into the life of grace has all of the sufficient helps available to him to resist sin *if* he chooses to cooperate with them. It is the grace of God which can enlighten the intellect and strengthen the will if we, as Mother Teresa so aptly said, give God permission.

SATAN'S TRIUMPH?

The greatest triumph of Satan is the *denial* of sin, the denial that he exists. The disobedience of our first parents resulted in their fall from grace. Original sin entered the world. The whole order of God's created good was rent asunder by original sin. Sin—the privation of good—is such an offense against the natural order of things that even the physical world was torn apart by it. The human being was made to be in harmony with God. The disruption caused by original and actual sin (each of our own sins committed after Baptism is an actual sin) is what accounts for human unhappiness. *If* human beings are made by God for God then it stands to *reason* that sin is a rebellion not only against God but against human nature itself. That is why a person might feel so cheap and tawdry when he sins. He knows, at least intuitively, that he has rebelled against his nature, and his *super*-nature bestowed upon him in the baptismal fount.

Serious sin cannot coexist with the life of grace. The two are incompatible. As a consequence of sin, our first parents lost the preternatural gifts that had been given to them by God. Their intellects were darkened and their wills weakened by original sin. That is, human beings from that time to the present have a very pronounced tendency to resist the known truth. We tend to think that we can determine right and wrong.

Yet, if thought is given to the matter, none of us created ourselves. It might therefore stand to reason that we do not determine right and wrong. However, the darkened intellect makes it difficult for us to accept objective truths—and Truth Himself. And even if we *do* come to an acceptance of objective truths by means of the enlightenment provided by God's grace, then the weakened will makes it difficult for us to *choose* to act in accord with what we know to be just.

GOOD BEINGS WHO ARE FLAWED

Human nature has been wounded by sin. We are weak vessels of clay inclined to maximize—and to rationalize—immoral behavior. Mind you, we are not evil. Martin Luther had it all wrong. We are not, as that unfortunate man would have it, "dungheaps covered with a few snowflakes of grace." No. God does not create junk. We are good beings who are flawed.

It is original sin which is at the root of all personal and societal problems: unhappiness, war, crime, disease, injustice, pain, rejection, racism, death. It is why there are dissenters from the teaching of Christ. That is why human problems remain unresolved. Human problems—individually and societally—can be resolved only by the free will acts of *individual* human beings who make an earnest effort to cooperate with the graces won for us on Calvary. No political ideology can resolve the problems of the world. There is no lasting solution which can produce peace and/or prosperity. The Kingdom of God must be built up in the soul of each human being on a daily basis. We can progress a bit on some days and then fall back on others. It is only when a society is rightly oriented toward God that it can progress toward a justice for all which is rooted in Him.

As the Holy Father noted in *Centesimus Annus* in 1991:

Moreover, humankind, created for freedom, bears within it the wound of original sin, which constantly draws persons toward evil and puts them in need of redemption. Not only is this doctrine an *integral part of Christian revelation*; it also has great hermeneutical value insofar as it helps one to understand human reality. The human person tends towards good, but is also capable of evil. One can transcend one's immediate interest and still remain bound to it. The social order will be all the more stable, the more it takes this fact into account and does not place in opposition personal interest and the interests of society as a whole, but rather seeks ways to bring them into fruitful harmony. In fact, where self-interest is violently suppressed, it is replaced by a burdensome system of bureaucratic control which dries up the wellsprings of initiative and creativity. When people think they possess the secret of a perfect social organization which makes evil impossible, they also think that they can use any means, including violence and deceit, in order to bring that organization into being. Politics then becomes a "secular religion" which operates under the illusion of creating paradise in this world.

STUBBORN HUMANITY

For reasons that are shrouded in mystery (is not human love shrouded with mystery frequently?), God chose Abraham and his stock to prepare the whole of humanity for His own Incarnation, Nativity, Life, Public Ministry, Death, and Resurrection. He raised up Moses to lead His Chosen People out of their bondage to the Egyptians as a foretaste of the Passover from the bondage to sin and death that He would celebrate at the Last Supper and consummate on Good Friday. Were the Chosen People grateful? No. They grumbled about not having enough water, food, and comfort. They worshiped the Golden Calf when Moses was being given the Ten Commandments, thinking that he had abandoned them. And subsequent generations refused to listen to the Prophets, preferring instead to tickle their own ears with what they considered expedient and useful. The fact that they paid a high price societally for their spiritual version of Alzheimer's disease never made much of an impression upon them. One self-made societal disaster would be followed by another in spite of God's constant displays of mercy. The Chosen People forgot God.

Not understanding the Suffering Servant songs of the Prophet Isaiah, the people of Ancient Israel envisioned that the long-awaited Messiah would thunderously manifest himself as a political leader who would liberate them from the shackles of Roman oppression. The Chosen People, still so very special to God (Who chose them to prepare the whole of humanity for the Gospel message)—and who have an important role yet to play in the economy of salvation—still await this kind of messiah.

SIGN OF CONTRADICTION

But God fooled most of them, except for Simeon and Anna in the Temple. He came on *His* terms, conceived by the power of the

Holy Spirit in the womb of a virgin, without for one second losing His Divinity, born as an outcast in a stable amidst farm animals, forced to be spirited away by His mother and foster father because of the jealousy of King Herod, living the first thirty years of His life in utter anonymity. He came in humility to live in a family which lived out the evangelical counsels of poverty, chastity, and obedience. He came in such a way that He would not be recognized as God. People would have to put *faith* in His words and in His deeds.

The preaching and the miracles of our Lord were acclaimed by the crowds. Misunderstanding His physical miracles—not realizing that they were manifestations of His power to heal the *inner* person from sin and selfishness—the crowds expected Him to lead them to their former political glory. They expected Him to correct all social evils. He did not meet their expectations. He was then—and remains today through His Mystical Body, the Church—a Sign of Contradiction.

The aged Simeon told the Mother of God at the Presentation that the little Baby he held in his arms would be a sign that would be contradicted. He was right. The God Who is made incarnate again and again on altars of Sacrifice in every celebration of the Mass came to contradict the expectations of the worldly wise. He came to teach us about self-denial and the *proper* use of the bodily and spiritual gifts we had been given. He came to teach us that *each* of our fellow human beings is a child of God; it is a violation of human dignity to reduce another person to being merely the instrument of the satisfaction of our own disoriented carnal desires.

SPEAKING TRUTH

Our Lord said things that people did not want to hear. He told them, "He who divorces his wife and marries another commits adultery" (Mk. 10:11). A closer look at this particular point is in order because there is such rampant misunderstanding, even among Catholics. "For this reason a man shall leave his father and mother [and be joined to his wife] and the two shall become one flesh. Therefore what God has joined together, no human being must separate" (Mk. 10:7–9). That is, the Sacrament of Matrimony leaves an indelible seal impressed upon the soul by the working of the Holy Spirit. It is broken only by death.

No civil court can decree the bond of sacramental marriage to be broken. A civil court has the power to end the *civil* effects of marriage; that the couple no longer has *legal* responsibility for each other. But the sacramental bond remains unless there is a determination by an ecclesiastical marriage tribunal that there never was a valid bond from the start of the marriage. That is why any Christian who divorces and remarries without a decree of nullity is said by our Lord to commit adultery. There is the presumption of a sacramentally valid bond until such time as that validity can be disproven.

Authentic love is meant to be permanent. The tragedy of the acceptance of divorce *and* remarriage without an annulment is in plain opposition to the words of our Lord. "Come, take up your cross, deny your very self and follow me!" He wasn't joking.

Our Lord also told them, "Everyone who looks at a woman with lust has already committed adultery with her in his heart" (Mt. 5:28). He told them that "Unless you eat the flesh of the Son of Man and drink His blood, you do not have life in you" (Jn. 6:53). Either He meant what He said or He was a liar. And if He is God He is not a liar.

AWAKENED CONSCIENCES

The crowds did not want to hear these words which disturbed their consciences. Christ was an inconvenience. He talked about things which forced them to reexamine the way in which they lived. He was forcing them to reject the "politically and socially correct" views of the day. He was considered to be a threat. He had to be done away with. (Abraham Lincoln, when debating Stephen Douglas on the issue of slavery in 1858, was faced with a heckler who demanded that the former Congressman not talk about the immorality of the *Dred Scott* decision. Lincoln shot back very wryly, "Oh, you want me to talk about something that don't hurt." Talking about things that hurt is not the best vehicle to popularity. But it might just be the way to Heaven.)

A vote was taken on Good Friday. Pontius Pilate did not want Christ's blood on his hands. Thus, the "courageous" governor (so symbolic of the sycophants who cater to public opinion in the name of the democratic ethos) let the crowd decide who was to be released as a token of Roman justice during the Passover observance. The crowd chose the political zealot, Barabbas, over Christ. Truth was rejected by the crowd then. Truth is rejected by the crowd today.

Christ hung on the Cross as a Sign of Contradiction. He stands in the world today in the person of His Church as a Sign of Contradiction. Now, as then, human beings think they know better. Now, as then, people mock and ridicule the successors of the Apostles (who went out into the known world to preach the Word in the midst of great persecution) who stand up in defense of Truth Himself. Now, as then, people believe that human redemption can be had by the acquisition of material goods, the gratification of carnal desires outside the context of the Sacrament of Matrimony, and by the quest for political power.

SLOW TO LEARN

It was not without reason that our Lord called us sheep. Sheep are dumb animals who are slow to learn. *We* are slow to learn, slow to follow the voice of the Chief Shepherd on earth, the successor of Saint Peter, the Pope.

When, for example, some "good Catholic" decries what is mistakenly considered to be "man-made rules" about human moral behavior, the whole of Christ's saving message is rent asunder. There is an integral *unity* to the message of Christ. The Beatitudes do not say, "Blessed are they whose heart is consumed with the lusts of one's own economic convenience." He said, "Blessed are the pure of heart!" He did not say, "Go, do your own thing and it won't make any difference on the Last Day." He said, "Come, take up your cross, deny your very self, and follow me."

PRIDE AND LUST

While the root of all heresies is pride, it is nevertheless true that that pride is manifested by a rejection of objective moral norms. As one famous theologian put it a few years ago, "The Reformation was principally about sex and divorce." Or, as Archbishop Sheen put it very succinctly, "When a person is having a problem with the teaching of the Church—which is nothing less than the teaching of Christ—my two-sentence response is:

45

'What's your sin?' 'What don't you want to surrender to our Lord?'"

How many Catholics understand that human conjugal intimacy is a profound participation in God's love for His Holy Church? Some even scoff and say that our Lord said little about conjugal love. What utter nonsense. Read the Beatitudes. Read the Sermon on the Mount. Read his condemnation of adultery and lust. The epistles of Saints Paul and Peter are full of admonitions against sexual immorality.

IMAGE OF CHRIST AND HIS CHURCH

For just as He espoused Himself to the Church born out of His wounded side on the Holy Cross, so does a man and a woman espouse themselves to each other in an unconditional surrender of self to self. Christ held nothing back on the Cross. He shed every drop of His Most Precious Blood. The most intimate of human encounters is meant of its nature to join husband and wife into a sacred bond of finding their authentic happiness by making the *other* happy, by dying to self and self-interest so that the other may have life to the full. This kind of authentic, unconditional love is limitless. It can be regenerated over and over again *if* couples choose to make use of the sacramental grace that *they* can bestow on each other—a sacramental grace which is strengthened by the medicine of God's forgiveness in Penance and nourished by the Eucharist.

MASTER OF LIES

The world does not know that kind of love today. Our Adversary has convinced us that we can engage in conjugal intimacy for any reason at any time with any person. He has convinced us that it is possible (and admirably necessary for a whole host of utilitarian reasons) to frustrate the natural ends of conjugal relations by the use of contraception—and that the fruit of such intercourse may be killed with legal impunity. He has convinced us that it is possible to lessen the chances of contracting a deadly disease if we make immoral behavior somehow "safe" (which is not only a philosophical absurdity—but an absolute impossibility. Evil acts can never be made free from consequences. It is a lie from the Master of Lies).

Satan hates God. He hates us because we are made in the image and likeness of God. And since he cannot hurt God he wants to do the next best thing: to destroy bodies and souls by appealing to our pride and to our passion. He wants to lead us away from God. He wants people to reject Christ as the fulfillment of the Old Testament prophecies. He has appealed to human pride to divide Christianity from the time of the Protestant Revolt to the present because he does not want people to receive the Sacraments; he despises the Real Presence of Christ in the Eucharist. From the prideful Luther to the syphilitic Henry VIII, the devil found willing vessels for his plan to lead people away from the one, true Church.

HELL

Satan wants to lead souls into Hell. Some people do not believe that a "loving" God would "send" a person to Hell. Well, the truth of the matter is that Hell exists. Our Lord was not joking when He spoke about the everlasting fires of Gehenna.

God will give us until our dying breath to respond to His love. But He will not—indeed, He *cannot*—force us to love Him. If we have not chosen Him freely in life, He is not going to force Himself upon us in death. *We* choose to go to Hell. It is that simple. A soul has until the moment of death to repent—and to know God's limitless mercy. An unrepentant soul goes to Hell. Our Lady told us in Fatima that there are souls in Hell. There is no possibility of repentance after death. That is why life is so precious. That is why our Lord warns us, "Stand on guard. Keep watch. You do not know the day or the hour. Your master comes like a thief in the night." He was not wasting His Theandric breath!

There is no end to the devil's desire to delude us. He wants people to think that they can follow Christ apart from the only Church which existed in all of Christendom for the first one thousand years after Christ's Death, Resurrection, and Ascension— and the only one that existed in Western Christendom for an additional five hundred years after the Greek schism in 1054. He wants people to point to the bad example of believers in order to provide an excuse not to persevere in the faith. He wants people to think that individuals do not need the guidance of the successor of Peter, to think that they are autonomous in the interpretation of Scripture.

AUTHORITY

As noted above, Satan desires also to divide the Church Christ created upon the Rock of Peter, the Pope. There are some today who reject almost all authority everywhere, religious or secular. They fail to understand the Divine nature of the Church—and that Christ speaks as clearly today as He did when He was on earth. They fail to understand that there are *two* sources of Divine Revelation: Sacred Tradition and Sacred Scripture. It was Saint John the Evangelist who said, "There are many other things that Jesus did, but if these were to be described individually, I do not think the whole world would contain the books that would be written" (Jn. 21:25).

Indeed, there was not even *one* book of the New Testament for at *least* thirteen years after our Lord's Resurrection and Ascension into Heaven. The Gospels did not appear until the year 60 A.D., at the earliest. How was the Word of God transmitted? Orally. Christ taught the Apostles—each of whom was personally endowed with the gift of infallibility—for forty days and forty nights before He Ascended to the Father in Heaven. Not one word of that is written down anywhere. We call this the *Deposit of Faith.* This deposit is protected by the Third Person of the Blessed Trinity, the Holy Spirit. If it was possible for the Second Person of the Blessed Trinity to become man in the womb of a virgin, if it was possible for Christ to rise from the dead, then it is indeed eminently possible and quite necessary for the Holy Spirit to protect the teaching of Christ from all error.

The Holy Spirit cannot contradict Himself. It is a philosophical absurdity to assert that God can teach one thing yesterday and another thing tomorrow. Yet that is precisely what those who favor women's ordination assert. These people fail to understand that our Lord Himself, Who broke every Pharisaical tradition (something that was brought up in His "trial" before the Sanhedrin in the early morning hours of Good Friday), instituted a male priesthood. He was the God-Man. He knew all things. He was not culture-bound. Indeed, when He suffered His agony in the Garden of Gethsemane and said, "Father, if it is possible, take this cup away from me," our Lord feared not death—but the knowledge that He, the God-Man, would have to come into physical contact with the very antithesis of His Divinity: sin. He knew full well what was ahead of Him.

Yes, the devil is very active. He wants to stir up dissent. But we know that Christ's victory on the Holy Cross has destroyed the power of the devil. We have nothing to fear from him. He has no power over us *unless we* find his appeals attractive. It is the sad reality that a society which has forgotten God has provided our adversary with fertile soil for planting the seeds of doubt and confusion within human hearts.

The confusion which we see within our society—and within our Church—is nothing new. Consider Saint Paul's letter to the Romans (written around 65 A.D.):

> Therefore, God has handed them over to impurity through the lusts of their hearts for the mutual degradation of their bodies. They exchanged the truth of God for a lie and revered and worshiped the creature rather than the Creator, who is blessed forever. Amen. Therefore, God handed them over to degrading passions. Their females exchanged natural relations for unnatural, and the males likewise gave up natural relations with females and burned with lust for one another. Males did shameful things with males and thus received in *their own persons the due penalty for their perversity*. And since they did not see fit to acknowledge God, God handed them over to their undiscerning mind to do what is improper. They are filled with every form of wickedness, evil, greed, malice; full of envy, murder, rivalry, treachery, and spite. They are gossips and scandalmongers and they hate God. They are insolent, haughty, boastful, and rebellious toward their parents. They are senseless, faithless, heartless, ruthless. Although they know the just decree of God that all who practice such things deserve death, they not only do them but give approval to those who practice them (Rom. 1:24–32).

What could be a more apt description of our own times. Can anyone, in all candor, *not* see the parallel here? Do we not remember what happened to *that* advanced civilization? Think about it.

The situation in our Church today was prophesied long ago by Saints Peter and Paul. We have been through periods like this before, of course. Indeed, ignorance of our spiritual history is one

reason why we are living through this period of ecclesiastical tur-
bulence at present. But pray over the words which follow:

> There were also false teachers among the people, just as there
> will be false teachers among you, who will introduce destruc-
> tive heresies and even deny the Master who ransomed them,
> bringing swift destruction on themselves. Many will follow
> their licentious ways, and because of them the way of truth will
> be reviled. In their greed they will exploit you with fabrica-
> tions, but from of old their condemnation has not been idle and
> their destruction does not sleep (2 Pt. 2:1–3).

> But these people, like irrational animals born by nature for cap-
> ture and destruction, revile things that they do not understand,
> and in their destruction they will also be destroyed, suffering
> wrong as payment for wrongdoing. Thinking daytime revelry a
> delight, they are stains and defilements as they revel in their
> deceits while carousing with you. Their eyes are full of adul-
> tery and insatiable for sin. They seduce unstable people, and
> their hearts are trained in greed. . . . For, talking empty bom-
> bast, they seduce with licentious desires of the flesh those who
> have barely escaped from people who live in error. They
> promise them freedom, though they themselves are slaves of
> corruption, for a person is a slave of whatever overcomes him.
> For if they, having escaped the defilements of the world
> through the knowledge of [our] Lord and savior Jesus Christ,
> again become entangled and overcome by them, their last con-
> dition is worst than their first. . . (2 Pt. 2:12–14; 18–20).

Saint Paul is equally explicit in his letters to Saint Timothy:

> We know that the law is good, provided that one uses it as law,
> with the understanding that the law is not meant for a righteous
> person but for the lawless and unruly, the godless and sinful,
> the unholy and profane, those who kill their fathers or mothers,
> murderers, the unchaste, practicing homosexuals, kidnapers,
> liars, perjurers, and whatever else is opposed to sound teaching,
> according to the glorious gospel of the blessed God, with which
> I have been entrusted (1 Tm. 1:8–11).

> Whoever teaches something different and does not agree with
> the sound works of our Lord Jesus Christ and the religious
> teaching is conceited, understanding nothing, and has a morbid
> disposition for arguments and verbal disputes. From these
> come envy, rivalry, insults, evil suspicions, and mutual friction
> among people with corrupted minds, who are deprived of the

truth, supposing religion to be a means of gain. Indeed, religion with contentment is a great gain. For we brought nothing into the world, just as we shall not be able to take anything out of it. If we have food and clothing, we shall be content with that. Those who want to be rich are falling into temptation and into a trap and into many foolish and harmful desires, which plunge them into ruin and destruction. For the love of money is the root of all evils, and some people in their desire for it have strayed from the faith and have pierced themselves with many pains (1 Tm. 6:1–10).

For the time will come when people will not tolerate sound doctrine but, following *their own desires and insatiable curiosity*, will accumulate teachers and will stop listening to the truth and will be diverted to myth (2 Tm. 4:3–5).

TRUTH AND REASON

The Catholic Church stands in the world as the Sign of Contradiction. If Christ is the Way, the Truth and the Life then it stands to *reason* that it is *impossible* for there to be alternate truths—or alternate *interpretations* of the Truth. If something is true it is impossible for an opposite statement to be true. It is not logical to think that God wants people to believe that all religious ideas have equal value. That would have made His work on earth entirely useless. Human beings have an equality of value because of the Redemption; but that does not mean that the ideas humans hold have equal value. There are true ideas and there are false ideas. In our egalitarian, democratic society we have deluded ourselves into thinking that one idea is as good as another. One religion is as good as another. But those are specious concepts. They defy logic—and they defy an understanding of Who God is.

Guided infallibly in matters of faith and morals by the Holy Spirit, the Bride of Christ wants all people to know the beauty and the wonder of all aspects of human life. Our Lord wants all of us—for whom He gave up His life—to see with the eyes of faith. He wants us to recognize a lie for a lie—and to recognize the prophetic voice of His Vicar on earth, the Holy Father. He wants all six billion people on this planet to receive His Body, Blood, Soul, and Divinity. He wants us to be the light of the world and the salt of the earth.

As our Holy Father noted to the American bishops in 1987:

It is sometimes reported that a large number of Catholics today

51

do not adhere to the teaching of the Church on a number of questions, notably sexual and conjugal morality, divorce and remarriage. Some are reported as not accepting the Church's clear position on abortion. It has also been noted that there is a tendency on the part of some Catholics to be selective in adherence to the Church's moral teaching. It is sometimes claimed that dissent from the magisterium is totally compatible with being a "good Catholic" and poses no obstacle to the reception of the Sacraments. *This is a grave error that challenges the teaching office of the Bishops of the United States and elsewhere.* . . . I wish to encourage you in the love of Christ to address this situation courageously in your pastoral ministry, relying on the power of God's truth to attract assent through the grace of the Holy Spirit, which is given both to those who proclaim the message and to those to whom it is addressed.

We must also constantly recall that the teaching of Christ's Church—like Christ Himself—is a "Sign of Contradiction." It has never been easy to accept the Gospel teaching in its entirety, and it never will be.

HUMANAE VITAE

If we begin to see with the eyes of faith, we can recognize the wisdom in what the Church offers to humanity as the *unchanging* truth of the natural law concerning sexuality—which, of course, is the most explosive issue among Catholics today. Pope Paul VI's encyclical letter *Humanae Vitae* is sneeringly dismissed by many even within the Church. But how many have taken the time to read the passages which follow, which sadly predicted the miserable state we are witnessing today:

> Responsible men can become more deeply convinced of the truth of the doctrine [against contraception] laid down by the Church on this issue if they reflect on the consequences of methods and plans for the artificial restriction of increase in the birth-rate. Let them first consider how easily this course of action can lead to the way being wide open to marital infidelity and a general lowering of moral standards. Not much experience is needed to be fully aware of human weakness and to understand that men—and especially the young, who are so exposed to temptation—need incentives to keep the moral law, and it is an evil thing to make it easy for them to break that law. Another effect that gives cause for alarm is that a man who

grows accustomed to the use of contraceptive methods may forget the reverence due to a woman, and, disregarding her physical and emotional equilibrium, reduce her to being a mere instrument for the satisfaction of his own desires, no longer considering her as his partner whom he should surround with care and affection.

Finally, grave consideration should be given to the danger of this power passing into the hands of those public authorities who care little for the precepts of the moral law. Who will blame a Government which in its attempt to resolve the problems affecting an entire country resorts to the same methods as are regarded lawful by married people in the solution of a particular family difficulty? Who will prevent public authorities from favoring those contraceptive methods which they consider more effective? Should they regard this as necessary, they may even impose their use on everyone. It could well happen, therefore, that when people, either individually or in family or social life, experience the inherent difficulties of the divine law and are determined to avoid them, they may be giving into the hands of public authorities the power to intervene in the most personal and intimate responsibility of husband and wife.

Consequently, unless we are willing that the responsibility of procreating life should be left to the arbitrary decision of men, we must accept that there are certain limits, beyond which it is wrong to go, to the power of man over his own body, and its natural functions—limits, let it be said, which no one, whether as a private individual or as a public authority, can lawfully exceed. These limits are expressly imposed because of the reverence due to the whole human organism and its natural function, in light of the principles, which we stated earlier, and according to a correct understanding of the so-called "principle of totality," enunciated by Our Predecessor, Pope Pius XII.

Have not Pope Paul's words proven to be very prophetic? Look what happens when just *one* teaching of the Church is denied: personal and societal disorder. Look at the wisdom of Wisdom Himself as taught by His Church.

OUR PLACE IN THE CHURCH

We need to take a step back from the polemics to remember that we are sheep. Those who are called to be catechists must follow the voice of the Chief Shepherd, Jesus Christ. We teach not with our own voice, but with that of our Master. As Pope John Paul II noted in a 1979 Apostolic Exhortation entitled *Catechesi Tradendae*:

> Christocentricity in catechesis also means the intention to transmit not one's own teaching or that of some other master, but the teaching of Jesus Christ, the Truth that he communicates, or, to put it more precisely, the Truth that he is. We must therefore say that in catechesis it is Christ, the Incarnate Word and Son of God, who is taught—everything else is taught with reference to him—and it is Christ alone who teaches—anyone else teaches to the extent that he is Christ's spokesman, enabling Christ to teach with his lips. Whatever be the level of his responsibility in the Church, every catechist must constantly endeavor to transmit by his teaching and behavior the teaching and life of Jesus. He will not seek to keep directed towards himself and his personal opinions and attitudes the attention and the consent of the mind and heart of the person he is catechizing. Above all, he will not try to inculcate his personal opinions and options as if they expressed Christ's teaching and the lessons of his life. Every catechist should be able to apply to himself the mysterious words of Jesus: "My teaching is not mine, but his who sent me." Saint Paul did this when he was dealing with a question of prime importance: "I received from the Lord what I also delivered to you." What assiduous study of the word of God transmitted by the Church's Magisterium, what profound familiarity with Christ and with the Father, what a spirit of prayer, what detachment from self must a catechist have in order that he can say: "My teaching is not mine!"

TO CHOOSE HEAVEN

Our Lord wants everyone to participate in the Triumph of the Holy Cross. He wants everyone to pass through the Gates of Heaven. However, people must *choose* to go to Heaven. They must awaken from the dark night of relativism which shrouds this country in order to see the bright love of God's boundless forgiveness. They must want to be cured of the disease of prideful spiritual blindness.

Pope John Paul II reminded us in *Reconciliatio et Paenitentia*, an apostolic exhortation issued in 1984, that the world's problems are the direct result of sinful choices. This is an unchanging reality of the human condition.

Whenever the Church speaks of *situations* of sin, or when she condemns as *social* sins certain situations or the collective behavior of certain social groups, big or small, she knows and she proclaims that such cases of *social sin* are the result of the accumulation and concentration of many *personal sins*. It is a case of the *very personal sins of those who cause or support evil or who exploit it*; of those who *are in a position to avoid, eliminate or at least limit certain social evils* but who fail to do so out of laziness, fear or the conspiracy of silence, through secret complicity or indifference; *of those who take refuge in the supposed impossibility of changing the world*, and also of those who sidestep the effort and sacrifice required, *producing specious reasons of a higher order*. The real responsibility rests with individuals.

Our Lady made possible the salvation of the human race by her humble obedience to the will of the Father. May we, the children entrusted to her care at the foot of the Cross by her Divine Son, fly to her tender patronage that *we* might be open to doing the will of the Father: to saying "Yes" to Christ and His Church. That will not solve all of the problems of the world. But it will give us the means to understand who we are, why problems exist—and how we can make a contribution to our fellow human beings by becoming faithful disciples of the Sign of Contradiction and His Holy Church.

CHAPTER FOUR

For Love of God and Love of Country

Knowing that the final victory belongs to our Lord, however, does not absolve us of our responsibility to pray and to work for the triumph of His social kingship over men and their societies right here and now. Although some would like to contend that we are in the "springtime of the Church" at the end of her second millennium, it is not to be a negativist to recognize the stark reality of our situation today. Our culture has rotted out as the all too natural consequence of the belief that it is possible for contingent beings whose bodies are destined for the corruption of the grave to govern themselves without reference to the true faith. And the decay of our culture has been expedited by the theological and liturgical revolutionaries within the Church herself, those "enlightened" ones who believe that the Deposit of Faith and the Church's entire living tradition must be wiped out in order to create a synthetic faith that corresponds to the beliefs of individualism, relativism, legal positivism, religious indifferentism, democracy, liberalism, socialism, communism, statism, redistributionism, materialism, egalitarianism, feminism, environmentalism, and nihilism. If you don't believe in Catholicism, folks, you're going to believe in one of the secular 'isms.

What we are witnessing is nothing other than a convergence of forces which threaten the very survival of Western civilization. As was explained in the previous chapter, all of the problems of the world are the consequence of original and actual sin. To a greater or a lesser extent, each of us contributes to the foul miasma of sin which tears apart the Mystical Body of Christ. But it is one thing to sin and to be sorry, to seek out the Divine Mercy in the Sacrament of Penance—and to offer that mercy freely to others who sin against us. It is quite another to *persist* in unrepented sin, to risk the fires of Hell by the *promotion* and *glorification* of sin as part of our law, our culture, our politics, our government, our education, our entertainment, indeed, of our own conversation and way of acting.

NO RIGHT TO SIN

The world in which we live at present is one that *glorifies* objectively sinful behavior. It seeks to codify such behavior in civil law as some kind of constitutional right, as we have seen so very clearly with divorce, contraception, and abortion. And it seeks to silence believing Catholics by the invocation of slogans, just as the Sophists of the Fifth Century before Christ did to those who *dared* to criticize *their* embrace of relativism and individualism and positivism and majoritarianism. We are told that it is not the American way to assert that one religion is better than another. One has to be sensitive to the demands of a pluralistic and multicultural society. It is not possible to "impose" morality upon others. You simply cannot use the Divine positive or the natural law as the basis of judicial decisions. To do so, obviously, would be to violate the American spirit of constitutionalism and majority rule.

All of this sloganeering has confused even a lot of believing Catholics in this nation. A lot of Catholics are confused about the relationship between their faith and public policy. A lot of Catholics are still trying to reconcile the irreconcilable: the founding of this *secular* republic—which is based upon the Masonic principle of religious indifferentism—with the true faith. Such an exercise has been—and will continue to prove to be—futile. For one cannot make an idol out of a secular government while at the same time seeking to serve our Lord and His Holy Church. It is not possible to both serve our Lord and at the same time refrain from using His Sacred Name as the basis for the just society.

TRUE LOVE

However, we either love our Lord or we do not. And we prove our love for Him by how we live. Authentic love is not an empty-headed sentiment. It is an act of the will. True love wills the good of another, the ultimate expression of which is the salvation of his immortal soul. No one loves another authentically who does or says anything, either by omission or commission, which impedes the salvation of that person's immortal soul.

Parents and Godparents have the obligation to correct their children and Godchildren. Not to do so could send those parents and Godparents to Hell for all eternity. And in like manner, a baptized and confirmed Catholic has the obligation—out of an authentic love for country, the *patria* written about by Saint Thomas Aquinas—to seek the good of one's country. And the ultimate good of any nation is to reflect in its laws and its culture the transcendent glory of Christ the King.

How is it possible to say that we love our Lord while we promote as a matter of public policy the very thing that caused Him to suffer in His Sacred Humanity on the wood of the Holy Cross, sin? Which one of us would vote for a candidate who said that he supported the execution of our parents or children or spouses or friends? Yet a large percentage of Catholics in this nation vote for candidates of *both* political parties who either support sex instruction, contraception, sodomy, and abortion—or who are indifferent about these evils. Our salvation is not in any political party or political candidate; it is found only in the Holy Roman Catholic Church. And it is time that Catholics in this nation, including those who say they are orthodox Catholics, stop being ashamed of Christ and His doctrine before men. It is time for everyone to proclaim from the rooftops that He is King and His Blessed Mother is Queen. Enough of trying to accommodate ourselves to an evil society which has not only not made any room for Him, but has made war against Him and His Holy Church.

THE APOSTOLIC ERA

It is during the Easter season every year that all of the Acts of the Apostles is read at the Holy Sacrifice of the Mass, the unbloody re-presentation of the Son's Sacrifice to the Father in Spirit and in Truth. The Acts of the Apostles records the unstinting zeal of the Apostles as they confronted all of the established religious and temporal authorities of the day. They did not fear to proclaim the Name of our Lord. They knew that they had been given a mandate to remake all things in Christ. And they rejoiced when they were deemed worthy of ill treatment for the sake of the Name. They trusted entirely in the power of the graces won for us on the wood of the Holy Cross by our Divine Redeemer. They did not engage in political strategies, and they did not compromise one little bit in their proclamation of the truth. Our Lord did not give them an "exceptions" clause to exempt them from speaking the truth plainly at all times.

Our Lord meant it when He told the Apostles to go out into the whole world, baptizing all men in the Name of the Father, and of the Son, and of the Holy Spirit. This is precisely what they did. All of them, save for Saint John the Evangelist, the one who stood valiantly by our Lady at the foot of the Holy Cross, died a martyr's death. Thousands of others did so as well, willing to risk even their very lives rather than worship the Roman Emperor as a god, rather than deny their belief in the Crucified and Risen Savior. Indeed, thousands marched happily to their deaths in amphitheaters and circuses and colossea throughout the Roman Empire off and on during the first three centuries of the Church. And over the course of time, you see, the Rome of the Caesars collapsed; the Rome of Peter, the Rome of Christ, arose. It stands to this very day—and it will stand until the end of time.

EVANGELIZATION

During the first millennium, missionaries went out to the far corners of the world. Barbaric peoples were confronted by the Cross of Christ. What was good in those barbaric cultures was baptized, so to speak. What was opposed to the Divine positive and natural law, such as human sacrifice and polygamy, was eradicated. An entire culture arose in Europe based around the faith. Yes, Christendom emerged. There was a time in human history when faith and culture were one and the same. Most of the foundation of Western civilization, which is under such fierce attack from the forces I listed above, emanates from the Church founded by our Lord upon the Rock of Peter, the Pope.

The fact that faith and culture were one and the same did not mean that the world was free from problems. Human nature is irreparably wounded by original sin. We have darkened intellects and weakened wills. Those intellects can be enlightened and those wills can be strengthened by supernatural grace. But every sin we commit darkens our intellect and weakens the will all the more, which is why we must recover by penance what we have lost by sin. No, there was no utopia in Christendom. There were wars and conflicts—and even corruption in the Church. Our ancient Adversary, who prowls about the world seeking the ruin of souls, seeks to discourage people from believing in the faith by the bad example of others, especially that provided by the clergy. But what distinguished Christendom from our own tragic era is that the people of the Middle Ages understood they were sinners! They knew they were in need of sacramental forgiveness for their sins in the confessional. They knew the problems of the world were caused by *them*—and that the only solution to the problems of the world was the daily conversion of self to the Cross of Christ effected by their cooperation with the graces won for us on Calvary.

SHATTERED UNITY

The unity of Christendom, however, was shattered by the lie of the Protestant Revolt. Just as man had rebelled against God in the Garden of Eden, so was it the case in the Sixteenth Century that disciples of Christ rebelled against His Mystical Body, believing that they could redefine His sacred truths to their own choosing, an utterly absurd proposition. You see, our Lord proclaimed Himself to be *the* Way, *the* Truth, and *the* Life. How is it possible for there to be multiple interpretations of truth? What Martin Luther unwittingly did was to unloose the forces which would produce the likes of Lenin and Hitler and Stalin and Mao and Bill and Hillary Clinton. For all of those petty tyrants believe in the absurd proposition of the Protestant Revolt: that nothing is absolutely true. And they have believed that nothing is absolutely true absolutely, proving the falsity and absurdity of that which they believe.

The Protestant Revolt promoted individualism and egalitarianism. It was a rejection of the hierarchical nature of the Church founded by the One who had submitted Himself in *humility* to the authority of His Blessed Mother and His foster father Saint Joseph in Nazareth. The Revolt came at a time when secularists and naturalists were promoting their own version of individualism and egalitarianism. The marriage of the theological relativists with the naturalists of the Age of the Enlightenment is what led directly to the political culture created by English settlers on these shores in the early 1600s: a culture that was—and remains—

committed to unbridled individualism, a rejection of hierarchical relationships (something that would be promoted in starker terms later on by the French and Bolshevik Revolutions), and the promotion of materialism as a sign of divine election.

CONVERTING THE NATIVES

The culture of the English colonies in what would later become the United States of America was in distinct contrast with the culture of *Catholic* America. The French and the Spanish and the Portuguese always sent *priests* to evangelize the native peoples, to expose them to the same Cross of Christ that had been introduced to the barbaric peoples of Europe a millennium before. A distinctly *Catholic* culture emerged, one that was reflected in the names of places (Saint Augustine, Santa Monica, Los Angeles, San Francisco, San Antonio, Corpus Christi, Santa Barbara, San Diego, Las Cruces, Santa Fe)—and in a way of life where *holy days* were celebrated with solemnity. In a truly *Catholic* culture, the faith comes first, not the bread and circuses that are treated in a sacred manner by *our* culture today.

Alas, the Catholics who made their way to these shores did not seek to Catholicize the former English colonies. No, they were content to go about their business of being accepted by the Protestant majority, of *proving* that they did not pose a threat to the American experiment in republican self-rule. What happened in this country was unique in the history of the Church up to that point. For the arrival of Catholics, right on from the Seventeenth through the early Twentieth Centuries, on these shores was the first time that Catholics did not seek to convert the land in which they lived to the true faith. Because Catholics did not evangelize this Protestant and Masonic land, you see, *they* were evangelized by the gospel of democracy, pluralism, and indifferentism. And that includes many, although certainly not all, of the bishops of the Nineteenth Century. Politics became the means of upward social mobility for Catholics. And, after all, is living out the American dream supposed to involve improving one's economic lot above and beyond all other considerations?

Pope Leo XIII commented on the way the naturalists and Freemasons were attempting to make politics the means of secular salvation, both in the United States and in Europe, in his encyclical letter *Humanum Genus*, issued in 1883:

> Then come their doctrines of politics, in which the Naturalists lay down that all men have the same right, and are in every respect of equal and like condition; that each one is naturally free; that no one has the right to command another; that it is an act of violence to require men to obey any authority other than that which is obtained from themselves. According to this, therefore, all things belong to the free people; power is held by the command or the permission of the people, so that, when the popular will changes, rulers may lawfully be deposed; and the source of all rights and civil duties is either in the multitude or in the governing authority when this is constituted according to the latest doctrines. It is held also that the State should be without God; that in the various forms of religion there is not reason why one should have precedence over another; and that they are all to occupy the same place. . . . Now, from these disturbing errors which We have described the greatest dangers to States are to be feared. For, the fear of God and reverence for divine laws being taken away, the authority of rulers despised, sedition permitted and approved, and the popular passions urged on to lawlessness, with no restraint save that of punishment, a change and overthrow of all things will necessarily follow.

Hasn't this happened? Hasn't this all happened?

AMERICANISM

Indeed, Pope Leo XIII recognized how the Catholic immigrants from Europe were being co-oped by the lie of Americanism. He wrote an apostolic letter, *Testem Benevolentiae*, to warn the bishops of the United States that they were not discharging their apostolic duties to teach the faith in all of its integrity. They were compromising the faith, with some of them, most notably Archbishop John Ireland of Saint Paul and Minneapolis, actually encouraging parents to send their children to the Masonic public schools as a means of educating them in democracy and egalitarianism! Listen to Pope Leo's prophetic words:

> The principles on which the new opinions We have mentioned are based may be reduced to this: that, in order the more easily to bring over to Catholic doctrine those who dissent from it, the

Church ought to adapt herself somewhat to our advanced civilization, and, relaxing her ancient rigor, show some indulgence to modern popular theories and methods. Many think that this is to be understood not only with regard to the rule of life, but also to the doctrines in which the *deposit of faith* are contained. For they contend that it is opportune, in order to work in a more attractive way upon the wills of those who are not in accord with us, to pass over certain heads of doctrines, as if of lesser moment, or to so soften them that they may not have the same meaning which the Church has invariably held. Now, Beloved Son, few words are needed to show how reprehensible is the plan that is thus conceived, if we but consider the character and the origin of the doctrine which the Church hands down to us. On that point the Vatican Council says: "The doctrine of faith which God has revealed is not proposed like a theory of philosophy which is to be elaborated by the human understanding, but as a divine deposit delivered to the Spouse of Christ to be faithfully guarded and infallibly declared. . . . That sense of the sacred dogmas is to be faithfully kept which Holy Mother Church has once declared, and is not to be departed from under the specious pretext of a more profound understanding."

A contemporary application of this firm rebuke to the American bishops means that you cannot be pro-life without openly opposing and working against all contraception. You cannot be pro-life without openly opposing and working against all abortions in all circumstances, no exceptions whatsoever. You cannot be pro-life without opposing all forms of sex instruction, including the so-called chastity education programs, which are nothing more than warmed over versions of the evils introduced into our mist by Planned Parenthood and SIECUS, evils specifically condemned by Pope Pius XI in *Divini Illius Magistri* in 1929. In a sentence, you cannot be pro-life unless you subscribe to everything the Church proposes as true—and unless you are willing to *proclaim* everything the Church proposes as true. It is the will of the Divine Redeemer that everyone be Catholic, the laws and culture of every nation be subordinated to Him and His Holy Church. Who are we in the United States at the end of the second millennium to think we are absolved of the sacred responsibility to so subordinate *our* laws and *our* culture?

AN AMERICAN CHURCH?

Pope Leo XIII knew that some of the bishops of the United States 99 years ago were attempting to remake the faith, something that has been done with astonishing speed in the last 35 years since the close of the Second Vatican Council. He addressed himself to this concern at the end of *Testem Benevolentiae*:

> But if [Americanism] is to be used not only to signify, but even to commend the above doctrines, there can be no doubt but that our Venerable Brethren the bishops of America would be the first to repudiate and condemn it, as being especially unjust to them and to the entire nation as well. *For it raises the suspicion that there are some among you who conceive of and desire a church in America different from that which is in the rest of the world. One in the unity of doctrine as in the unity of government, such is the Catholic Church, and since, God has established its centre and foundation in the Chair of Peter, one which is rightly called Roman, for where Peter is there is the Church.* Wherefore he who wishes to be called by the name of Catholic ought to employ in truth the words of Jerome to Pope Damasus, "I following none as the first except Christ am associated in communion with your Beatitude, that is, with the Chair of Peter; upon that Rock I know is built the Church; whoever gathereth not with thee scattereth."

As we know all too tragically, the reality of our own times is that many of the bishops of the United States do not gather with the Vicar of Christ; they scatter. Again, it is not to be negativist to point out the simple reality of our situation. We know that the Church is going to last until the end of time. We know that the jaws of Hell will not prevail against her. Sure. Granted. However, our Lord does not want us to sit on the sidelines while souls are being driven into Hell because of doctrinal heresy and liturgical irreverence. The late Archbishop Fulton Sheen talked much about the fact that the laity has always been the salvation of the Church in times of ecclesiastical crisis. Well, behold a time of almost unparalleled ecclesiastical crisis. There will be no improvement in our temporal situation, you see, unless bishops teach the faith in all of its undiluted purity—and until they exercise their governing authority to firmly and publicly excommunicate every Catholic in public life who supports and promotes contraception, sodomy, and abortion. Without compromise and without delay.

CONFUSING THE SACRED WITH THE PROFANE

There is an old saying: the state of the world depends upon the state of the Church. That is, confusion and disarray in the Church leads to souls being in states of sin and/or states of error. Individual souls which are at war with God by means of unrepented sin become instruments of injustice in their own lives—and in the life of society. And if our liturgy does not reflect and communicate the fullness of the splendor of Truth Incarnate, Truth Crucified and Resurrected, then people are going to profanize the sacred and sacralize the profane. Yes, we must face with manly Christian courage the simple truth that although there have been forces at work in the world to undermine the faith for over four centuries now, those forces have been aided and abetted by kindred spirits within the Church herself, especially within the hierarchy of the United States.

We have witnessed an incredible spectacle in this country: the American bishops have become closely allied with almost all of the statist and redistributionist policies of the Federal government of the past 65 years. They have abandoned the principle of subsidiarity enunciated so clearly by Pope Pius XI in *Quadregesimo Anno*. They have looked—and they continue to look—to government programs as the solutions to the problems caused by the systematic destruction of the family engineered by the social engineers who started to populate the bureaucracy of the Federal government as early as the administration of President Woodrow Wilson. Rather than teach the simple truth that all social problems are ultimately the consequence of personal sins, the bishops have embraced the false notion that it is the inequitable distribution of wealth and goods that produces society's problems, a thoroughly Marxist proposition. They have sought "liberation" in the forces of this world, creating an ecclesiastical apparatus that is an eerie parallel of our bloated Federal government. Bishops have been reduced to the role of functionaries, serving the whims of their ecclesiastical bureaucrats, just as elected officials, especially at the state and local levels, are pretty much at the mercy of non-appointed Federal bureaucrats.

RECENT CHANGES

This reliance of the American bishops upon our statist government paved the way for many of them to try to redefine the faith in the wake of the close of the Second Vatican Council. What was old, including the liturgy and the *Baltimore Catechism*, had to be discarded. Even older priests, those who refused to be "re-educated," had to be put out to pasture or stigmatized with some sort of psychological disorder. And many younger men applying for priestly study were turned down precisely because they were deemed to be pre-conciliar, that is, because they were authentically Catholic, men who knew the faith and had a deep interior life of prayer.

The synthetic religion created by these bishops and liturgists and Scripture scholars and pastoral ministers, *et al.*, was *not* intended to create a Catholic culture. Quite the contrary. It promoted indifferentism. It sought to reaffirm people in their sins; after all, we're only human, right? It sought to take the Cross out of Christianity. This new religion sought an accommodation with the world, eager to accept the privatization of religion, eager to embrace Catholics in public life who work against the unchanging truths of the Divine positive law and the natural law. This new religion sought to marginalize as irrelevant fanatics anyone who refers to the older encyclical letters which emphasize the primacy of the social reign of our Lord.

Consider the wisdom of Pope Pius XI. As had Pope Leo XIII before him, Pope Pius XI knew that there were people in the Church who were seeking to replace the faith with secular political ideologies. He wrote in *Urbi Arcano* in 1925:

> In view of this organized common effort towards peaceful living, Catholic doctrine vindicates to the State the dignity and authority of a vigilant and provident defender of those divine and human rights on which the Sacred Scriptures and the Fathers of the Church insist so often. It is not true that all have equal rights in civil society. It is not true that there exists no lawful social hierarchy. Let it suffice to refer to the Encyclicals of Leo XIII, already cited, especially to that on State power, and to the other on the Christian Constitution of States. In these documents the Catholic will find the principles of reason and the Faith clearly explained and these principles will enable him to defend himself against the errors and perils of a communis-

tic conception of the State. The enslavement of man despoiled
of his rights, the denial of the transcendental origin of the State
and its authority, the horrible abuse of public power in the service of a collective terrorism, are the very contrary of all that
corresponds with natural ethics and the will of the Creator.
Both man and civil society derive their origin from the Creator,
Who has mutually ordained them one to other. Hence neither
can be exempted from their correlative obligations, nor deny or
diminish each other's rights. The Creator Himself has regulated
this mutual relationship in its fundamental lines, and it is by an
unjust usurpation that communism arrogates to itself the right
to enforce, in place of the divine law based on the immutable
principles of truth and charity, a partisan political program
which derives from the arbitrary human will and is replete with
hate.

Pope Pius XI's words have great currency as they relate to the
contemporary state of politics in the United States, where most
people, including most baptized and confirmed Catholics, have
no understanding that the State is meant to be subordinate to the
Divine and natural laws. Indeed, as Pius XI pointed out in
Quadregesimo Anno in 1931, the belief in the ability of the State
to resolve all human problems, the nexus between liberalism and
communism, is a violation of the principle of subsidiarity, which
insists that problems be resolved in the units closest to the individuals involved, starting with the family. The wholesale usurpation of the responsibilities proper to the family, for example, has
been the cause of much of the breakdown of family life, not to
mention the cause of dependency upon government programs.

Pius XI also noted in *Divini Redemptoris*:

In teaching this enlightening doctrine, the Church has no other
intention than to realize the glad tidings sung by the Angels
above the cave of Bethlehem at the Redeemer's birth: "Glory
to God . . . and . . . peace to men . . ." true peace and true happiness, even here below as far as it is possible, in preparation
for the happiness of heaven—but to men of good will. This
doctrine is equally removed from all extremes of error and all
exaggerations of parties or systems which stem from error. It
maintains a constant equilibrium of truth and justice, which it
vindicates in theory and applies and promotes in practice,
bringing into harmony the rights and duties of all parties. Thus
authority is reconciled with liberty, the dignity of the individ-

ual with that of the State, the human personality of the subject with the divine delegation of the superior; and in this way a balance is struck between the due dependence and well-ordered love of a man for himself, his family and country, and his love of other families and other peoples, founded on the love of God, the Father of all, their first principle and last end. The Church does not separate a proper regard for temporal welfare from solicitude for the eternal. If she subordinates the former to the latter according to the words of her divine Founder, "Seek ye first the Kingdom of God and His justice, and all these things shall be added unto you," she is nevertheless so far from being unconcerned with human affairs, so far from hindering civil progress and material advancement, that she actually fosters and promotes them even in the most sensible and efficacious manner. Thus even in the sphere of social-economics, although the Church has never proposed a definite technical system, since this is not her field, she had nevertheless clearly outlined the guiding principles which, while susceptible of varied concrete applications according to the diversified conditions of times and places and peoples, indicate the safe way of securing the happy progress of society.

The Church finds herself today in a situation that is the direct result of the rejection of her divinely-instituted authority to direct the civil affairs of men and their societies as it relates to the fundamental principles of human dignity. As *Donum Vitae* pointed out in 1987:

The inalienable rights of the person must be recognized and respected by civil society and the political authority. These human rights depend neither on single individuals nor on parents; nor do they represent a concession made by society and the state; they belong to human nature and are inherent in the person by virtue of the creative act from which the person took his origin. Among such fundamental rights one should mention in this regard every human being's right to life and physical integrity from the moment of conception until death.

The moment a positive law deprives a category of human beings of the protection which civil legislation ought to afford them, the state is denying the equality of all before the law. When the state does not place its power at the service of the rights of each citizen, and in particular of the more vulnerable, the very foundations of a state based on law are undermined. . . . As a consequence of the respect and protection which must be ensured for the unborn child from the moment of conception, the law must provide appropriate sanctions for every deliberate violation of the child's rights.

Pope John Paul wrote about this most emphatically in *Evangelium Vitae*, issued in 1995:

> There is an even more profound aspect which needs to be emphasized: freedom negates and destroys itself, and becomes a factor leading to the destruction of others, when it no longer recognizes and respects *its essential link with the truth*. When freedom, out of a desire to emancipate itself from all forms of tradition and authority, shuts out even the most obvious evidence of an objective and universal truth, which is the foundation of personal and social life, then the person ends up by no longer taking as the sole and indisputable point of reference for his own choices the truth about good and evil, but only his subjective and changeable opinion or, indeed, his selfish interest and whim (*Evangelium Vitae*, No. 19).

This view of freedom *leads to a serious distortion of life in society*. If the promotion of the self is understood in terms of absolute autonomy, people inevitably reach the point of rejecting one another. Everyone else is considered an enemy from whom one has to defend oneself. Thus society becomes a mass of individuals placed side by side, but without any mutual bonds. Each one wishes to assert himself independently of the other and in fact intends to make his own interests prevail. Still, in the face of other people's analogous interests, some kind of compromise is found, if one wants a society in which the maximum possible freedom is guaranteed to each individual. In this way, any reference to common values and to a truth absolutely binding on everyone is lost, and social life ventures on the shifting sands of complete relativism. At that point, *everything is negotiable, everything is open to bargaining*: even the first of the fundamental rights, the right to life.

This is what is happening also at the level of politics and government: the original and inalienable right to life is questioned or denied on the basis of a parliamentary vote or the will of one part of the people—even if it is the majority. This is the sinister result of a relativism which reigns unopposed: the "right" ceases to be such, because it is no longer firmly founded on the inviolable dignity of the person, but is made subject to the will of the stronger part. In this way democracy, contradicting its own principles, effectively moves towards a form of totalitarianism. The State is no longer the "common home" where all can live together on the basis of principles of fundamental equality, but is transformed into a *tyrant State*, which arrogates to itself the right to dispose of the life of the weakest and most defenseless members, from the unborn child to the elderly, in the name of a public interest which is really nothing but the interest of one part. The appearance of the strictest respect for legality is maintained, at least when the laws permitting abortion and euthanasia are the result of a ballot in accordance with what are generally seen as the rules of democracy. Really, what we have here is only the tragic caricature off legality; the democratic ideal, which is only truly such when it acknowledges and safeguards the dignity of every human person, *is betrayed in its very foundations*: "How is it still possible to speak of the dignity of every human person when the killing of the weakest and most innocent is permitted? In the name of what justice is the most unjust of discriminations practiced: some individuals are held to be deserving of defense and others are denied that dignity?" When this happens, the process leading to the breakdown of a genuinely human co-existence and the disintegration of the State itself has already begun.

To claim the right to abortion, infanticide and euthanasia, and to recognize that right in law, means to attribute to human freedom a *perverse and evil significance*: that of *an absolute power* over *others and against others*. This is the death of true freedom: "Truly, truly, I say to you, every one who commits sin is a slave to sin (Jn. 8:34)" (*Evangelium Vitae*, No. 20).

It is not an imposition of anything upon anyone merely to insist that the order of things created by God be recognized as the only legitimate basis of the just society. Baptized Catholics have the obligation to stand up in defense of Christ's holy truths, and to use those truths as the basis by which to judge the actions of those in public life. It is no work of "peace" to remain silent for the sake of not wanting to hurt the feelings of others; authentic Christian discipleship involves the willingness to run the risk of rejection as a means to disturb the consciences of those who are in error about right and wrong, who do not understand the proper role of government in the economy of God's creation.

As Pope John Paul II noted in *Centesimus Annus*:

But freedom attains its full development only by accepting the truth. In a world without truth, freedom loses its foundation and people are exposed to the violence of passion and to manipulation, both open and hidden. The Christian upholds freedom and serves it, constantly offering to others the truth which he has known, in accordance with the missionary nature of his vocation. While paying heed to every fragment of truth which he encounters in the life experience and in the culture of individuals and of nations, he will not fail to affirm in dialogue with others all that his faith and the correct use of reason have enabled him to understand. . . .

Even in countries with democratic forms of government, these rights are not always fully respected. Here we are referring not only to the scandal of abortion, but also to different aspects of a crisis within democracies themselves, which seem at times to have lost the ability to make decisions aimed at the common good. Certain demands which arise within society are sometimes not examined in accordance with criteria of justice and morality, but rather on the basis of the electoral or financial power of the groups promoting them. With time, such distortions of political conduct create distrust and apathy, with a subsequent decline in the political participation and civic spirit of the general population, which feels abused and disillusioned. As a result, there is a growing inability to situate particular interests within the framework of a coherent vision of the common good. The latter is not simply the sum total of particular interests; rather it involves an assessment and integration of those interests on the basis of a balanced hierarchy of values; ultimately, it demands a correct understanding of the dignity and the rights of the person (*Centesimus Annus*, Nos. 46–47).

Our obligations are quite clear. We belong to Christ and His Holy Church, not to the world. Our obligation is to lift high the Cross in the midst of an unbelieving world, not shrink from our apostolic duties out of the fear of offending the multitudes.

The new religion created by the theological and liturgical revolutionaries has failed. It has failed the Church, and, as a consequence, it has failed the world. For the world needs the fullness of the splendor of Truth Incarnate, as Pope Leo XIII wrote in all of his great encyclical letters on society and the state. To be a good American, therefore, one *needs* to be a faithful Catholic, one who is working assiduously in the pursuit of personal sanctity so that he might be an instrument, no matter how unworthy, of bringing this nation under the banner of Christ the King.

Pope Leo XIII wrote in *Sapientiae Christianae*:

> Christians are, moreover, born for combat, whereof the vehemence, the more assured, God aiding, the triumph. "Have confidence: I have overcome the world." Nor is there any ground for alleging that Jesus Christ, the Guardian and the Champion of the Church, needs not in any manner the help of men. Power is certainly not wanting to Him, but in His loving kindness He would assign to us a share in obtaining and applying the fruits of salvation procured through his grace.
>
> The chief elements of this duty consist in professing *openly and unflinchingly the Catholic doctrine*, and in propagating it to the utmost of our power.

CHRIST IS KING

Establishing the social reign of our Lord, which is the full expression of love of one's country, is made more difficult, however, by the fact that most of our bishops do not want such a thing. Even some of the bishops who are personally orthodox (but who would never impose it upon anyone else) are afraid of losing their much-vaunted tax-exempt status. Well, it is time for bishops to have the courage of Saint John Fisher in England, the only bishop who remained faithful to Rome in the wake of King Henry VIII's revolt against the Church. Like the Apostles themselves, John Fisher was not afraid of losing his life, no less any material benefit provided to him by the State. Why in the world are our bishops afraid of losing the tax-exempt status? We need *Apostles*, not cowards who believe that all is well. All is *not* well. Bishops need to govern.

Therefore, I believe, out of love of God and love of country, the following needs to be done:

1. The Holy Father must do what Pope Pius XI did: publicly remove bishops (Kenneth Untener, Matthew Clark, Howard Hubbard, John R. McGann, Daniel Ryan, Joseph Imesch, Roger Mahony, Rembert Weakland) who are at war with the Church, men who promote theological heresy and liturgical irreverence. Sure, the Church will be around until the end of time. But what about the souls that are being lost here and now? We need help, Holy Father, and we need it now.

2. We plead with the Holy Father to erect the *Ecclesia Dei* Commission as a Personal Prelature of his, giving the Traditional Latin Mass a canonical protection it does not now enjoy. The faithful have the *right*, as Pope Pius XII noted in *Mediator Dei* over 50 years ago, to this glorious liturgy. The Traditional Mass needs to be in every parish in every diocese in the world. We pray that a personal prelature will help to expedite the restoration of the liturgy which fully and completely communicates the Christocentric, sacerdotal nature of the Holy Sacrifice of the Mass. The sooner our Lord is recognized as King in the Mass, the sooner his Kingship will be realized in society—as is explained in a succeeding chapter herein.

3. As noted earlier, bishops must publicly excommunicate Catholics in public life who support contraception and abortion. Period. No exceptions. And the bishops must dismiss any teacher (at any and every level of education) who does not accept everything the Church teaches as true.

4. Home-schooling—and private, independent Catholic schools—must be encouraged, not persecuted by the bishops. Home-schooling is one of the true bright spots in the Church today. New soldiers for Christ are being trained in the truth. They are going to take their place— and they are going to make their voices heard both within the Church and within the world.

5. Catholics must stop compromising the truths of the faith, believing that we are only one election away from turning the corner on abortion. Both major political parties are opposed to us. Don't kid yourselves. We have to catechize our own people before we have even a ghost of chance to have a truly Catholic candidate elected to public office, one who will be unafraid to invoke the Holy Name in public debate. Do not participate in the mistaken belief that our salvation will come from politics. It will not. That is why we must vote for candidates of conscience regardless of their ability to win. We need individuals who will stand up in defense of the truths of the

faith, no matter how much they will be criticized by the media and their political opponents for doing so.

6. The insidious lie of classroom sex instruction must be stopped posthaste. This is a matter of tremendous urgency. The innocence and purity of souls has been harmed by this evil, even in *Catholic* schools.

7. Finally, each of us must be serious about saving our own souls. We must be people devoted to the Sacrifice of the Mass, people who spend much time in prayer before our Eucharistic King, people who are consecrated to the Sacred Heart of our Lord and the Immaculate Heart of Mary. We should be ever mindful of our Lady's Fatima requests, praying the Rosary earnestly each day for our needs and those of the world. And we must be people who have recourse to the Divine Mercy in the Sacrament of Penance—and who offer that mercy to others.

SAVING OUR LAND

Even though it is difficult for many people to accept, we have to understand that the Constitutional underpinnings of our secular, indifferentist republic *are* the root cause of the problems we face today in the United States. Yes, many of the men who wrote the American Constitution believed in transcendent truths that could not be abrogated licitly by a majority vote of any civil institution. Yes, they expected that statesmen would present themselves as candidates for office, people who were willing to sacrifice electoral success in order to articulate and to defend the principles of the just society. But what they did not understand, coming from a Protestant and rationalistic background, was that no written document can provide the foundation of a just society if people do not have recourse to the sacraments instituted by our Lord and administered to men by the Church He created upon the Rock of Peter, the Pope.

The American Constitution has no defense against the rise of sentimentality and egalitarianism and materialism and majoritarianism. Admitting of no ultimate arbiter—and not recognizing the Sovereignty of Christ the King—it is of its nature open to the attacks of the relativists and sentimentalists. As will be examined later in the book, a political and governmental system which does not honor Christ as King nor looks to His Vicar as the ultimate guide on matters of fundamental justice is destined to disintegrate as ours is doing at present.

As Pope Pius XI wrote in *Quas Primas*:

> While nations insult the beloved name of our Redeemer by suppressing all mention of it in their conferences and parliaments, we must all the more loudly proclaim His kingly dignity and power, all the more universally affirm His rights. . . . Nations will be reminded by the annual celebration of this feast [of Christ the King] that not only private individuals but also rulers and princes are bound to give public honor and obedience to Christ. It will call to their minds the thought of the last judgment, wherein Christ, who has been cast out of public life, despised, neglected, and ignored, will most severely avenge these insults; for His kingly dignity demands that the State should take account of the commandments of God and of Christian principles, both in making laws and in administering justice, and also in providing for the young a sound moral education.
>
> The faithful, moreover, by meditating upon these truths, will gain much strength and courage, enabling them to form their lives after the true Christian ideal. If to Christ our Lord is given all power in heaven and on earth; if all men, purchased by His precious blood, are by a new right subjected to His dominion; if this power embraces all men, it must be clear that not one of our faculties is exempt from His empire. He must reign in our minds, which should obey the laws and precepts of God. He must reign in our hearts, which should spurn our natural desires and love God above all things and cleave to Him alone.

Blessed Miguel Augustin Pro was executed by the Masonic revolutionaries in Mexico because he lived and worked to promote the social reign of our Lord in our Lady's country, Mexico. May we, who invoke our Lady's intercession as patroness of this country under the title of her Immaculate Conception, be ever ready, for love of God and for true love of country, to utter with Blessed Padre Pro: *Viva Cristo Rey!*

CHAPTER FIVE

The Consequences of Defying the Divine and Natural Laws

The United States is paying a high price for defying the Divine and natural laws. As noted in the last chapter, the United States Constitution has been read by legal positivists in such a way as to justify every manner of vice, beginning with contraception, which paved the way for the legalized killing of the pre-born in the *Roe v. Wade* decision of January 22, 1973.

The broad acceptance of contraception which characterizes social life in Western society has its roots in the Protestant Revolt of the Sixteenth Century. The theological relativism of the Revolt led logically to the moral relativism and legal positivism of the Twentieth Century. Even secular commentators were able to understand the ramifications of such subjectivity on social life. Responding to the Anglican Church's Lambeth report of 1931, which sanctioned contraception, *The Washington Post* editorialized:

> It is impossible to reconcile the doctrine of the divine institution of marriage with any modernistic plan for the mechanical regulation of human birth. The church must either reject the plain teachings of the Bible or reject schemes for the "scientific" production of human souls. Carried to its logical conclusion, the committee's report if carried into effect would sound the death-knell of marriage as a holy institution, by establishing degrading practices which would encourage indiscriminate immorality. The suggestion that the use of legalized contraceptives would be "careful and restrained" is preposterous.
>
> It is the misfortune of the churches that they are too often misused by visionaries for the promotion of "reforms" in fields foreign to religion. The departures from Christian teachings are astounding in many cases, leaving the beholder aghast at the

76

willingness of some churches to discard the ancient injunction to teach "Christ and Him crucified." If the churches are to become organizations for political and "scientific" propaganda they should be honest and reject the Bible, scoff at Christ as an obsolete and unscientific teacher, and strike out boldly as champions of politics and science as modern substitutes for the old-time religion (March 22, 1931).

PLANNED BARRENHOOD

Much of mainline Protestant Christianity *has* forsaken the unchanging Gospel of Jesus Christ and placed its trust in politics and science as the "modern substitutes" for the old-time religion. By so doing, however, the Christian advocates of contraception (which today include many heterodox Catholic theologians) helped to unleash a tidal wave of consequences responsible for most societal and economic problems. To be sure, Margaret Sanger and her allies in the Birth Control League (later to become the Planned Parenthood Federation of America and the International Federation of Planned Parenthood) helped to spade the political and religious ground for the Lambeth committee's report "legitimizing" contraception. It was Sanger who wrote to numerous Protestant ministers around the world to encourage them to use their pulpits to preach the "gospel" of birth control. But that was only part of Sanger's strategy. She desired to use religious leaders as a means of influencing public policy both in the United States and internationally.

Sanger, termed *The Father of Modern Society* by Elasha Drogin, elicited the support of academicians, scientists, physicians— and the then emerging caste of social engineers—to try to devise policies which would encourage, if not mandate, the use of contraception. Part of Sanger's strategy was patently racist: she desired the elimination of the "weaker" races that were a "drain" on the financial resources of society. She sought to encourage "colored" ministers to preach about birth control in order to eliminate "this unfortunate people." Sanger also corresponded with the eugenicists of the Weimar Republic in Germany—*and* with officials of Adolf Hitler's Third Reich. She laid the groundwork for separating the unitive and procreative aspects of marital love as the basis of politics, law, education, culture, and economics.

SOCIAL ENGINEERING

Although the social engineers moved tendentiously at first, Rexford Guy Tugwell, President Franklin Delano Roosevelt's appointee as Governor of the then Territory of Puerto Rico, suggested that voluntary sterilization be encouraged on the island he was assigned to govern. Such a voluntary sterilization program *was* introduced in Puerto Rico by Governor Luis Munoz Marin in the late-1940s. Puerto Rico was therefore used as a laboratory of social experimentation, out of the view and consciousness of the rest of the nation, much in the same manner as the black family become a laboratory of social engineering during the Great Society program of President Lyndon Baines Johnson.

At the root of the early efforts to "engineer" contraception into the public policy of the United States was a Marxist view of sexuality and the family. Karl Marx considered the family to be a bourgeois institution which was not in the best interests of the state; women were therefore "enslaved" by having to bear children. They were inhibited from participating in the full economic life of a society, deprived of fulfilling themselves in a "meaningful" career. As Pope Pius XI noted in *Divini Redemptoris*:

> Refusing to human life any sacred or supernatural character, such a doctrine logically makes of marriage and the family a purely artificial and civil institution, the outcome of a specific economic system. There exists no matrimonial bond of a juridico-moral nature that is not subject to the whim of the individual or of the collectivity. Naturally, therefore, the notion of an indissoluble marriage-tie is scouted. Communism is particularly characterized by the rejection of any link that binds woman to the family and the home, and her emancipation is proclaimed as a basic principle. She is withdrawn from the family and the care of her children, to be thrust, instead, into public life and collective production under the same conditions as man. The care of home and children then devolves upon the collectivity.
>
> Finally, the right of education is denied to parents, for it is conceived as the exclusive prerogative of the community, in whose name and by whose mandate alone parents may exercise this right.

A ROGUE SUPREME COURT

The social engineers in the United States could not have had such success in translating their "visions" into public policy without the cooperation of the United States Supreme Court. In a series of decisions in the 1950s and 1960s, under the tutelage of Chief Justice Earl Warren, the Court ruled that most pornography was protected "speech" under the Justices' "interpretation" of the First Amendment to the United States Constitution. Giving cover to the likes of Hugh Hefner, the Court therefore made it possible for pornographers to proselytize the ethic of contraception, adultery, fornication, masturbation, sodomy—and abortion. If human sexuality is reduced to the level of pleasure alone, divorced from its procreative *and* unitive ends, then the conception of a child must be perceived as somehow unnatural, an accident. It would be a mistake to discount the impact of pornography in the 1950s as a contributing factor to the acceptance of contraception and the "sexual revolution" in the 1960s.

Permissive Supreme Court decisions sanctioning pornography were only the initial assaults made by government against the sanctity of human sexual love in the 1950s. After all, no public official was *then* publicly supporting the idea that sexual relations outside of marriage was acceptable. Married couples had a "right to privacy" when "deciding" how many children to have. And the United States had a duty to encourage married couples in other nations to use contraception so that they would not be mired in poverty. Thus the Rockefeller Commission proposed to President Dwight D. Eisenhower in 1956 that foreign aid programs should be tied to the acceptance of contraceptives and contraceptive policies. Puerto Rico was the first laboratory; the world was now ready for the spread of contraceptive pills and devices as a matter of United States foreign policy. The myth of overpopulation, a myth perpetrated to this very day, became the "rationale" for mandating contraceptive policies abroad in order to promote "economic development" (and, in our own today, "to save the environment").

CHILDREN: A CAPTIVE AUDIENCE

Employing a strategy devised by the Sex, Information and

Education Committee of the United States (SIECUS), Planned Parenthood Federation of America began its assault upon public education in the United States in 1963. Believing that children needed to be educated about contraception in order to be "responsible" parents—and in order to stem an alleged crisis in teen pregnancy which did not exist at that time, Planned Parenthood and the National Education Association (NEA) joined forces to force sex education into the curricula in secondary schools. It would not be too long after that until the same forces were militating for such education from kindergarten through twelfth grade. The fact that teen pregnancies and venereal disease soared after these programs were introduced does nothing to dissuade the contemporary proponents of sex education and "school-based" clinics, such as United States Surgeon General Joycelyn Elders, from advocating the expansion of that which has failed miserably. Children are now educated to believe that sexual intercourse has almost nothing to do with a sacred bond elevated to a sacrament by the Second Person of the Blessed Trinity made Man at Cana. The resulting increase in teen suicide, depression, alcoholism, drug addiction, violence, divorce, abortion, and social irresponsibility is directly related to the public education policies fostered by the SIECUS forces.

The same Supreme Court which sanctioned pornography in the 1950s and early 1960s gave its *imprimatur* to contraception in the famous *Griswold v. Connecticut* case in 1965, paving the way for *Roe v. Wade* in 1973. The judicial invention of a "right to privacy" which is nowhere to be found in the American Constitution provided elected officials (and those *seeking* election to public office) a convenient rhetorical device to use when defending the rapidly decaying moral life of American society. Although Associate Justice Hugo Black did not like the long unenforced Connecticut statute banning the sale of contraceptives to married couples, he did note in his dissenting opinion that:

> I repeat so as not to be misunderstood that this Court does have power, which it should exercise, to hold laws unconstitutional where they are forbidden by the Federal Constitution. My point is that there is no provision of the Constitution which either expressly or impliedly vests power in this Court to sit as a supervisory agency over acts of duly constituted legislative bodies and set aside their laws because of the Court's belief

that the legislative policies adopted are unreasonable, unwise, arbitrary, capricious or irrational. The adoption of such a loose, flexible, uncontrolled standard for holding laws unconstitutional, if it is ever finally achieved, will amount to a great unconstitutional shift of power to the courts which I believe and am constrained to say will be bad for the courts and worse for the country. Subjecting federal and state laws to such an unrestrained and unrestrainable judicial control as to the wisdom of legislative enactments would, I fear, jeopardize the separation of governmental powers that the Framers set up and at the same time threaten to take away much of the power of States to govern themselves which the Constitution plainly intended them to have.

I realize that many good and able men have eloquently spoken and written, sometimes in rhapsodical strains, about the duty of this Court to keep the Constitution in tune with the times. The idea is that the Constitution must be changed from time to time and that this Court is charged with a duty to make those changes. For myself, I must with all deference reject that philosophy. The Constitution makers knew the need for change and provided for it. Amendments suggested by the people's elected representatives can be submitted to the people or their selected agents for ratification. That method of change was good for our Fathers, and being somewhat old-fashioned I must add it is good enough for me.

Griswold and the case in 1972 which struck down laws prohibiting the sale of contraceptives to *unmarried* persons (*Eisenstadt v. Baird*) made possible the most sweeping exercise of judicial review in legal history in the case of *Roe v. Wade* on January 22, 1973. Abortion-on-demand up to and including the day of birth became the law of the United States as a direct result of the societal and *legal* acceptance and legitimization of contraception. Millions of women—who do not know that Mercy Incarnate stands ready to forgive them for killing their children—have been victimized spiritually, psychologically, and physically by a prevailing culture which has, in effect, aborted our Lord from its midst. Millions of mangled bodies of dead babies have been discarded in a national rush to assert and exercise non-existent rights which are opposed to the Divine and natural laws.

OUR LORD IS MARGINALIZED

Contraception and abortion have become accepted evils. Children are educated by teachers, parents, the media, and by the law that they can do with their bodies as they see fit. The preoccupation with genital pleasure divorced from its supernatural beauty—and divorced from the indissoluble bond which is part of that beauty—has led to the breakdown of family life, the abuse of women and children, the feminization of poverty, adultery, fornication, teen pregnancy, suicide, and now the propagandizing in behalf of active homosexual and lesbian behavior. But it is not "politically correct" to point out any of this. One is termed a "religious zealot" if one attempts to state that most of our national problems relate to the theological relativism begotten four and one-half centuries ago. A relativism which has relativized Christ and His Holy Church to the margins of human consciousness, especially among baptized members of the one, true Church.

Women who stay home to have children are excoriated by many public educators for being "selfish" or "lazy." Young girls are told that they *must* have a career in order to be fulfilled. Divorce, once a stigma in Western society, is now made legally easy—encouraging the adultery and abandonment of women and children, which is the natural consequence of the contraceptive mentality. National leaders from the likes of Bill Clinton in the United States to one-time Canadian Prime Minister Kim Campbell exhibit the attitudes of a generation which came to age during the sexual revolution of the 1960s. Their ilk propound that the proliferation of AIDS must be stopped by educational programs such as the Rainbow Curriculum advanced by former City of New York Schools Chancellor Joseph Fernandez, even though AIDS is a disease transmitted almost exclusively by voluntary behavior. (Its transmission via blood transfusions and the accidental mingling of body fluids occur now only because the militant homosexual community lobbied against efforts to screen blood donors in the 1980s and to reveal medical personnel who are HIV-positive in the 1990s.)

UTILITARIANISM

Contraception has become such an accepted fact of social life and public policy that Associate Justice Sandra Day O'Connor noted in the case of *Planned Parenthood of Southeastern Pennsylvania v. Casey* in 1992 that:

> Abortion is customarily chosen as an unplanned response to the consequence of unplanned activity or to the failure of conventional birth control. . . . To eliminate the issue of reliance that easily, however, one would need to limit cognizable reliance to specific instances of sexual activity. But to do this would be simply to refuse to face the fact that for two decades of economic and social relationships, people have organized intimate relationships and made choices that define their views of themselves and their places in society, in reliance on the availability of abortion in the event that contraception should fail. The ability of women to participate equally in the economic and social life of the Nation has been facilitated by their ability to control their reproductive lives.

Utilitarianism has become the yardstick by which this society now measures the worth of one human life. Justice O'Connor, joined by Associate Justices Anthony Kennedy and David Souter, plainly demonstrates the consequences of contraception: the reductionism of human sexual activity to a cost/benefit analysis of access to "participation" in the economic life of the nation. Margaret Sanger and her descendants are indeed the victors at this present stage of human history.

CONSEQUENCES

All of the multifaceted social and political consequences of contraception could have been avoided if *Catholics* had heeded the prophetic words of Pope Paul VI in *Humanae Vitae* as quoted in Chapter Three.

The social and economic consequences of contraception are many. One of the most telling is the triumph of mediocrity in our national life, resulting in an untold chain of economic consequences.

If one can deny the sovereignty of God over human conjugal love, then one is willing to define human life in terms of convenience, "wantedness," utility. A child must be planned, wanted, perfect. This disregards God's clear will, expressed in the Book of Genesis, "Be fruitful and multiply." (As far as I know, He has not repealed that injunction.) God intends that human beings use the conjugal gifts only in a valid, sacramental marriage, and that marriage of its nature is meant to be open to the fruition of the conjugal union, children. Period. A child need not be planned. And properly formed parents have to understand that a child is wanted by God as the natural fruit of their conjugal intimacy, which is meant to be used in imitation of Christ's selfless, unconditional love on Calvary.

THE ONLY TRUE HUMAN DEFECT

Insofar as "perfection" is concerned, the sort of defect that God cares about is sin. Each of us is deformed spiritually because of our sins, which is why we must do much penance to try by God's grace to repair the damage that sins do to our souls. Physical or mental deformity do not lessen a person's humanity in the slightest. Even a person who is permanently incapacitated, who may not be able to be economically "productive," who may "cost" his family a great deal of money, is precious. He has an immortal soul, purchased by the shedding of our Lord's Most Precious Blood on Calvary. A person who suffers from some chronic deformity (whether by heredity or by an accident) is a source of grace for us; the love we offer to them helps to build up the whole Body of Christ, and they, in turn, offer their love to us. God provides all of the grace necessary for the one suffering from a deformity, and for the ones who suffer *with* them through their pain, to carry the cross they have been asked to bear.

Those who promote contraception and abortion would do so frequently under the "aegis" of preventing suffering. Which one of us can guarantee to an expectant mother that the child she is carrying will never know any suffering whatsoever? Her child will never know any physical pain, will never suffer any romantic rejection, will never be ridiculed, will never fail an examination, will never have a tragic accident, will never lose a job, will never have financial worries. Obviously, suffering is part of the human condition. And it comes in many forms. To try to use the canard that contraception and abortion are necessary to prevent "suffering" is a self-serving attempt to justify the pursuit of a life which is as convenient as possible.

POPULATION CONTROL

That very mentality results in a depletion of a nation's population. The only reason that the United States is gaining population at present is because of immigration. Otherwise, this country would be in almost exactly the same position as many European nations (particularly Italy and Germany) which have birth-rates for women of child-bearing years well below that necessary to *replace* their current populations. As a consequence, European nations are very dependent upon immigrant workers just to keep their economies functioning; there are not enough native-born citizens to do so.

The Social Security and Medicare systems in the United States are in such difficulty at present because of the consequences of contraception and abortion. We have permitted the slaughter of over 37 million children in abortuaries around this nation, about 7 million of which either would be in the work force or in colleges today. Countless other children's conceptions have been prevented by all manner of insidious devices and pills, with millions of others aborted as the result of contraceptives (most of which abort most of the time). There are two very observable results of this, with others stemming from them.

Naturally, it can be argued rather successfully that there would be no *need* for either Social Security or Medicare—or any other government program which violates the principle of subsidiarity—if we had a truly Catholic culture. For in a truly Catholic culture married couples would welcome children generously as the natural fruit of their conjugal love. Such children would see it as their solemn responsibility to provide for their parents if they became unable to provide for themselves. The concept of the *extended* family which provides for its own is something that has been devastated by divorce and contraception—and by the subsequent statism and redistributionism that have arisen as a consequence of divorce and contraception.

AGING POPULATION

Contraception and abortion have resulted in the "graying" of America. The median age in this nation is projected to be 60 years of age in 2020. That would not be the case if all the children who have been killed in abortuaries, and the others whose births have been prevented by contraception, had been permitted to be born.

The current trends, however, are such that both the Social Security and Medicare systems will be incapable of sustaining themselves; there will simply be too little money coming from too few workers to provide the "benefits" expected by the large number of who will be eligible for them in just thirty years (as the baby boomers begin to retire). There will be calls, as came from former Colorado Governor Richard Lamm in 1984, for a mandatory age for death, or for some utilitarian test to determine who is considered "useful" enough to be permitted to continue living beyond a certain age.

One should not doubt such a possibility. After all, very few people a mere forty years ago would have thought it possible that most of the perversities which are accepted as a part of everyday life (rampant teen promiscuity, sodomy, abortion, "victimhood" as a means of excusing personal sins) could ever come to characterize our national life. Only a scant few people would have thought it possible in the 1950s that this country would permit the legal destruction of innocent human life in the womb up to and including the day of birth itself. A mandatory age for death, or the adoption of a policy of euthanasia for the chronically and terminally ill (such as exists in a *de facto* manner in the Netherlands, where national laws against "medically-accepted" practices of taking such lives are not enforced). This country is much too eager to solve its social problems by killing people. It will be no different with the elderly and disabled if we do not stand up to make a difference by the way we cast our votes.

MEDIOCRITY

Contraception and abortion have also resulted in a spirit of mediocrity which is responsible for many of our social and economic problems. This is particularly the case as it relates to private college education, as there is a much smaller pool of available applicants today than there was just thirty years ago. The very same colleges which could be very selective in admitting students in the 1960s now admit anyone and everyone who applies, as they are desperate for cash to keep their institutions alive. When coupled with the independent (though related) phenomenon of brainwashing people into thinking that life is one giant entitlement, the acceptance of unqualified applicants, usually under the guise of providing "equal opportunity," convinces young people that they do not have any responsibility to pursue excellence, no less a realization that we are to pursue it as befits children of God.

Colleges are not only desperate to admit students, they are desperate to retain them. To that end, all manner of pressure is put on professors not to grade students too harshly, as that might affect their self-esteem to such a degree that they would consider transferring elsewhere. "Retention" becomes the buzzword of many of these colleges; students are considered little other than "cash cows" whose tardiness, inattentiveness, lack of qualifications, illiteracy, rudeness, and irresponsibility must be tolerated in order for the institution to survive. And if a student is not challenged to pursue excellence, to learn how to think and reason clearly, to take responsibility for his actions, to have a love for the things of the mind, then he is going to graduate into the work world believing that an employer has no right to "force" him into doing anything other than that which he wants to do at a given moment.

Only a society which recognizes the sovereignty of Christ and His Holy Church is able to combat the temptation to succumb to the allure of the contraceptive mentality. The blindness which covers our national eyes at present prevents most people, including many Catholics, from realizing how a denial of God's sovereignty over the human body has resulted in so many of our social and economic problems. And that blindness is what leads otherwise decent people to think that all we need is some kind of political program to "fix" things. But it is only when people try to live in accordance with the Divine and natural laws, when they submit themselves in humility to the teaching authority of the true Church, that problems begin, piece by piece, to be ameliorated. Politics is not salvific; and a politics which glorifies sin, particularly the sins of contraception and abortion, ultimately destroys a nation.

CHAPTER SIX

Obstacles from Within the
American Hierarchy

One of the reasons that Catholic Americans have had such difficulty seeing the world through the eyes of faith is because there has been quite an alliance between the American hierarchy and the left wing of the Democratic Party. Moreover, there has been a long history of the American hierarchy's seeking to accommodate itself to the spirit of pluralistic democracy that, as has been demonstrated, is one of the major flaws of the American Constitutional system.

The alliance between the American bishops and the Democratic Party is such that many of the slogans that pass for political "dogma" today (affirmative action, separation of Church and State, the role of government in helping the poor) are almost advanced as if they have been received from the hand of God Himself. The contemporary expression of this alliance is to be found in the utter silence of the National Conference of Catholic Bishops, never slow to criticize Ronald Reagan or other Republicans, about the policies of evil being pursued by President William Jefferson Blyth Clinton.

Even historians favorable to the concept of an "American Church" have documented the fact that the American hierarchy, under the auspices of the National Catholic Welfare Conference (which became the NCCB in 1966), has long been committed to the social engineering policies begun in earnest by Franklin Roosevelt in the 1930s—and which were multiplied and expanded in grandiose terms by Lyndon Johnson thirty years later. We are now at the point where the whole apparatus of the Catholic hierarchy in this country is enmeshed in a web of fiscal and social relationships with the very people who are promoting programs which are at odds with the dignity of the human being as a child of God. The ecclesiastical bureaucracy in this country has quite shamelessly promoted one failed social program after another, openly endorsing the Clintons' monstrous government takeover of the health care industry in 1993–94 (with only a mild expression of concern about abortion).

ECCLESIASTICAL BUREAUCRACY

The bishops (and the bureaucrats who dictate policy to them) criticized Ronald Reagan at every possible opportunity, using a variety of intellectually dishonest inventions (such as the "seamless garment," to be elaborated upon below) and pastoral letters to help elect Democrats to the White House and Congress. They made divine mandates out of their own prudential policy decisions (most of which were simply flat out wrong, and a number of things all too curiously in line with the Kremlin position on nuclear arms and the conflict in Central America), while downplaying the restoration of legal protection for the preborn.

The NCCB/USCC's silence during the Clinton administration, as it has promoted all manner of evil, is scandalous. For this is only *part* of what has happened since William Jefferson Blyth Clinton became this nation's 42nd President.

1. Fetal research has been authorized.

2. Fetal transplant research has been authorized.

3. RU–486 is being tested; some women are deliberately getting pregnant in order to test the abortion pill.

4. Sterilization drugs are being put into immunization and tetanus shots administered in the Third World, as close to our own borders as Mexico. There is even some evidence that pharmaceutical companies are distributing such potions here. No word of criticism from the bishops.

5. The Freedom of Access to Clinic Entrance bill was passed. This has resulted in the formation of a special task force under the control of Janet Reno, who has used FACE to try to intimidate even those people who merely write letters to abortionists to plead with them for their conversion.

6. Ruth Bader Ginsburg and Stephen Breyer have been nominated—and confirmed—as Supreme Court Associate Justices. These militant pro-aborts were not opposed massively by efforts of the U.S. Catholic Conference.

7. As noted above, the International Conference on Population and Development in Cairo in 1994 received only perfunctory criticism (prompted by the Holy See, it should be noted) from the NCCB/USCC.

8. Joycelyn Elders and Henry Foster received virtual free passes from the ecclesiastical bureaucracy in Washington and in chancery offices around the country. The scandal that is public school "sex education" (and most such programs in Catholic schools) is allowed to undermine the innocence of our children without any pastoral letter from our bishops.

9. Sodomy has been promoted as a legitimate civil right. Not only has the NCCB/USCC failed to issue a clear condemnation of the promotion of this evil, some bishops have even supported "homosexual rights" legislation. And the notorious pastoral letter, "Always Our Children," issued in 1997, sought to denigrate the seriousness of a sin that cries out to Heaven for vengeance. Lincoln, Nebraska, Bishop Fabian Bruskewitz called the document "evil" in its denigration of sin.

The list could go on and on. But this list contains matters that are not inconsequential for the salvation of souls, and hence for the right order of relations in society. Apart from the brave souls in the bishops' pro-life secretariat, who issue some excellent reports and newsletters, most of the NCCB/USCC apparatus does not want to criticize Clinton because they actually agree with this scandalous list of "accomplishments" just provided. There are no other explanations for their silence.

AMERICAN CHURCH

There can be no question that the "American Church" is a reality in the minds of many in the hierarchy. To wit, the Bishop of Fort Worth, the Most Reverend James Delaney, told a laywoman who was begging him not to appoint a "liberal" pastor to head St. Patrick's Cathedral parish, "You don't understand, ma'am. This is the American Catholic Church." An American Catholic Church, it has to be noted, which has developed a very close working relationship with the statism of the past eighty years, especially as the Campaign for Human Development has been used to fund programs inimical to the splendor of Truth Incarnate.

The sense that there is an "American Catholic Church" goes back to the beginning of the Republic. All historians who have studied this topic, including those who are not noted for their fealty to the Holy See, understand that the basic tension which has existed between the American hierarchy and the Holy See is caused by the prevailing ethos of democracy which exists in American politics and culture. There has been such an exaltation of democracy and egalitarianism from the very beginning of the Church in this country, dating right back to Archbishop John Carroll himself, that it is no wonder the faithful now find themselves in a situation where there has been an actual transposition of democracy into the Church herself in this country. Instead of the Church serving as the force by which culture is shaped and directed, she has been shaped and directed by the prevailing culture norms of democracy and positivism.

Most Catholics therefore tend to view the Church into which they were baptized as little more than yet another human institution, quite analogous to Congress or the Supreme Court, which makes up rules that can be changed from time to time. There is no sense of transcendent truths which do not depend upon human acceptance for their validity, for their binding force. The Calvinist notion of the strict equality of all believers has had such a strong impact on our culture that almost all notion of hierarchical relationships, which were the particular objects of destruction by the French and Bolshevik Revolutions, from the Church to the family to the State, has been lost. We are thus faced with a situation where the average Catholic will say, "Who's that Pope to tell me what to think? Who's that Cardinal O'Connor to tell off Mario Pilate or Pontius Cuomo? Who are my parents to tell me there is a right and a wrong."

REBELLION

The average Catholic can utter such inanities because he is mimicking, however, unconsciously, a rebellion against the Divinely-instituted hierarchy of Christ's Mystical Bride, the Church that is being exhibited with a great deal of boldness right now by at least forty bishops. *They* are asking, in essence, "Who is that Pope to tell *us* what to do? Doesn't he know his place? What right does Cardinal Ratzinger have to interfere with the way we want to print a *Catechism*, or the way we want to *do* liturgy (sort of like doing lunch, eh?)?" It is no wonder that the faithful have no respect for or understanding of the hierarchical nature of the Church, is it?

Truth be told, of course, this rebellion, to a greater or lesser extent, goes back to the very beginning of the Church in this country. Although Archbishop John Carroll—and the other pastors of souls who served under him following the founding of the infant Republic in the late Eighteenth Century—had a genuine solicitude for the salvation of souls, they nevertheless resented what they believed was "Roman interference" in the affairs of the American Church. Carroll himself praised the democratic ethos, believing that the American spirit of religious tolerance and pluralism could set an example for Europe itself. Although scrupulously faithful to the authority of the Pope in matters of faith and morals, he wanted as much autonomy as possible insofar as the internal governance of the American Church was concerned.

NO THREAT TO PROTESTANTS

That having been said, however, it must be noted that however much Carroll and others wanted to accommodate the Protestant majority by making Catholicism appear as safe as possible to them, he was a Roman Catholic. They may have desired to create what one author, Joseph Agonito, called "a truly national, American Catholic Church." But "neither John Carroll nor his co-religionists ever forgot that the Catholic Church in America was part of a universal, ancient, highly structured body whose center was Rome" (Joseph Agonito, *The Building of an American Catholic Church: The Episcopacy of John Carroll*, p. 276). It was this understanding that prevented them from doing what they were tempted to do: create an autonomous Church.

While Carroll and the clergy wanted the American Catholic Church free from all temporal foreign jurisdiction, they never intended the Church in America to be removed from the spiritual authority of Rome, the center of ecclesiastical unity and the faith itself. Furthermore, recognizing as he must the spiritual primacy of the Holy See over the whole Church, Carroll was compelled to accept (though with reluctance) Rome's right to appoint episcopal candidates to American bishoprics. And, it was this sense of belonging to a universal church, under Rome's leadership, that ultimately prevented Carroll from changing the liturgy from the Latin to the vernacular, a change he earnestly desired (Agonito, p. 277).

LITURGY

Indeed, as will be discussed at length later in this chapter, the liturgy really is at the essence of the American hierarchy's occasional opposition to the Holy See in the Nineteenth Century—and its almost persistent opposition to it in the past 30 years. Although he understood he did not have the authority to change the liturgy on his own—a little fact that many of our pastors and liturgists have overlooked in the past twenty-five years or so—Carroll believed early on that a Mass in English would help to blunt Protestant prejudice against the tiny Catholic minority here in the late Eighteenth Century.

As Agonito reports, "While Carroll may have agreed with the Council of Trent's decision in the Sixteenth Century to retain use of Latin in the liturgy, he no longer felt the compelling need to do so in the Eighteenth. Its retention was of no advantage to the religious life of Catholics in America. He said as much in 1787 to Joseph Berington, a well-known English Catholic author. Carroll stated to Berington that one of the principle obstacles ". . . to Christians of other denominations to a thorough union with us, or at least to a much more general diffusion of our religion, particularly in North America," was the use of Latin in the liturgy (Agonito, p. 126). With respect to this point, Carroll exclaimed:

> I cannot help thinking that the alteration of the Church discipline ought not only to be solicited, but insisted on, as essential

to the service of God and benefit to mankind. Can there be anything more preposterous, than for a small district in extent no more than Mount Libanus and a trifling territory at the foot of it, to say nothing of the Greeks, Armenians, Coptics, etc. to have a liturgy in their proper idiom, and on the other hand for an immense extent of countries, containing Great Britain, Ireland, all North America, the West Indies, etc. to be obliged to perform divine services in an unknown tongue. In spite of all evasions, the Latin is an unknown tongue, and in this country, either for want of books, or inability to read, the great part of the congregations must be utterly ignorant of the meaning and sense of the public offices of the Church. It may have been prudent, for aught I know, to refuse a compliance in this instance, with the insulting and reproachful demands of the first reformers; but to continue the practice of the Latin liturgy in the present state of things must be owing either to chimerical fears of innovation or to indolence or inattention in the first pastors of the national churches in not joining to solicit, or indeed ordain the necessary alteration (Agonito, p. 127).

LOYALTY TO THE CONSTITUTION

Yes, Carroll—and the first diocesan synod of the Clergy in November of 1791—retained Latin, and even more stringently so nineteen years later. He was a son of the Church. But the very democracy which he exalted so much was to result eventually in the situation we find ourselves in today: where bishops and liturgists and pastors have *no* regard for ecclesiastical authority, implementing all manner of unauthorized liturgical changes— and proposing others that they *insist* Rome approve in a mere clearinghouse capacity. The democracy loved so much by Archbishop Carroll became the *modus vivendi* for the life of the Church in the United States to such an extent that the Church finds herself today in a position of near-congregationalism: every parish having its own liturgical rite.

AUTONOMY FROM ROME

This worshipful attitude about democracy was actually praised by one of Carroll's most powerful successors, James Cardinal Gibbons:

The dominant idea in the mind of Bishop Carroll, who was as great a statesman as he was a churchman, an idea that has remained the inspiration of the Church, and has dictated all her policy of the last century . . . was absolute loyalty to the letter and the spirit of the Constitution of the United States (James Cardinal Gibbons, *A Retrospect of Fifty Years*, p. 248–249).

There you have it. Not loyalty to the mind of our Lord. Loyalty to the letter and the spirit of the Constitution of the United States.

Bishop Carroll did not wish to see the Church vegetate as a delicate exotic plant. He wished it become a sturdy tree, deep rooted in the soil, to grow with the growth and bloom with the development of the country, inured to its climate, braving its storms, invigorated by them and yielding abundantly the fruits of sanctification. His aim was that the clergy and the people should be thoroughly identified with the land in which their lot is cast; that they should study its laws and political constitution, and be in harmony with its spirit (Gibbons, pp. 248–249).

A spirit, it should be noted, that rejected the authority of the Vicar of Christ as the ultimate interpreter of the natural law. As Jay P. Dolan put it, quite admiringly:

Carroll and his co-religionists understood that the very survival and growth of the Catholic Church in the United States depended upon its ability to accept, and become a part of the American way of life. In many ways Catholics labored to create an American Catholic Church.

Ever sensitive to the charge that they were too dependent on a foreign power, and concerned lest such an indictment revive anti-Catholic legislation, Catholics wanted their Church to be independent of all foreign jurisdiction save the spiritual authority of the Holy See. It was for this reason that they opted for the establishment of the more autonomous diocesan bishopric, the position to be filled by an American elected by the clergy in this country, rather than have Rome appoint a vicar-apostolic who would be too dependent on the Congregation of Propaganda. This goal achieved, the American clergy—and later the bishops—tried to assert their control over the future selection of the American hierarchy. They were unsuccessful, but the attempt indicated their commitment to the idea of a

CHRIST IN THE VOTING BOOTH

national church (Dolan, *The American Catholic Experience*, pp. 110–111; cf. Agonito above and Annabelle Melville, *John Carroll of Baltimore*).

We can see very clearly, can we not, that this nascent spirit of autonomy from Rome is what drives many bishops today, who sincerely believe that Rome has no business telling them what to do. To paraphrase the title of a movie with a very immoral theme, many of our bishops today are asserting, "Whose Church is it anyway?" Christ's, we dare add. Christ's.

PAPAL INFALLIBILITY

The doctrine of papal infallibility proved to be in the Nineteenth Century one of the major stumbling blocks between the American bishops and the Vatican, as it is today. As early as the late Eighteenth Century, some Catholics in this country were very much opposed to any solemn proclamation of this doctrine, partly out of disbelief, and partly out of a fear of the reaction of the Protestants (who interpreted the claims to Papal infallibility to extend to any utterance of the Pope, something that *is* characteristic in our own day of ultramontanists, who believe the Pope cannot err on anything, including matters of prudential judgment, such as the appointments of bishops). This controversy would break out in full force in 1870, when the first Vatican Council proclaimed this doctrine solemnly.

One of the stalwart opponents of this proclamation was Peter Richard Kenrick, the Archbishop of St. Louis. He was joined by John B. Purcell, the Archbishop of Cincinnati. Kenrick believed that papal infallibility was a theological opinion, going so far as to publish his thoughts on the matter in a newspaper in Naples, expressing his reservations also about the doctrine of the Immaculate Conception. After much correspondence and maneuvering, Kenrick eventually submitted to the *authority* of the proclamation, but wrote several of his friends to say that he took back not one blessed word of his opposition to the doctrine itself. Nobody could make him believe it, he wrote.

AMERICANIST BISHOPS

The Americanist heresy—which is to this day denied by apologists of the American Church as ever having existed—in the late Nineteenth and early Twentieth Centuries, was eerily prophetic of the controversy that would be caused by John Courtney Murray's *We Hold These Truths* in 1960. Led by Archbishop John Ireland of St. Paul and Bishop John Keane of Richmond, with more than adequate direction received from Monsignor Dennis O'Connell, the rector of the North American College, Americanism sought to make an accommodation with liberal democratic thought. There was a de-emphasis on parochial schools and ethnic consciousness. Catholics in this country had to adapt themselves to the schema presented by a democratic republic. We had much to learn from participatory governance and the like. It was not our job to direct society. No, we could learn from what society had to offer us. *Testem Benevolentiae* was a ringing condemnation of Americanism, yet the heresy lives on in our own midst today.

Bishop John Lancaster Spaulding, the Bishop of Peoria in the late–Nineteenth Century, exemplified much of the Americanist spirit when he wrote in opposition to the appointment of a Papal delegate to the United States:

This opposition arises in part from a fixed and strongly-rooted desire, which exists throughout the English-speaking world, to manage as far as possible one's own affairs. The firm determination of the American people to permit no needless foreign interference is shown in the Monroe Doctrine, and it was more practically demonstrated by the overthrow and death of Maximillian. Catholics who live here, and who, wherever they were born, are true American citizens, feel the impulse of this desire and wish to manage as far as possible their own affairs. They are devoted to the Church; they recognize in the Pope Christ's Vicar, and gladly receive from him faith and morals; but for the rest, they ask him to interfere as little as may be (from a letter written by Bishop John Lancaster Spaulding, cited in Robert Leckie, *American and Catholic*).

To be sure, there were bishops and priests and lay Catholics who were very *Roman* in their Catholicism in the Nineteenth Century. But the Americanist spirit was present, especially in the glorification of democracy and pluralism, traps which would eventually wind up ensnaring most Catholics in the United States by the last part of the Twentieth Century. There is a wealth of material demonstrating how a handful of bishops in the Nineteenth Century were trailblazers of an American Church—Amchurch, if you will—for many of the men who serve as bishops in the United States at present.

World War I also posed a problem concerning the relations between the American hierarchy and the Vatican. Cardinal Gibbons wanted to be loyal to the Holy See, but also wanted to demonstrate Catholic patriotism when the United States got involved in Woodrow Wilson's efforts to make the world safe for democracy. What poor Cardinal Gibbons did not understand was that Wilson—a Mason who hated the Catholic Church and referred to His Eminence as "Mister Gibbons"—used the slogan of "making the world safe for democracy" as a cover to once and for all eliminate the influence of the Church in Central Europe. He wanted to replace the Austro-Hungarian Empire with a series of republics wherein laws would be made democratically, not dictated by the Church he hated so much. As the quintessential Lockean liberal, Woodrow Wilson believed he had the formula to provide for peace in the world: the League of Nations and democratic republics in Europe, a formula that gave us World War II and the mess in Yugoslavia we are eyewitnesses to in our own day. Yet the American bishops wanted to demonstrate patriotism. They had made their commitment to the Democratic Party.

Wilson, however, had made no commitment to them, other than to make the new National Catholic Welfare Council (which became the National Catholic Welfare *Conference* shortly after its birth) beholden to the Federal government. As a perverse prelude to the extensive involvement of the National Conference of Catholic Bishops and United States Catholic Conference (and Catholic Charities and the Campaign for Human Development) with the statists and pro-aborts who populate our Federal government today, Wilson provided Federal funds to the NCWC during World War I. The bishops did not realize how they were being co-opted by the statist, anti–Catholic Wilson.

Wilson was so anti–Catholic that he was oblivious to the suffering of Catholics in Mexico at the hands of the Masonic revolutionaries there in 1916 and 1917. A man committed to the principles of liberal egalitarianism, which were let loose on the world as a result of the French Revolution, Wilson dismissed the execution of Catholics in Mexico as simply an exercise to promote the "progressive ideas" being advanced by the anti–Catholic revolutionaries in the country our Lady converted to the true faith in 1531.

> Wilson replied [to a Father Kelley]: "I have no doubt but that the terrible things you mention have happened during the Mexican revolution. But terrible things happened also during the French revolution, perhaps more terrible things than have happened in Mexico. Nevertheless, out of that French revolution came the liberal ideas which have dominated in so many countries, including our own. I hope that out of the bloodletting in Mexico some such good yet may come."
>
> Having thus instructed his caller in the benefits which must perforce accrue to mankind out of the systematic robbery, murder, torture and rape of people holding a proscribed religious conviction, the professor of politics [Wilson] suggested that Father Kelley visit Secretary of State William Jennings Bryan, who expressed his deepest sympathy. Obviously, the Wilson administration was committed to supporting the revolutionaries (Leckie, p. 274).

In other words, Wilson believed that the shedding of Catholic blood in Mexico was a good thing. The less Catholics in the world, the better. All revolutions devoted to the eradication of the influence of the Catholic Church in the politics and culture were things from which "good" would come. And it was *his* intention, as noted earlier, to destroy the influence of the Church in Europe by the proselytizing of democracy and religious indifferentism, as well as by the creation of the League of Nations as the means to supplant the diplomatic power of the Church. This was the man to whom the American bishops had hitched their new bureaucratic apparatus.

ALIGNED WITH ANTI–CHURCH FACTIONS

Indeed, one of the principal sources of the current friction between the American hierarchy and the Holy See is precisely the marriage of its bureaucratic apparatus—conceived during World War I and born afterward (the National Catholic Welfare Conference, which became the National Conference of Catholic Bishops in 1966)—with the Democratic Party. The slavish adherence to

99

Franklin Roosevelt's social engineering was such that one bishop, including Bishop Hurley, came to Roosevelt's defense when the latter proposed direct aid to the Soviet Union in 1941, claiming that Pope Pius XI's *Divini Redemptoris*, which barred Catholics from aiding communism, did not apply in this special instance, that Nazism was a far worse enemy than communism. One of the reasons Father Charles Coughlin was silenced was that he understood, after an initial flirtation of his own with Roosevelt, that the policies of the New Deal were violative of the principles of subsidiarity enunciated so clearly by Pius XI in *Quadregesimo Anno*.

Cardinal Alfredo Ottaviani took on John Courtney Murray in the 1950s, at a time when the Catholic hierarchy was praising John F. Kennedy. Catholics had finally arrived. Catholics were now considered "safe" enough to be elected to the Presidency. As we know, what Kennedy made possible was a veritable army of Catholic politicians who continue to posit a false notion of the "imposition" of morality upon society. The bishops failed in their understanding of the basic mission of the Church, to convert souls, to establish the social reign of Christ the King.

THE REVOLUTION AGAINST THE LITURGY

As noted earlier, however, it is in the realm of the liturgy that the American hierarchy has been most rebellious with respect to the Holy See. And it is in this regard that we see the tragic results of the liturgical reform, which permitted the very ethos of democracy so loved by John Carroll to profanize the sacred mysteries.

True, there has been an open rebellion against the mind of Christ on matters of sexual morality, the infallibility of the Church, the nature of Sacred Scripture, the practical application of Church teaching in education and health care, to mention only a few areas. All of these, however, are directly related to the liturgy. And there is a direct connection between liturgical reverence and social order. If Christ is not honored in the liturgy as the God-Man, then there is little chance that Catholics will see in others the Divine impress. Although the spirit of Americanism and modernism had corrupted the underpinnings of the faith in this country long before the liturgical reform was implemented in 1970, that reform unwittingly (or wittingly?) hastened a wholesale embrace of all things modern, both secular and religious.

A PROPHECY

The subject of the liturgical reform is too broad to be examined in detail here. Suffice to say that we are witnessing the most fatal flaw in the whole process of liturgical change which was inaugurated by *Sacrosanctum Concilium* in 1963: the devolution of control over the liturgy from Rome to the individual episcopal conferences—*and* to bureaucracies such as ICEL. Such a devolution of control has resulted in the placing of substantive decision-making on liturgical matters in the hands of liturgists and theologians who were only too eager to ignore the wise counsel offered by Pope Pius XII on the liturgy in *Mediator Dei* in 1947. Much as has become the case in civil government throughout the world in this century, we find that the religious bureaucrats have more actual authority over matters of faith, morals, and worship than those who are their nominal superiors—the bishops, the successors of the Apostles.

Pope Pius XII warned in *Mediator Dei* that any liturgical reform should proceed slowly. He noted that there are Divine and human elements in the Mass, the latter of which are subject change.

> The sacred Liturgy does in fact include divine as well as human elements. The former, instituted as they have been by God, cannot be changed in any way by men. But the human components admit of various modifications, as the needs of the age, circumstance and the good of souls may require, and as the Ecclesiastical Hierarchy under guidance of the Holy Spirit, may have authorized. This will explain the marvelous variety of Eastern and Western rites. Here is the reason for the gradual addition, through successive development, of particular religious customs and practices of piety only faintly discernible in earlier times. Hence likewise it happens from time to time that certain devotions long since forgotten are revived and practiced anew. All these developments attest the abiding life of the Immaculate Spouse of Jesus Christ through these many centuries. They are the sacred language she uses, as the ages run their course, to profess to her divine Spouse her own faith, along with that of the nations committed to her charge, and her own unfailing love. They furnish proof, besides, of the wisdom of the teaching method she employs to arouse and nourish constantly the "Christian instinct."

Several causes, really, have been instrumental in the progress and development of the sacred Liturgy during the long and glorious life of the Church.

Thus for example, as Catholic doctrine on the Incarnate Word of God, the Eucharistic Sacrament and Sacrifice, and Mary the Virgin Mother of God *came to be determined with greater certitude and clarity,* new *ritual forms were introduced* through which the acts of the Liturgy proceeded to reproduce the brighter light issuing from decrees of the teaching Authority of the Church, and to reflect it, in a sense so that it might reach the minds and hearts of Christ's people more readily.

The subsequent advances in ecclesiastical discipline for the administering of the Sacraments, that of Penance for example; the institution and later suppression of the Catechumenate; and again, the practice of Eucharistic Communion under a single species, adopted in the Latin Church; these developments were assuredly responsible in no little measure for the modification of the ancient ritual in the course of time, and for the *gradual introduction* of new rites considered more in accord with prevailing discipline in these matters.

RAPID CHANGE

Pope Pius stated quite explicitly that only the Roman Pontiff could promulgate changes in the liturgy. He believed that rapid change for its own sake was neither wise nor laudable. He did not say these things *could* not be done. He was warning the bishops that they *should* not be done. The rejection of his sound pastoral advice has resulted in what the late Dietrich von Hildebrand called *The Devastated Vineyard.* Reverence has been lessened, if not eradicated altogether, in many Catholic parishes around the world. Doctrinal integrity is nonexistent in many places.

There is an inexorable nexus between liturgical reverence and doctrinal fidelity. Liturgical reverence begets personal piety. Personal piety opens one's soul to receive the transmission of the true faith in all of its integrity. Such a reception of the true faith leads one, when enlivened by the graces made available in each Mass, to scale the heights of personal sanctity. And personal sanctity is the basis of the just society.

A newly formed religious community dedicated to the promotion of the traditional Latin Mass and the renaissance of classical learning, the Society of Saint John, notes this matter in its foundational document:

> Another significance of the liturgical decadence is the evident decline in the moral, intellectual, and social life throughout our civilization. The moral decline takes root in liturgical decadence because the Church teaches most efficaciously through her liturgy. All the virtues find in the liturgy an organic and cyclical exposition. Moreover, perseverance in the practice of virtue requires the help of grace, and the liturgy is the principal source of that grace.
>
> The liturgy, further, is prior by nature to any Catholic intellectual endeavor, just as life and experience are prior to reflection and study. This is particularly true of theological studies. "*Lex orandi; lex credendi.*" The liturgy is the true and ultimate "mystagogy," i.e., the teaching of the divine mysteries. This teaching is based not so much on a rational demonstration as on the sacramental, experiential knowledge of the divine mysteries. These august truths, which are the main object of contemplation for a truly Catholic intellectual, are wholly contained and efficaciously re-presented in the liturgy. The spirit of contemplation, if true and objective, necessitates the opening to and the experience of the higher realities offered by the sacred rites.
>
> Finally, in what concerns the social life, through the liturgy the individual shares in the life of the Church and assumes his place in the new and definitive order of redeemed creation, the order of the Mystical Body. Thus, the liturgy is the forming factor and the ultimate expression of Catholic society, supernatural and natural (Society of Saint John, *The Founding Document*, No. 41).

EXCLUSIVELY INCLUSIVE

The unity of the Catholic Church in matters of worship has been lessened dramatically by the implementation of the liturgical reforms. We have become a congregational church, with many parishes having their own rites and customs—regardless of anything sanctioned by Rome or the NCCB. A lot of very good people have become so disgusted with the idiosyncratic celebrations of the Mass (and the denial—by priests—of the Real Presence and the sacrificial nature of the Mass) that they have jumped from the Ship of Peter. And this is really one of the goals of the ideologues; although they call themselves "inclusive," they actually want to *exclude* those who believe in "pre-conciliar" notions about the Mass and the priesthood Christ instituted to perpetuate His sacrifice for men until His Second Coming.

The ideologues are not going to stop with revisions approved almost on an annual basis by the American bishops. They are going to continue to experiment as they see fit, continuing to bewilder the faithful. They push out the boundaries with each passing year, hoping that the average Catholic will go along with liturgical abuses quite passively. Anyone who "dissents" from liturgical innovations is to be dismissed as "disruptive" and "divisive."

KEY PROBLEM

The key problem with *Sacrosanctum Concilium* lies not in modernism, *per se*. The key problem, as I see it, with *Sacrosanctum Concilium* is the fact that it called for the *de-centralization* of decision-making on liturgical matters noted above. Oh, yes, it emphasized the primacy of the Holy See; however, it envisioned significant decision-making authority being exercised by what would become the national conferences of Catholic bishops around the world. It called for *diocesan* liturgical commissions in every diocese around the world. That kind of de-centralization is what gave the liturgists who were bent on doing everything Pope Pius XII warned about in *Mediator Dei* an opportunity to *shape* the implementation of the liturgical "renewal" before the *Consilium* (the council appointed by Pope Paul VI to "reform" the liturgy, headed by the notorious friend of the Masons, Archbishop Annibale Bugnini) had made its recommendations to Pope Paul VI.

As stated earlier, the de-centralization of liturgical decision-making, more than any other development ushered in by the Second Vatican Council, is what would embolden modern theologians who desired to stake out positions at odds with the "institutional" Church's teachings. If sweeping liturgical reforms could be introduced in a *blitzkrieg*, so to speak, then it might be possible to convince the faithful that moral teaching also was subject to rapid "change" and "renewal." Liturgical changes, coupled with changes in centuries-old disciplinary practices of the Church—practices which had been promulgated to keep weak human nature in check—would so bewilder, it was reasoned, the people that they might be willing to look to local theologians for moral guidance, rather than look to the Vicar of Christ. And this, in turn, results in Catholics being willing to vote for candidates who support all manner of moral evils; after all, if the Church has changed her liturgy, why cannot moral teaching change?

One of the very reasons that Pope Pius XII warned against changing the human elements in the Liturgy was that he knew that most of the laity would not be able to distinguish between discipline and doctrine. A rapid change of discipline, he knew, could lead some to the erroneous conclusion that doctrine was subject to change. This is precisely what happened.

OPEN FLOODGATES

The devolution of decision-making to the national episcopal conferences made it possible for a whole bureaucracy of theologians and liturgists, in conjunction with the likes of the International Commission for English in the Liturgy, to become the shepherd of the shepherds, if you will. Pronouncements drafted by the United States Catholic Conference, for example, become the basis for catechetical instruction and pastoral practice, with *pro forma* attention being paid to Vatican documents (at best; at worst, of course, Vatican documents are merely ignored). Rome is, in the view of many who populate this strange life-form, a "clearing-house" that occasionally gets in the way of a "free development" of liturgy and doctrine.

What *Sacrosanctum Concilium* unwittingly did, therefore, was to provide the *structure* by which both the Liturgy and doctrine could be undermined and subverted. It is time to admit this reality. The doctrinal dissenters needed to capture control of the Liturgy in order to prepare the way, as perverse John the Baptists, for the coming of the New Age.

Adding to this reality was the fact that the *Consilium*, also an outgrowth of *Sacrosanctum Concilium*, was populated by individuals who were very much in sympathy with the liturgists scattered across the world. There were those at the Council—and those in charge of the enforcement and interpretation of conciliar and post-conciliar documents—who had an agenda alien to the Cross of our Lord. These people, whose names are better left unmentioned, recognized the value of abolishing the old Mass as a means of destroying the faith. For the Mass is the great teacher of the faith. If Theocentricity and Christocentricity could be replaced by *anthro*pocentricity, then there was the possibility of "opening up" Catholics to the ideas of the world, ideas that are in direct contradiction to the Sign of Contradiction Incarnate, Jesus Christ. If the sacerdotal nature of the Mass and the priesthood could be de-emphasized—or obliterated altogether—then there was the possibility that the faithful would see themselves as the true ministers of the Eucharist.

SANDBAGGING

This was not the intent of the reform. Indeed, the Holy See issued document after document to prepare the way for the reform—and to *try* to make mid-course corrections once it had gotten underway (a process which proved futile because of the power that had been assumed by the national episcopal conferences). *Sacram liturgiam, Inter oecumenici, Ecclesiae semper, Eucharisticum mysterium,* the *Missale Romanum, Actio Pastoralis Ecclesiae, Memoriale Domini, Cenam Paschalem, Liturgiae Instaurationes,* and *Conferentiarum episcopalium* are just *some* of the documents issued in the immediate aftermath of the reform. A several-thousand-page book, published in 1979, contains an encyclopedia of documents that had been issued from 1963 to that point. This is not even to mention *Dominicae Cenae* or *Inaestimabile Donum,* issued April 17, 1980. And there have been other documents since then, including ones in 1994 and another in 1997 (yet additional efforts to "reinforce" norms which are ignored in many dioceses around the world).

To be sure, the *Novus Ordo* is valid. It was validly promulgated by a Successor of Saint Peter. And it can be celebrated with great solemnity, as is the case at Monsignor Richard Schuler's St. Agnes parish in St. Paul, Minnesota. The typical experience, however, is far more pedestrian than that of Monsignor Schuler's parish (where priests face a high altar, celebrate the Mass in Latin—and are accompanied by an orchestra and choir). The experience can range from the bizarre to the sacrilegious elsewhere, with novelty replacing the approved liturgical rites.

PERSONAL PRELATURE?

Many observers believe that it is necessary for the good of the faith to raise the *Ecclesia Dei* Commission, created to promote the Tridentine Mass, to the rank of a Personal Prelature of the Holy Father. The faithful should not have to be subjected to ICEL's concoctions. Those who desire solemnity and reverence, who want a Christocentric Mass, should have the ability to attend the Mass of our fathers, substantial parts of which date back over a thousand years. The permanence of the old rite gave rise to an understanding that the truths of the faith were unchanging. It would be a tremendous service to the Church for the Holy Father to make the Mass in which he was ordained to the priesthood available to those who desire the peace that is their right when they attend the Sacrifice of Calvary.

As Pope Pius XI noted in *Quas Primas* in 1925:

> For people are instructed in the truths of the faith, and brought to appreciate the inner joys of religion far more effectually by the annual celebration of our sacred mysteries than by any pronouncement, however weighty, of the teaching of the Church. Such pronouncements usually reach only a few and the more learned among the faithful; feasts reach them all; the former speak but once, the latter speak every year—in fact, for ever. The Church's teaching affects the mind primarily; her feasts affect both mind and heart, and have a salutary effect upon the whole of man's nature. Man is composed of body and soul, and he needs these external festivities so that the sacred rites, in all their beauty and variety, may stimulate him to drink more deeply of the fountain of God's teaching, that he may make it a part of himself with profit for his spiritual life.

Moreover, there was a cycle of preaching. Pope Pius XI recognized the Church could produce all types of marvelous documents to teach the faith. However, most people have neither the time nor the inclination to read papal encyclical letters. They learned the faith from the annual cycle of preaching at Holy Mass. They were reminded in Mass of the Ten Commandments and the Beatitudes. Yes, the Mass is the great teacher.

REIGN OF CHRIST THE KING

It is not possible to end our social problems if we do not recognize the social kingship of Jesus Christ and His Holy Church as the only basis of true justice. And it is not possible to establish the reign of Christ the King if there is confusion in the Body of Christ. That confusion will not end as long as we make a mockery of Christ's Holy Sacrifice, the Mass.

We can hold all manner of protests against abortion. We can wring our hands about the horrible nature of the Clinton administration. But we are not going to stop these outrages if our liturgy does not reflect the social and eschatological kingship of Jesus Christ.

Every human being is going to see our Lord as his King at the moment of his particular judgment. The world is going to see Jesus Christ return in *glory* as King at the end of the world. There will be no mistaking his Kingship then. There will be no hiding places. The just will acknowledge his Kingship with jubilation; the unjust will flee in fright.

None of us knows the exact day or hour of our death, no less when the world is going to end. We have a fundamental obligation, therefore, to work with all of the strength afforded us by the grace won for us on Calvary to establish His reign here and now. All of our culture—politics, education, law, literature, music, entertainment—must be subordinated under His reign. There is no other answer to the problems of our era.

Christ's reign in our own hearts must be renewed every day. Every choice we make either moves us closer toward Christ—or farther away from Him. Similarly, His social reign must be renewed day in and day out. We must recognize His sovereignty at all times and in all circumstances. We must insist that our laws and politics reflect His unchanging teaching. But we can only do that if we encounter Him as our Lord and King in the sublime mystery of Holy Mass. And it is only the Mass of our fathers that faithfully communicates this Kingship.

THE MYTHOLOGY OF THE TAX-EXEMPT STATUS

One of the reasons given by some orthodox bishops for their relative timidity in matters of politics is a concern they have over losing the Church's tax-exempt status. Others among the episcopate and in chancery offices are only too happy to use the tax-exempt status as a dodge to avoid discussing contraception and abortion at all. The Cardinal Archbishop of Los Angeles, Roger Mahony, said during the 1992 campaign that there are "other" issues besides abortion.

The response that the Cardinal Mahonys in the Church use is that it is not possible to change behavior by law. No? 1.5 million women were not seeking abortions prior to the decision in *Roe v. Wade*. As Dr. Bernard Nathanson has documented both in *Aborting America* and *The Abortion Papers*, the most accurate statistics for the pre-*Roe* period indicate that about 100,000 illegal abortions were performed in the United States each year. There has been a ten-fold increase in that number since the legalization of abortion-on-demand until the day of birth. Women are having abortions because they believe, erroneously, that it is their constitutionally guaranteed right to do so. A plethora of Catholic politicians *reaffirm* them in the existence of this bogus right. What do some of our bishops do and say? They say that there is nothing that can be done.

Law *does* change behavior. Those of us committed to the restoration of legal protection to our preborn brothers and sisters recognize the fact that the *mere* overturning of *Roe* (as unlikely as that seems at present) is not going to end the demand for abortions. Much needs to be done to change hearts and souls. But changing the law is a necessary first step; Saint Thomas Aquinas tells us that a law which sanctions a grave moral evil is unjust and illegitimate. There is much work of evangelization and catechesis to be done within our own Catholic ranks to assure that such a change in law would be met with enthusiasm and prayers of thanksgiving to the Father through the Son in Spirit and in Truth.

POLICY AGREEMENT

The truth is that some bishops and chancery officers—and many people within the headquarters of the NCCB/USCC—find the programs of the Democratic Party appealing. They believe in the illusion of secular salvation through the quasi-socialist policies of Clinton and his ilk. *That* is why they are so happy to acquiesce to the guidelines of the Internal Revenue Service. Failing to understand the problems of humanity are caused by original sin and can be remedied only by a constant metanoia on the part of each person in cooperation with God's grace, many of our clerics look to government for the "solution" to our national problems. They buy into the class-envy arguments of the left, believing in all tragic error that the "poor" will be helped out of their material poverty by massive redistribution of income through government taxation policies. The failure of this formula to have worked previously in our national history does little to dissuade these people from believing in social engineering with the sort of religious fervor and conviction that should be reserved solely for the Holy Faith.

Some bishops would contend that it is an act of prudence to submit to the IRS guidelines. But the unpleasant truth is that all of the Church's efforts in this country to cooperate with the government (particularly in the work of Catholic Charities, the Campaign for Human Development) results in greater government demands for adherence to its bureaucratic agenda of social engineering. The Archdiocese of New York several years ago was on the verge of severing its ties with the City's foster child-care program because bureaucrats demanded that birth control and abortion information be provided to children entrusted to the Archdiocese. A compromise was reached where the children receive this information from the bureaucrats—and not directly from any Catholic social service agency. There is the refusal to face facts: the Church is under siege, albeit by slightly more sophisticated and subtle means than employed by Nero, by the state to cease being a force for spiritual and moral reform in society.

SUBMIT OR CHALLENGE

It is therefore no act of prudence to submit to the tax terrorists. It is not even good constitutional law to do so. For it is the contention of this professor trained in constitutional law that all of the guidelines imposed upon the Church are unconstitutional (and duplicitly enforced). The bishops of the United States could challenge these guidelines successfully on the grounds of the clear language of the United States Constitution. True, the legal positivists who comprise much of U.S. District Courts and Circuit Courts of Appeal would probably not agree with the case which will be made below. But the Supreme Court, as currently constituted, *might* accept the following argument:

The First Amendment to the United States Constitution states that Congress shall pass no law respecting the establishment of religion—nor of prohibiting the free exercise thereof. This is a double-edged sword. As has been well-documented in other places, the reason the establishment clause was inserted in the amendment was because of the rivalry and distrust among all of the various Protestant sects; there could be no agreement about which of those sects should be the state church. There was thus the agreement to have none. This does not mean, however, that religious ideas were to be excluded from public policy discourse—or that religious leaders were to be denied the exercise of free speech in attempting to *persuade* society about the relevancy of supernatural truths. However, this is *precisely* what most people, including many Catholics, *do* believe: that it is somewhat unjust, undemocratic, and authoritarian for a bishop or priest to take a stand on public policy.

HYPOCRISY

Even *that* warped understanding of the first amendment admits of exceptions. It is "politically correct" for bishops to oppose the build-up of nuclear weaponry or to condemn economic injustice or to seek the eradication of the death penalty. But dare any one of them speak out on an issue touching upon personal morality, then the cries of "separation of Church and State" are invoked with solemn tones of apoplexy and indignation. What hypocrisy! There can be no social justice or world peace unless *we* are at peace with God by virtue of our being in a state of sanctifying grace.

How is it that Bill Clinton, Al Gore, Jesse Jackson—and other Democratic politicians—can openly campaign, from the pulpit, in black Baptist churches and no one talks about removing *their* tax exempt status? How is it that the *Reverend* Jesse Jackson is considered an appropriate public figure and the courageous Bishop Fabian Bruskewitz of Lincoln, Nebraska, is not? How is it that Bill Clinton can quote Scripture and be hailed as a hero while a Pat Buchanan is termed a religious zealot when doing so? We know how. Hypocrisy and duplicity of the highest order.

Religious leaders have a constitutionally protected right of free speech. They also have a duty, as part of their constitutionally protected right of free exercise of religion, to speak the truth as they see it. But the churches they represent have an *inherent* constitutional right to be tax-exempt! We do not have to rely upon Congressional statutes and the rules written by the IRS. There is an inherent constitutional right of churches to be exempt from taxation.

CHURCH RIGHTS

If churches have a right to exist and to exercise their religious duties, it stands to reason that any attempt to interfere with that exercise constitutes an unconstitutional infringement on religion. Chief Justice John Marshall noted in *McCulloch v. Maryland* in 1819 that the power to tax is the power to destroy. He was speaking of the State of Maryland's imposition of a transactions tax upon the branch Bank of the United States in Baltimore. But the principle is a solid one: the power to tax is the power to destroy. The state has no legitimate right to seek to destroy churches by means of taxation. It is a simple argument. It is constitutionally unassailable.

WORTH THE RISK

Instead of acquiescing to the Internal Revenue Service, the United States Catholic Conference would do well to *challenge* the appropriate federal statutes—and all guidelines written to enforce them—on the grounds stated herein. But even if they should lose, so what? So what? Is not the immortal soul of a woman seeking an abortion worth risking material benefits for? Is not the life of a little baby created in the image and likeness of God worth being disliked by the intelligentsia, the bureaucratic elite, and the media?

The Apostles did not take personal comfort and security into consideration when they traveled to the far corners of the known world to preach the Gospel. We should have the courage to stand by the foot of the Cross with our Lady to say that no government can legitimately silence us from proclaiming the Truth Who is her Divine Son.

We need our shepherds to stand up in defense of the faith, to be of one mind and one heart with the Chief Shepherd on earth, the Vicar of Christ. The sheep need to hear from their shepherds words of prophetic, apostolic zeal, not silence, a lot of which implies support for the very people (such as Clinton) who are opposed to the splendor of Truth Incarnate.

CHAPTER SEVEN

How We Got from Christendom to Clintondom

As has been demonstrated in previous chapters, one must understand government and politics in light of a true understanding of human nature. And human nature can only be understood authentically in light of Original Sin and Christ's Redemptive Act. The only real way to ameliorate the problems of the world is by individual spiritual and moral reform made possible by the graces won for us on Calvary.

Nevertheless human beings still live in specific institutional arrangements, the chief of which is the family. The hierarchical structure of the family is, as has been noted before, in imitation of the sovereignty of the Triune God over all of His creation, and in imitation of the hierarchical nature of Holy Mother Church herself. But society also needs to be structured in a hierarchical manner, beginning with a fundamental respect for the rights of Christ's Holy Church to guide men in matters of faith and morals.

ORDER IN SOCIETY

Church fathers have been reflecting since before the collapse of the Roman Empire on the institutional arrangements in society which are most conducive to helping foster those conditions necessary for the salvation of individual souls. One constant in Catholic political philosophy, however, has been the realization that there is no perfect society attainable here on earth; there is no one political arrangement and/or ideology which is going to resolve the problems of humanity. Human problems are the result of the free will choices made by individual human beings; order in society is the result of order within individual souls. And order within individual souls is the consequence of being in a state of sanctifying grace. The more holiness there exists within the souls of individuals in a society, the more likely it is that that society will reflect the order desired by God for the proper functioning of civil government. That is, the Kingdom of God needs to be built up in individual souls on a daily basis. One mortal sin can kill the life of grace in the soul until it is restored in the hospital of Divine Mercy, the Sacrament of Penance. As most people fight a daily struggle of good and evil, and as even venial sin can darken the intellect and weaken the will, order within individual souls is an ongoing process. Spiritual growth is usually gradual, as good habits are hard to form and very easy to break; bad habits are very easy to form and very difficult to break. That is why there is no once-and-for-all solution to the problems of a society; the pursuit of an authentic justice based upon Justice Himself requires our constant attention.

FIRST AND LAST THINGS

What the age of Christendom demonstrated was that it was possible for people to be rightly directed to First and Last Things, even though the frailties of human nature were all too evident. All manner of wars were fought. Corruption was frequently rife within the members of Holy Mother Church, with much bad example having been given. But people had a common frame of reference, the Faith, to understand why problems exist, and how problems can be resolved by individual spiritual and moral reformation.

During the Age of Christendom (also referred to as the Middle Ages), people gave unto God what was God's, and they gave unto Caesar what was Caesar's. What belongs to God are the principles of the just society, starting with the defense of innocent human life. As will be demonstrated in a later chapter, the attempt to overthrow the sovereignty of God in matters of human sexuality, particularly as it relates to contraception and abortion, has led to all manner of individual and collective confusion. Deny God in just one thing as it relates to the fundamental dignity of the human being, and the process is set in motion for a whole range of consequences which can lead to the undermining of all order in a given society.

115

However, God has a role to play even in the things of Caesar. While there is no "Catholic" way to build a highway or a bridge, or to perform a particular type of surgery, a properly-formed Catholic does everything for the greater glory of God. Such a Catholic is going to build the best highway he can, as he realizes he is doing everything in the Divine Presence—and for the good of his brothers and sisters in the Lord. Such a Catholic recognizes that the salvation of his immortal soul depends in large measure on how well he fulfills the obligations imposed by his freely chosen state in life. One of the reasons, for example, there are so many economic problems in the world today is because people no longer pursue excellence as befits a child of God; they are working merely to make money, and to do that as a means to enjoy leisure time as the ultimate end of human existence. While the enjoyment of leisure time is legitimate, the pursuit of mediocrity on the job—and the belief that life is one giant entitlement—both run contrary to the dignity of human work, to the honor that we owe the Triune God. There was a frank recognition of that during the Middle Ages; many commentators in the world today are aghast if there is even the mention of such a perspective, no less an earnest effort to try to base a sound economy on the individual pursuit of personal excellence for the honor and glory of God.

MONARCHY

Similarly, monarchs in the Middle Ages were required, albeit more than a little reluctantly on occasion, to recognize that civil law must be conformed to the Divine and natural laws, that they were to be judged by the Divine Judge on the basis of how just they had been to the subjects entrusted to their care. Consider the words of Saint Louis IX, King of France, in a letter written to his son:

> My dearest son, my first instruction is that you should love the Lord your God with all your heart and all your strength. Without this there is no salvation. Keep yourself, my son, from everything that you know displeases God, that is to say, from every mortal sin. You should permit yourself to be tormented by every kind of martyrdom before you would allow yourself to commit a mortal sin.
> If the Lord has permitted you to have some trial, bear it

willingly and with gratitude, considering that it has happened for your good and that perhaps you well deserve it. If the Lord bestows upon you any kind of prosperity, thank him humbly and see that you become no worse for it, either through vain pride or anything else, because you ought not to oppose God or offend him in the matter of his gifts.

Listen to the divine office with pleasure and devotion. As long as you are in church, be careful not to let your eyes wander and not to speak empty words, but pray to the Lord devoutly, either aloud or with the interior prayer of the heart.

Be kindhearted to the poor, the unfortunate and the afflicted. Give them as much help and consolation as you can. Thank God for all the benefits he has bestowed upon you, that you may be worthy to receive greater. Be just to your subjects, swaying neither to the right nor left, but holding the line of justice. Always side with the poor rather than with the rich, until you are certain of the truth. See that all your subjects live in justice and peace, but especially those who have ecclesiastical rank and those who belong to religious orders.

Be devout and obedient to our mother the Church of Rome and the Supreme Pontiff as your spiritual father. Work to remove all sin from your land, particularly blasphemies and heresies."

PROTESTANT REVOLT

There was a fusion between faith and culture during the Middle Ages that made it possible for there to be the social reign of Christ the King. That fusion would come under attack by some of the forces of the Renaissance, many elements of which promoted the relativism that had been fought by Socrates, Plato, Aristotle, and Cicero in the pagan world of Greek and Roman antiquity. Michel de Montaigne said, "We can know nothing with certainty." (It is interesting how those who deny absolute truths do so absolutely.) But those elements of the Renaissance which promoted relativism in the social and political orders only paved the way for the theological relativism of Martin Luther, which unwittingly made it possible for political ideology to replace Christianity as the drive force of culture.

Augustinian monk Martin Luther was a profoundly troubled man. The father of the Protestant Revolt could not accept the fact that he was loved by God. This simple fact led to a chain of events which culminated in the division of Western Christendom. And it is the division of Christendom which is the reason for most of the chaos in society today.

Luther suffered from what spiritual directors call "scruples." Scruples—derived from the Latin word *scrupulus*, meaning "small unit of measure"—is a condition involving decrees of compulsive behavior *and* a strong lack of the sense of self-worth. The manifestations of scruples in Father Luther's life were many.

1. As noted above, Luther did not believe that he was loved by God. This mistaken notion became the entire basis of the Protestant Revolt: that the human being was evil by nature. John Calvin would echo this quintessential Lutheran conviction. Luther said, "The human being is a dungheap covered with a few snowflakes of grace." As Catholics, we know that God makes nothing but that which is good; *all* human beings are good—but flawed because of original sin. Luther contended that human nature was entirely corrupted by original sin. Wrong.

2. Luther was a man plagued by feelings of guilt for the sins he had committed. It stands to reason that a man who does not believe in God's love for him is going to doubt that God could forgive His sins. Luther would go to confession every day, but he did not "feel" forgiven. This led to profound conflicts within him. His inability to accept forgiveness resulted in the Protestant rejection of the Sacrament of Penance, a sacrament clearly instituted by our Lord in Saint John's Gospel.

3. Luther believed that his love for God was unrequited. It was therefore difficult for him to pray, particularly to engage in liturgical prayer. He would deliberately not pray the Divine Office for periods of up to one month, thirty days. Then, consumed by guilt, he would stay up for thirty hours making up the Office he had missed. (A priest is required, under penalty of sin, to pray the Divine Office each day; a missed day is gone. It cannot be made up. Luther thought that the penance given him by his confessor was inadequate; *he* would *add* the penance on his

own by making up the days that had already passed by into the pages of history.)

4. Luther was a man of tremendous pride. Although he was gifted with an unquestionably keen intellect, Luther was a strange combination of a man: one who was insecure and consumed by guilt—but who at the same time had feelings of massive superiority and pride. This is not an uncommon German characteristic. Transcending his feelings of inadequacy, Luther believed that his theological insights were the most profound in the history of Christianity. That is quite a leap for a man who did not believe he was a lovable creature of the Loving God.

PROBLEMS IN THE CHURCH

Luther saw real problems within the Body of Christ in the Sixteenth Century. The clergy had become very corrupt in many parts of the world. The sale of indulgences to finance the construction of the Basilica of Saint Peter in Rome was scandalous. There were abuses of temporal power and authority by some bishops and pastors.

What Luther failed to recognize was that problems had *always* existed in the Church. The first bishops ran away from their Divine Master on Good Friday. They refused to believe that He had risen from the dead. Many bishops and priests in the Fourth Century were Arians, men who did not believe in the Divinity of Christ. The clergy of the Twelfth Century was about as corrupt as that of the Sixteenth Century.

In each of these troubled eras, however, God raised up individuals to lead the reform of the Church from *within*. Saint Francis of Assisi, for example, was one of the greatest reformers in Church history. But he worked from *within*, trusting in the power of God's grace to effect *internal* reform with the souls of individual human beings. Francis, like so many before (and after) him, realized that the Church is the property of no one man. The Church was founded by our Lord and Savior Jesus Christ upon the Rock of Peter, the Pope. He promised that the gates of Hell would not prevail against her; He said that He would be with us until the end of time. Francis knew, therefore, that the problems that existed because of the weak human beings who composed the Church Militant on earth would have to be worked out in the framework of a humble faith.

Humility was not a word which could be used to describe Father Martin Luther. He was impatient, strong-willed, prideful—yet plagued with self-doubt. He overcame his self-doubt to confront the problems that he perceived existed in the Church. In so doing, however, Luther began to reject practically every aspect of the Catholic faith. He said that human beings did not need any guide for the interpretation of Scripture, and he gave us the belief that it is Scripture *alone* which leads to faith in Christ (and hence salvation).

What Luther did was revolutionary. He was saying that the previous fifteen hundred years of Christian thought and development had been erroneous. Revelation had been given to him. Or had it? His break with Rome prompted a mad scramble for the gold in the former Catholic churches which had gone over to Lutheranism. He was frightened and depressed that all the common man seemed interested in was gold and silver, not in his theological "insights."

IMPURITY AND DIVORCE

Living the Cross of Christ is always difficult. Fallen human nature works against our desire to build a more intimate relationship with God. But God's grace is always sufficient for us to live a life of sanctity *if* we choose to cooperate with it by our own free will choices. Luther, in essence, denied much of human freedom (although not to the degree that Calvin did; Calvin denied human freedom in its entirety). Human beings are always looking for reasons not to live out the Gospel message. As a scrupe, Luther did not believe it was possible to live by the light of the Catholic faith. Breaking the bond of unity with the See of Peter, Luther gave free rein to human depravity.

Father John Hardon has written that the Protestant Revolt was principally about sex and divorce. The theological relativism of the Revolt reinforced the moral relativism of the Renaissance, which has become preeminent in our own time. Human beings were deprived of the Sacraments that Christ Himself had instituted for the salvation of each human being. The division of

Christendom is what makes it possible for the neopagans to have such influence on our society in this last decade of Christianity's second millennium.

BROKEN FROM ROME

It is no accident that the land of pride which spawned Luther would later spawn the ideas of Marx, Nietzsche, and Hitler. The land of the Revolt later became the land of the social engineering and eugenics which would lead to the Nazi genocide. This is not what Luther intended, but it is the natural result of what happens when humanity strays from the one, true Sheepfold of Peter.

Another interesting facet of Luther's complex personality was his anti-Semitism. His book *Table Talk* is replete with hateful references to Jews. He blamed Jewish people for many of the problems of the world—and for many of his own personal problems. *Table Talk* is as much an embarrassment to Lutherans as Margaret Sanger's writings are to her disciples.

The break with Rome prompted by Luther begat a series of revolts. If no one is the pope, then everyone is the pope. The state of affairs which exists in Christianity today is not what Christ prayed for at the Last Supper. He prayed that all of his disciples would be one. He was not joking.

Luther's belief that human beings were saved by faith alone gave rise, however unwittingly, to the belief that all a person has to do to enter the Kingdom of Heaven is to *profess* faith in Christ. This heresy is what prompts many "evangelical" Christians to think that "being saved" is a once and for all proposition; they do not see the need for *living* out the Gospel message on a daily basis.

The net effect of Luther and Calvin was a profound fission between faith and culture in European society. The unity which had characterized Europe for over a thousand years was rent asunder. This had a direct impact upon the Christian conception of the State—and gave rise to political ideologues peddling their wares as the logical substitute for the "fraud" of Christianity.

As Pope Pius XII noted in his encyclical letter *Ad Summi Pontificatus* (*On the State in the Modern World*):

The denial of the fundamentals of morality had its origin, in

Europe, in the abandonment of that Christian teaching of which
the Chair of Peter is the depository and exponent. That teaching had once given spiritual cohesion to a Europe which, educated and ennobled, and civilized by the Cross, had reached
such a degree of civil progress as to become the teacher of
other peoples, of other continents. But, cut off from the infallible teaching authority of the Church, not a few separated
brethren have gone so far as to overthrow the central dogma of
Christianity, the Divinity of the Savior, and have hastened
thereby the progress of spiritual decay.

The Holy Gospel narrates that when Jesus was crucified
"there was darkness over the whole earth" (Mt. 27:45); a terri-
fying symbol of what happened and what will happen spiritually wherever incredulity, blind and proud of itself, has suc-
ceeded in excluding Christ from modern life, especially from
public life, and has undermined faith in God as well as faith in
Christ. The consequence is that the moral values by which in
other times public and private conduct was gauged have fallen
into disuse; and the much vaunted civilization of society, which
has made ever more rapid progress, withdrawing man, the family, and the State from the beneficent and regenerating effects
of the idea of God and the teaching of the Church, has caused
to reappear, in regions in which for many centuries shone the
splendors of Christian civilization, in a manner ever clear, ever
more distinct, ever more distressing, the signs of a corrupt and
corrupting paganism. "There was darkness when they crucified
Jesus."

There is much prophecy in this passage from Pius XII's
encyclical letter. The division of Christendom has led to all of our
problems today. The "state" has replaced the Church as the guiding force of society. Indeed, the state is considered by the social
scientists and social engineers to be better equipped than the family to educate children. The breakdown of the family, chronicled
herein, is the direct result of the collapse of unity in Christendom.
Divorce, adultery, child abuse, contraception, abortion, selfish
careerism, feminism all spring from the tree of Luther and Calvin.

BREAKDOWN OF THE FAMILY

The reason, for example, that the inner city family has lost its
stability in the contemporary United States is because the reli-

gious faith of families has been attacked by social workers and government bureaucrats. Margaret Sanger and Rexford Tugwell were just two of the leading proponents of eliminating religious faith from the "colored" people so that blacks and other non-whites would not "reproduce" themselves. "More from the fit, less from the unfit. *That* is the chief issue of birth control," read the masthead of Sanger's *Birth Control Review* in 1919. And when a society such as ours is founded on a defective under-standing of Christianity, the results are nothing less than personal disorder and social chaos.

The problems we face in the United States as a result of the Revolt and the rise of political ideology are multifaceted and inter-related. Drug abuse, worker under-productivity, student lazi-ness—in a word, the sloth exhibited by so many in society—is the result of people not understanding that they live every moment of their lives in the Divine presence. If we understood that we have to answer to Almighty God for how we have spent every moment of our lives, and if we were truly in Love with Love Incarnate, *then* many of our societal problems would be ameliorated.

The recognition of the Chair of Peter as the binding force of the world is not a panacea. Human nature remains wounded as a result of original sin. As Pope Pius XII noted in the encyclical let-ter referred to above:

> With the weakening of faith in God and in Jesus Christ, and the darkening in men's minds of the light of moral principles, there disappeared the indispensable foundation of the stability and quiet of that internal and external, private and public, order, which alone can support and safeguard the prosperity of States.
>
> It is true that even when Europe had a cohesion of broth-erhood through identical ideals gathered from Christian preach-ing, she was not free from divisions, convulsions, and war which laid her waste; but perhaps they never felt the intense pessimism of today as to the possibility of settling them, for they had then an effective moral sense of the just and of the unjust, of the lawful and of the unlawful, which, by restraining outbreaks of passion, left the way open to an honorable settle-ment. In our days, on the contrary, dissensions come not only from the surge of rebellious passion, but also from a deep spir-itual crisis which has overthrown the sound principles of pri-vate and public morality.

ENDS V. MEANS

Political ideologues capitalized on the divisions within Christendom. Niccolo Machiavelli paved the way to amorality in statecraft with *The Prince*. Cleverly disguising his own arguments, the Italian political philosopher argued that morality and politics must be separated. The ends therefore justify the means. There is no need for a "prince" to agonize over the morality of particular decisions; all he needs to do is what is *expedient* for his own ends. This is the foundation of utilitarianism—an ideology which characterizes American government and politics in the last decade of the Twentieth Century.

But it is John Locke who gave birth to an ideology, liberalism, which instituted the specious notion of secular self-redemption. The analysis of Locke which follows is closely allied with that of Joseph de Maistre and Russell Kirk.

Although much of his *Second Treatise on Civil Government* is ambiguous, Locke seems to say that democracy could be defined as a form of government wherein the people voluntarily relinquish their claim to total liberty in order to enjoy the protection of their basic rights and liberties by a government they create, elect, and participate in.

Locke based his philosophy upon the following false premises:

a. that, at one time, there existed something called a state of nature. There was no law, no organized society or government. In such a situation, man was incapable of realizing the protection of his basic right to life, liberty, and property.

b. since groups of individuals could therefore violate with impunity the rights of others, Locke concluded that reasonable men banded together to improve or perfect the state of nature.

c. these reasonable men, drawing their strength in a majoritarian manner, would conclude that the state of nature was defective and required improvement.

d. the price of protecting basic rights and liberties would be the forfeiture of the claim to total liberty.

e. the reasonable majority would therefore devise the structures of government necessary to afford the protection of basic rights and liberties and to perfect the state of nature.

f. if, for whatever reason, the consensus of the majority was lost—or if the structures failed to perfect the state of nature, a new majority of reasonable men could arise to once again perfect the state of nature.

Locke's ideas may appear romantically attractive. But the plain fact of the matter is that he was attempting to provide a secularized version of Genesis. His account of the creation of society is patently false and contains within it the following problems:

a. the state of nature never existed. According to Russell Kirk, the human being has always lived in the framework of a moral covenant. All societies at all times have had codes of conduct and have penalized members for not living in accord with those codes. The state of nature is pure Lockean mythology.

As Kirk points out in *The Roots of American Order*:

All the aspects of any civilization arise out of a people's religion: its politics, its economics, its arts, its sciences, even its simple crafts are the by-products of religious insights and a religious cult. . . . Thus all order—even the ideological order of modern totalist states, professing atheism—could not have come into existence, had it not grown out of general belief in truths that are perceived by the moral imagination.

b. Locke confused liberty with license. Having the physical freedom to perform an act does not mean that one has the moral right to commit that act! Thus, one does not have the freedom morally to push his neighbor in front of a subway train. How can it be said, then, that one is giving up his "freedom" not to perform an act of violence?

c. Locke wrongly concludes that government is an artificial imposition upon human society. Government is *not* an artificial imposition upon human society. It is a natural response to the phenomenon of politics. Locke concluded that since humans had to surrender their claim to total freedom, government was unnatural. For Locke, government took humans out of the state of nature. But since the state of nature never existed (and since he confused liberty with license), government is not an artificial evil.

d. Locke trusts infallibly in the reasonableness of the majority. Locke could not conceive of a situation whereby the majority would not be composed of anyone other than reasonable humans. As we know, the crowd is often wrong. Mobocracy is *not* the basis for just government. Majorities have rationalized practically every perversion of the natural order.

e. Locke wrongly believes in the ability of structural reform to perfect the state of nature. This is the fundamental belief of all modern liberalism (and most modern conservatism). The liberal belief is that a majority of reasonable persons can devise those structures which will resolve societal problems. Such a belief, while held most sincerely by many people, treats the symptoms of problems rather than problems' root causes. Without understanding that the root cause of societal problems is fallen human nature (and hence remediable only by constant personal conversion to holiness on daily basis), the human being becomes convinced that he can create THE solution to the problems of war, poverty, homelessness, drug abuse, AIDS, economic injustice, racism, greed, environmental pollution, and the like. The fact that such solutions never work does nothing to convince committed Lockeans of the rightness of their position. For example, we are told by Planned Parenthood that the "solution" to teen pregnancy is *more* birth control! Never mind the fact that it was precisely the proliferation of birth control which made conjugal relations outside of marriage attractive to teenagers (and apparently "safe" from its natural end during the fertile years: pregnancy). Planned Parenthood contends that young people cannot control themselves. But human beings are endowed with reason which can control our disordered passions. But the anti-chastity crowd contends that we need more of a solution that has failed to work.

Similarly, there are those who believe that the mere

expenditure of funds on social problems will result in the resolution of those problems. The failure of such programs to work (urban poverty remains high, homelessness is on the rise) does nothing to cause such ideologues to rethink their basic premises. The same is true of those who believe that the mere expenditure of money will produce a stronger defense (or those who think that the elimination of weapons by itself will produce peace). There were wars long before there were nuclear weapons. As Albert Einstein said, when asked what the next war would be fought with, "I don't know what the next war will be fought with. The one after the next one, however, will be fought with sticks and stones."

The belief in structural reform as the means to resolve societal problems leads the human being to believe in self-redemption. That is, adherents to a secular political ideology believe that it is possible to realize real social improvement without individual moral reform. It is possible to lessen the *effects* of injustice in the world—but only as a result of humans who cooperate with God's grace and who recognize the limitation of governmental actions.

f. Locke's system leads to frustration. If one believes that structural reform in and of itself is the means to perfect the state of nature, then one is bound to lead a life of utter frustration. The person who believes that "others" are responsible for their problems get divorced frequently, are rootless and restless—and are constantly searching for "external" solutions to ease their sense of unhappiness (an unhappiness which has internal origins). Similarly, a society seeking in good faith to deal with serious problems will find itself quite frustrated when the problems remain despite the "best" efforts to eradicate them. New solutions are therefore proposed as the next step to resolve problems. Marx saw the failures of liberalism and proposed what he considered to be the ultimate solution: communism (a system designed theoretically to produce "peace" and "justice"). The unraveling of communism in Eastern Europe leaves hardline left-wingers shaking their heads in disbelief.

Locke's influence on modern thought is profound. Although most of the men who framed the American Constitution had made a break with Locke's simple-minded majoritarian formula for secular self-redemption, it is the Lockean view of government that prevails in education and politics today. As noted in earlier chapters, people have come to believe that the government can somehow resolve all of the problems of human society without any moral and spiritual reformation of individual lives.

REVOLUTIONS

As will be discussed in the next chapter, the French Revolution had its own influence on the American experiment in self-government (and upon the implementation of totalitarian rule in the former Soviet Union by the Bolsheviks in 1917). The French Revolution unleashed what can be called the ideology of hatred upon the human race.

Unlike the American Revolution (which was a revolt against British colonial rule), the French Revolution was a social revolution which sought to overthrow all existing order in society. Its leaders blamed—and hated—others for causing injustice and poverty. Motivated by a spirit of what the late Father Vincent Miceli referred to as "anti-Theism" (the hatred of God), it was a short step to hate human beings who are made in the image and likeness of God.

The French Revolutionaries substituted sloganeering for religious faith. The Twentieth Century has been a time in which sloganeering has become the basis of education, communication, politics, and jurisprudence. As Simone Weil once noted, "It is as though we had returned to the age of Protagoras and the Sophists, the age when the art of persuasion—whose modern equivalent is advertising slogans, publicity, propaganda meetings, the press, the cinema, and radio—took the place of thought and controlled the fate of cities and accomplished *coups d'etat*. So the ninth book of Plato's *Republic* looks like a description of contemporary events."

Thousands were put to death in revolutionary France because they were deemed to be "enemies of the people." "The people." Sound familiar? Sure. The *People's* Republic of China. The highest title: *citizen*. How did President Clinton begin his inaugural address? "My fellow citizens. . . ." He did not want to use the phrase, "my fellow *Americans.*"

THE "COMMON MAN"

The spirit of the French Revolution infects American politics in a number of ways. It is from the French Revolution (*not* the American Revolution) that we find a societal commitment to simple-minded majoritarian egalitarianism as the basis of politics and government. Andrew Jackson, no "common" man, perverted the whole notion of the statesmanship envisioned by the Founding Fathers of this nation. Jackson believed that it did not take any particular experience or education to hold public office; any person, the common "citizen," could handle the responsibilities of the public trust.

Jackson popularized anti-intellectualism as a distinguishing characteristic of American social life. Anyone who uses words too difficult for the "common man" to understand is not trustworthy enough to hold public office. Closely allied with careerism (the commitment to career success by whatever means prove expedient, a variation on Machiavelli's theme), anti-intellectualism reduces democracy to a pandering to the lowest common denominator. Rather than attempt to *elevate* the level of national debate during an election year, the ethos of anti-intellectualism seeks to use plebiscitary polls as a means of gauging national "feelings" as the only legitimate basis of public policy.

The demagogues who exploited these themes were only too eager to serve as evangelizers of the Jacksonian spirit of democracy to the immigrants who arrived on these shores in the middle of the Nineteenth Century. The Irish and German immigrants, many of whom were Catholics, learned quickly that the road to political and economic success in the New World followed the path of American materialism and careerism, thereby developing an alliance with the Democratic Party, particularly when the latter supported public funding of parochial schools in the State of New York in the 1860s.

ANTI–CATHOLICISM

Anti–Catholicism, which has deep roots in the American

129

character, unwittingly forced the immigrants into seeking success in politics as the means of upward mobility, most other avenues being closed to them. Even this had to be stopped.

Growing out of Calvinist materialism—and the native individualism that is a hallmark of Protestantism—anti–Catholicism in the Nineteenth Century led to organized efforts to keep Catholics out of politics. Much of the thrust of the "Good Government" movement of the 1880s was a thinly-disguised effort to prevent big-city political "bosses" from using their new-found source of electoral support, the Catholics, as a springboard for a Catholic president.

MATERIALISM

Unfortunately for us in the last decade of the *Twentieth* Century, the plain fact is that most of the Catholics who came here in the two major waves of immigration (the second occurring in the 1870s and 1880s) were not seeking to serve as missionaries in their adopted home. Not at all. They wanted to get a piece of the American *material* pie. And while it is true the culture from which they came was losing its Catholic influence, there was certainly more societal support for living the Catholic faith in Europe than in the United States.

The practice of the Catholic faith, therefore, became something that was a "religious obligation" on Sundays and holy days, but most Catholic immigrants saw little need to bring their faith out into the marketplace. Indeed, there were some bishops who attempted to *discourage* Catholics from being too overtly Catholic, encouraging their sheep to become as American as possible. This movement, called Americanism, preached a belief in American pluralistic democracy as the basis of the just society, going so far as to call Catholic elementary and high schools a possible threat to peace among people belonging to different religious denominations.

Not all immigrants succumbed to the Americanist spirit; the faith *was* handed on very successfully by two generations of parents. But the corrupting influence of the culture (and the fissions that would take place in the Church in the United States as a result of the recrudescence of Modernism following the close of the Second Vatican Council) proved so corrosive that a large plurality of Catholics today have no understanding of the relationship between their faith and public policy. All the immigrants of the Nineteenth Century wanted was to be "good" money-making Americans. They were not, regrettably, the "threat" to social order feared by the leaders of the reform movement. The Democratic Party became the vehicle by which the new immigrants were socialized into the mainstream of American political life. This explains the almost religious-like adherence of many Catholics to a political party which now champions every perversion of the Divine and natural laws imaginable.

POLITICAL SOCIALIZATION

Long before the advent of government welfare programs, social assistance was provided in the Nineteenth Century by the urban political machines. New arrivals to these shores would be given jobs, places to live, food, clothing—and other benefits *if* they were willing to do what the "bosses" desired (stuffing ballot boxes, intimidating opponents, canvassing for votes). Politics quickly became the means of socialization into the United States.

Edwin O'Connor's novel, *The Last Hurrah*, depicted the conflict between a typical big city boss (a thinly disguised version of Mayor James Francis Curley of Boston) and the Protestant "bluebloods" who opposed him. Prescient in so many ways, the novel is a very good portrayal of the resentment felt by those who were being outnumbered by Catholics. The Republican candidate for President of the United States in 1884, James G. Blaine, condemned the Democratic Party for being the party of "rum, Romanism, and rebellion."

It is because the Democratic Party served as the vehicle of political socialization (and acculturation in the norms and folkways of Protestant America) that there remains today a slavish devotion to it as the means of redressing the social ills of society. There are countless examples of Democratic office-holders who profess a sense of regret over the reality of abortion, for example, but who say that there are "larger" issues that need to be resolved. Too bad for the preborn. These politicians have bought into the ideology that government is *the* means to redress problems; they, like Locke before them, have lost sight of the fact that the prob-

CHRIST IN THE VOTING BOOTH

lems of human society are the result of the *sinful* choices made by individual human beings.

TODAY

When confronted with the current commitment of the Democratic Party to abortion, radical feminism (an off-shoot of Marxism), and sodomy, many Catholics shrug their shoulders and say that the "Church" has no business being involved in politics. A logical consequence of the Revolt and the Age of the Enlightenment, this misconception has led to the phenomenon of even Church-going Catholics allying themselves with those who hate Christ's Holy Church—and everything she teaches.

As Arthur Schlesinger, Sr., noted in the 1920s, "Anti-Catholicism is the anti-Semitism of the intellectual elite." In other words, anti–Catholicism is the only "acceptable" prejudice in the United States. It is "politically correct" to keep a believing, faithful Catholic from attempting to influence public policy. Religion is something that one does in "private"; it is to have no impact in a society-at-large.

The belief that religion is to be kept closeted away out of public view (and therefore incapable of disturbing consciences) is one closely connected to Calvinism, Lockeanism, the French Revolution, and Marxism. Americanism is the heresy which closely parallels these beliefs. The United States Supreme Court has even given implicit sanction to it in cases involving school prayer (*Engel v. Vitale*), the reading of Bible passages in public schools (*Abbingdon v. Schemp*), public aid to parochial schools (*Lemon v. Kurtz*), and Nativity scenes on public property.

This is all so very similar to the naked war against the Church waged by the Bolsheviks in 1917 when they seized control of the former Czarist Russia. Marxism promised humanity the illusion of total secular salvation by the eradication of the root cause of all problems: class warfare promoted by the capitalists (or bourgeoisie). Wedding Lockean liberalism with the hatred of humanity of the French Revolution, the Bolsheviks believed that they had discovered the "scientific" way to build a "better world," a world free of conflict, a world of "peace and justice." Mankind would be liberated from the superstitions of Christianity—and live lives of usefulness and productivity for the good of the State.

Marxism–Leninism

Pope Pius XI noted:

> Communism, moreover, strips man of his liberty, robs human personality of all its dignity, and removes all the moral restraints that check the eruptions of blind impulse. There is no recognition of any right of the individual in his relations to the collectivity; no natural right is accorded to human personality, which is a mere cog-wheel in the Communist system. In man's relations with other individuals, besides, Communists hold the principle of absolute equality, rejecting all hierarchy and divinely-constituted authority, including the authority of parents. What men call authority and subordination is derived from the community as its first and only font. Nor is the individual granted any property rights over material goods or the means of production, for inasmuch as these are the source of further wealth, their possession would give one man power over another. Precisely on this score, all forms of private property must be eradicated, for they are at the origin of all economic enslavement.

Sound familiar? The characteristics of a communist society listed above in the quotation from Pius XI's encyclical letter, *Divini Redemptoris*, read like a litmus test for what is considered "politically correct" in American society today. At its base, feminism is a construct of Marxism designed to eradicate "emotional, bourgeois" ties to the family. The state—public education—has the responsibility for training children, according to the Marxists. Is this not the battle cry of the National Education Association and its apologists today in the United States?

Social Engineering

The belief that the state could resolve all social problems received expression in the United States in the administration of President Franklin Delano Roosevelt. Roosevelt himself was not an ideologue of any stripe; he was a stereotypical John Dewey pragmatist who was concerned about resolving the problems of the Great Depression. However, he oversaw the creation of a mammoth federal bureaucracy (to be expanded anew by Lyndon Johnson thirty years later) which was composed of social engineers inebriated, at the very least, with the breath of socialism.

The problems of the Great Depression were multi-faceted. But they were the byproducts of the immorality and materialism of the 1920s. The invention of the assembly line made consumer goods available for mass consumption for the first time. People became entranced with adult toys; banks and other lending institutions extended easy credit for this new life-style. The automobile changed the way families lived, paving the way for the suburbanization of the country which took place after World War II (thus breaking down the extended family). And the availability of contraceptive devices "freed" families from the "burden" of more children; it also paved the way for adultery and fornication in an era of "good feelings."

Rather than recognize the Depression as a sign of the things that had gone wrong in the decade before, Roosevelt believed that it was possible for government to restore and *extend* the material prosperity that had been lost. Aided by the social engineers he placed in the government, Roosevelt changed the very definition of government. As political scientist Morton Frisch noted, Abraham Lincoln once defined the purpose of American government as the elevation of the condition of man; Roosevelt defined those *conditions* principally in material terms.

REDISTRIBUTIONISM

There was quite a degree of coincidence, therefore, between the New Deal of Franklin Roosevelt and Marxism: the attempt to engineer, via government structures and bureaucracies, a re-distribution of the wealth to produce human happiness. Research has documented the fact that some within the Roosevelt administration, particularly Rexford G. Tugwell, agreed with Margaret Sanger that the best way to eliminate poverty was to reduce the number of poor people! How to do that? Simple. Teach them to use contraceptive devices and/or force them to undergo sterilization.

As the appointed Governor of the then Territory of Puerto Rico, Tugwell actually considered doing the latter (which had been proposed by some states—and was dealt with by the United States Supreme Court in the 1927 case of *Buck v. Bell*).

The 1930s, therefore, was the decade in which all of the rotten fruit sown by the seed of the Revolt came to sprout above the ground. They would not come into full bloom until the 1960s.

However, we began to see the pattern that would emerge: the killing of "useless," "unwanted," or "inconvenient" persons. The masthead of Margaret Sanger's *Birth Control Review* in 1919 boasted, "More from the fit. Less from the unfit. *That* is the chief issue of birth control."

The New Deal captured the imagination of intellectuals throughout the United States. And while it is certainly true that Roosevelt desired to *prevent* a communist takeover of the United States, he did so by adopting much of what is at the basis of Marxism: the reduction of government activity to the realm of materialism. This was to imbue the culture and ethos of the United States from that point to this.

LEGAL POSITIVISM

Roosevelt not only put social engineers into the bureaucracy. He put legal positivists onto the United States Supreme Court and the lower courts of the federal judiciary. Legal positivism, popularized in the United States at the beginning of the Twentieth Century by Associate Justice Oliver Wendell Holmes, contends that law in and of itself connotes moral legitimacy. An action is moral because it is legal. This is the prevailing mindset concerning law in the United States.

If true, however, that must mean that slavery was legitimate—as the United States Supreme Court sanctioned this evil in the case of *Dred Scott v. Sanford* (1857). Segregation was also sanctioned by the Court (*Plessy v. Ferguson*, 1896). It was legal in Nazi Germany to kill the elderly, the deformed, the "useless," Jews, Catholics—and whoever else was deemed to be politically and culturally expendable. It was legal in the Soviet Union to kill and imprison whoever was deemed to be an enemy of the State— just as it had been legal in revolutionary France to kill those who were enemies of "the people."

An entire generation of young people, who could be called the *Roe v. Wade* generation (or the "MTV" generation), has grown up believing that anything that is legal must be right. Sadly, there are many *older* Americans who have been duped into believing this, too. A woman in her eighties recently remonstrated a priest for condemning abortion. She said, "Father, abortion is legal. It *must* be right!"

BUREAUCRACY

The legacy left by Franklin Roosevelt was one that would become "gospel" in the Democratic Party. Roosevelt had "ended" the Depression! A generation of Catholic Democrats came to "revere" Roosevelt's legacy. The Democratic Party had not only become the means to political socialization; it had become the means of social salvation. Even now, in the 1990s, the legacy of Roosevelt is being reaffirmed by the Republican-controlled Congress, ever eager to please focus groups—and so very much afraid to criticize Clinton. Pope John Paul II commented in *Centesimus Annus* on the growth of the bureaucracy:

> In recent years the range of such intervention has vastly expanded, to the point of creating a new type of state, the so-called "Welfare State." This has happened in some countries in order to respond better to many needs and demands by remedying forms of poverty and deprivation unworthy of the human person. However, excesses and abuses, especially in recent years, have provoked very harsh criticisms of the Welfare State, dubbed the "Social Assistance State." Malfunctions and defects in the Social Assistance State are the result of an inadequate understanding of the tasks proper to the State. Here again the principle of subsidiarity must be respected: a community of a higher order should not interfere in the internal life of a community of a lower order, depriving the latter of its functions, but rather should support it in case of need and help to coordinate its activity with the activities of the rest of society, always with a view to the common good.
>
> By intervening directly and depriving society of its responsibility, the Social Assistance State leads to a loss of human energies and an inordinate *increase of public agencies, which are dominated more by bureaucratic thinking than by concern for serving their clients,* and which are accompanied by *an enormous increase in spending.* In fact, it would appear that needs are best understood and satisfied by people who are closest to them who act as neighbors to those in need. It should be added that certain kinds of demands often call for a response which is not simply material but which is capable of perceiving the deeper human need.

To criticize the failed, bankrupt Welfare State policies of the Democratic Party is not to say that there is salvation in the Republican Party. A common mistake made by those who defend the moral relativism of the Democratic Party is to think that their critics are reflexive Republicans. There is salvation in no political party. There is salvation only in the Church founded by Christ upon the Rock of Peter, the Pope. But therein lies the rub: many Catholics have transferred their faith from the Rock of Peter to the Democratic Party.

APPEASING THE PROTESTANTS

Then Senator John Kennedy sent a tragically mistaken signal in 1960 when campaigning for the Democratic presidential nomination. He told a group of Protestant religious broadcasters at a convention in Houston, Texas, that if there was ever a conflict between his faith and his constitutional duties he would resign. This was to allay the fears of those who believed that a Catholic president would take his commands from the Vicar of Christ.

What Kennedy did, however, was to send the signal to another generation of Catholic politicians that it was politically expedient to say, in effect, that the Catholic faith has little or no impact upon one's public policy positions. If the late president had understood that the Constitution was written in the framework of the natural law—and that the Church is the guardian of the natural law—then he would have realized that there could never be, properly interpreted, a conflict between the Constitution and his faith. But he chose to present a false dichotomy to give him "respectability" in the eyes of Protestant America.

John Kennedy's pursuit of "human respect" is what characterizes most of the Catholic politicians in public life in the 1990s. Having accepted the agenda of the social engineers and legal positivists, the Edward Kennedys, Mario Cuomos, Daniel Patrick Moynihans, Christopher Dodds, George Mitchells, Jim Florios, Thomas Foleys, Vic Fazios, Barbara Mikulskis, Richard Daleys, and Joseph Bidens all beat their breasts self-righteously by claiming that they cannot impose "morality" upon society. This is something that will be examined in depth in the next chapter.

ENGINEERING THE GREAT SOCIETY?

However, what *was* imposed upon society in the 1960s was

an even more radical spirit of social engineering than had been seen thirty years earlier in the New Deal. Lyndon Johnson, determined to outdo his mentor Franklin Roosevelt, unleashed the scourge of social scientists upon the United States. Intent upon making the relationship between the national government and the states a unitary one, Johnson's Great Society programs were designed to preempt the states and localities from pursuing archaic policies based on the "old morality."

A central part of the agenda of the social engineers schooled in the quasi-Marxist disciplines of the social sciences (and supported by "mainline" Catholic politicians and office-holders) was to promote sex instruction, contraceptive use, and abortion. Dr. Bernard Nathanson, a one-time leader of the abortion-rights movement, documents the fact in *Aborting America* and *The Abortion Papers* that it was the goal of the social engineers to lie about the number of women who had illegal abortions—and to make the Catholic Church the enemy. This served the purposes of the Johnson administration very well; it was their goal to seek to eliminate the influence of religion from public life. America needed to be "liberated" from the "shackles" of religious thought and practice; the "sexual revolution" of the 1960s was in part the result of the bureaucratic support given to the organization founded by the racist-eugenicist, Margaret Sanger's Planned Parenthood.

The killing which is taking place here is only the logical consequence of a Catholic culture in the United States that was but a myth. Catholic culture in this nation was, at best, little more than a means of socializing with other Catholics. It is the failure of Catholics to take their faith seriously, a failure to try to convert this nation to the truths of the one, true Church, that made it possible for the social engineers and moral relativists, and not Christ the King, to be triumphant.

CHAPTER EIGHT

A Catholic Understanding of the Law

Which is superior, the United States Constitution or the Divine positive law? Can a man who sits on the United States Supreme Court use the natural law to interpret the Constitution? Is a Catholic who serves as a judge bound to observe the dictates of Congress and/or state legislatures without regard to their conformity with the objective norms of justice?

Such questions would appear to be relatively easy for a believing Catholic to answer. No human institution or document is superior to the law written on the very flesh of our hearts by God Himself. It is the duty of each man, especially those who serve in public life, to recognize that the Divine positive law and the natural law impose limits upon them that they are not morally free to transgress, either individually or corporately. And it is especially the duty of a Catholic to see to it that civil law *is* in conformity with the objective norms of justice. Simple enough. Or so it would seem.

However, we live at a time when even exemplary Catholics can give answers to the questions posed above that are derived from the spirit of Americanism, not from the teaching of the Church which our Lord and Savior Jesus Christ founded upon the Rock of Peter, the Pope. Such is the case with United States Supreme Court Justice Antonin Scalia, who addressed a communion breakfast in 1997 sponsored by Father John Perricone's ChristiFidelis organization at the Marriott Marquis Hotel in New York City.

Justice Scalia has the sharpest mind of anyone serving on the Court at present. He has been known to be scathing in his criticism of his fellow justices, particularly Justice Sandra Day

O'Connor. He is very blunt when questioning the attorneys who argue cases before the Court. But he is also a serious-minded Catholic who is devoted to the Traditional Latin Mass. One of his sons was recently ordained to the priesthood. And he is responsible for helping to bring Associate Justice Clarence Thomas back into the faith.

Scalia gave a fine talk at the communion breakfast, which was attended by over 600 people (testimony to Father Perricone's organizational efforts and Scalia's own star power). He discussed the concept of the Christian as "cretin." That is, believing Christians are considered to be simple-minded in the eyes of the world. We are, he said, truly fools for the sake of Christ. He cited the example of Saint Thomas More to demonstrate how a man of faith chose to give up everything he had, including life itself, rather than surrender on a matter of faith.

As good as the talk was, Scalia turned around a full one hundred eighty degrees once written questions were asked of him. Responding to one question, Scalia reiterated what he had said at Thomas Aquinas College and at the Gregorian University in Rome last year: that while he believes in the natural law he is an American judge who must rely upon the American Constitution. "God enforces the natural law. It is not my job to enforce the natural law." He went on to say that he is bound to interpret legislation which appears before him solely on the basis of its constitutionality, a finding he discovers by looking at the text of the Constitution and the intent of the framers. He cannot use anything extraneous, including the natural law, to interpret the Constitution. Scalia did say that he viewed the role of a judge in different terms than he viewed the role of a legislator or an executive or a voter, individuals who might very well have the duty to consider and to use the natural law.

But he reiterated that a judge in this country has to respect the dictates of legislative majorities. Assuming that something is not prohibited by the Constitution, Scalia said, "You write it, I'll enforce it." This is consistent with the view he expressed in *Webster v. Planned Parenthood* eight years ago, wherein he asserted that since abortion is nowhere mentioned in the Constitution it is up to state legislatures to determine what legislation, if any, to make on the matter. He implied that abortion is a matter of states' rights, that is neither permitted nor prohibited by the Constitution.

He would be bound to uphold legislation passed by a state legislature permitting abortion. That is why he has voted rather consistently to uphold applications of the Freedom of Access to Clinic Entrances Act. Yes, Scalia has voted that Congress has the power to protect abortuaries by sending peaceful rescuers to Federal prisons and subjecting them to monstrous fines.

(Associate Justice John Paul Stevens, certainly no friend of the right to life, saw the intellectual inconsistency of this argument. *He* does not believe that unborn babies have any right to life. If a person *did* believe that, however, how is it possible for him to contend that *any* legislature had the authority to permit their destruction? Good question. And it is one that continues to plague Justice Scalia.)

Scalia was pressed to discuss the role of the Church in matters of public policy. He responded by saying that he believes the Church had no role to play in public policy, apart from forming souls so as to make proper decisions which concern both themselves and their society. He was especially caustic when discussing the role of the Church in policy debates over issues such as welfare reform, and he went on to say that our Lord had little to say about government, that He seemed not to care about the subject very much at all.

The Justice's comments actually raised more questions than they answered. Given his own scholarship and standing, his views need to be examined carefully. A critical review of those comments by anyone engaged in Catholic scholarship, however, has got to take into consideration the social teaching of the Church on the state, especially as it relates to the limits which exist in the very nature of things upon men and their societies.

THE NATURAL LAW AND THE AMERICAN FOUNDING

Saving an examination of Justice Scalia's seemingly dismissive view of the Church's social teaching on the state, especially as it relates to the social reign of Christ the King, for the end, suffice to say at this point that he is simply wrong about his understanding of the natural law and the United States Constitution. One need not declare himself to be a practicing Catholic to understand that the Constitution, although a defective document (for reasons to be elaborated upon later), was written in the framework of the natural law, and that it is only in the context of the natural law that it can be properly interpreted.

The Constitution was not written on a *tabula rasa*. The concepts which went into it were the result of the entire patrimony of the development of Western political institutions. Indeed, the late Russell Kirk examined the contributions made by the thought of four cities (Jerusalem, Athens, Rome, London) to our constitutional regime in his mammoth work, *The Roots of American Order*. While the Founding Fathers were influenced by the ethos of the Protestant Revolt, which had started just about 260 years prior to the Constitutional Convention, and the Age of the Enlightenment, many of them were influenced by Socrates, Plato, Aristotle, Cicero, Saint Ambrose, Saint Augustine, Saint Thomas Aquinas, and Saint Robert Bellarmine, whether directly or indirectly.

MIGHT V. RIGHT

As the Minority Report of a Senate Subcommittee which examined the utility of the electoral college in 1970 concluded, "If anything is clear about the thought of the Founders it is this: they believed that the mere weight of numbers—be those numbers fifty percent or ninety percent of the whole—could never make legitimate that which is otherwise illegitimate." In other words, the patrimony of the Greco-Roman and Judeo-Christian heritage was so strong upon them that they understood that the might of the majority could never make that which was of its nature evil right.

Indeed, the whole reason we have a complex form of government (Federalism, bicameralism, separation of powers, checks and balances) is to make it difficult for passion to triumph over reason in the passage of legislation. The Founders knew that majorities could be wrong. As James Madison wrote in *The Federalist*, Number Ten, a democracy could turn into a thinly-disguised dictatorship of the majority if there are not sufficient safeguards to protect against the vagaries of fallen human nature.

The Constitution was an attempt to provide a balance between the responsible, restrained exercise of human free will (in accord with the dictates of right reason and the natural law) and the need for social order. The Founders knew that human nature was such that men would abuse their liberty, necessitating a social arrangement—government—to impose penalties upon those who did that which was wrong of its nature. They recognized that government did not create or invent rights, that neither a government nor a constitution made actions right or wrong. They believed that it was the purpose of government to pursue justice, to *apply* the precepts of the natural law in concrete circumstances according to the specific institutional framework created by the American Constitution.

The Church has consistently taught, right from Augustine through Pope John Paul II's *Centesimus Annus* (and a host of treatises on political philosophy and Papal encyclical letters in between), that she has no specific models to offer men as to how to constitute a civil society. What she does have, as will be discussed later, are the *principles* of the just society which must govern men in their relations with each other. However, there is a great deal of latitude with respect to how men arrange their affairs civilly.

For example, there is nothing in either the Divine positive law or the natural law which informs us as to which is better, a Presidential-Congressional system or a Parliamentary-Ministerial one. Similarly, it is an open question as to whether a Federal or a Confederal or a Unitary system is the best way to divide power between a central government and sub-national governments. The same is true concerning the adoption of the adversarial or the inquisitorial system of justice. Indeed, there are significant procedural differences in the pursuit of justice in Western democratic republics that have similar systems, whether adversarial or inquisitorial. These are all open questions. Men of good will are free to choose any of them, keeping in mind always the greater glory of God, something, sadly, that governments ceased doing during the Age of Enlightenment (and something not at all addressed by our thoroughly secular Constitution).

BILL OF RIGHTS

Scalia, therefore, would be right in asserting that the Constitution is what informs a judge when deciding matters touching on the specific institutional arrangements that exist among the three branches of the Federal government (or in the interpretation of the powers granted to those branches). But he is wrong when stating flatly that the natural law is irrelevant to Constitutional interpretation. For the natural law is *very* relevant when it comes to the interpretation of the provisions of the amendments which constitute what we call the Bill of Rights, most of which merely protects inherent rights against arbitrary government action.

One could, for example, use a strict natural law approach to strike down all laws permitting legalized baby-killing in this nation. The Fifth and Fourteenth Amendments guarantee that the right to life (along with the rights of liberty and property) shall not be infringed without due process of law. There is no right in the natural law to deliberately will to kill an innocent human being. All that the two named amendments do is to *recognize* the simple fact that neither Congress nor state legislatures have any authority to arbitrarily deny the right to life to innocent human beings.

Furthermore, the Ninth Amendment reserves to the people those rights not enumerated in the Constitution. That is, the Founding Fathers understood that the Bill of Rights was not an exhaustive summary of human rights and responsibilities. However, the legal positivists of this century have seized upon this amendment as the means of establishing a bogus "right to privacy," thereby giving Constitutional sanction to both contraception (*Griswold v. Connecticut*) and abortion (*Roe v. Wade*). But this is worse than nonsense. One schooled in the natural law knows that no one has any right to contracept or to choose to kill an innocent baby. No one has the right to sell or to distribute or to own pornography. No one has the right to commit or to promote sodomy. No one has the right to do that which is wrong. Yes, one may have the physical *ability* to do that which is wrong, but one is not morally free to do it. And the good order of civil government *demands* that what is necessary for order within the soul be the basis of positive law and of legal interpretation.

APPLYING THE NATURAL LAW

Justice Scalia is simply wrong. The natural law was the basis of Western civilization. It is the basis of the American constitution. He should have the courage to draw upon the experience of judges in *Catholic* England during the Middle Ages, men who merely *applied* the precepts of the Divine positive and natural law in concrete circumstances to cases brought before them for judgment. Even a written Constitution is subordinate to the law of God; it must be interpreted as such. And it was interpreted as such by the United States Supreme Court on occasion.

Pope Pius XI recognized this in his 1929 document on Christian education, *Divini Illius Magistri*:

> This incontestable right of the family has at various times been recognized by nations anxious to respect the natural law in their civil enactments. Thus, to give one recent example, the Supreme Court of the United States of North America, in a decision [*Pierce v. Society of Sisters*] on an important controversy, declared that it is not in the competence of the State to fix any uniform standard of education by forcing children to receive instruction exclusively in public schools, *and it bases its decision on the natural law*; the child is not the mere creature of the State; those who nurture him and direct his destiny have the right, coupled with the high duty, to educate him and prepare him for the fulfillment of his obligations.

The natural law has even been recognized in the realm of international law and war crimes trials. For example, even though the Nuremburg trials after World War II were loathe to invoke the law of God, the late Morris Abram, an aide to Supreme Court Justice Robert Jackson, said that the judges who took part in those trials found German judges and soldiers guilty because they had violated the natural law. If positive law is the basis of a judge's decision, then by what authority were the judges and soldiers and officials of Nazi Germany, who were carrying out orders that were fully legal under the emergency powers clause of the 1919 Weimar Constitution, judged at all? There *is* a law above written law. If that law is not respected, then society is subjected to the arbitrary whims of passing majorities, and contingent beings get to play God.

THE SPLENDOR OF TRUTH

Pope John Paul II noted in *Veritatis Splendor* the binding force of the natural law on men and their institutions:

> The Church has often made reference to the Thomistic doctrine

of the natural law, including it in her own teaching on morality. Thus my Venerable Predecessor Leo XIII emphasized the essential subordination of reason and human law to the Wisdom of God and to His law. After stating that "the natural law is written and engraved in the heart of each and every man, since it is none other than human reason itself which commands us to do good and counsels us not to sin," Leo XIII appealed to the "higher reason" of the divine Lawgiver: "But this prescription of human reason could not have the force of law unless it were the voice and the interpreter of some higher reason to which our spirit and our freedom must be subject." Indeed, the force of law consists in its authority to impose duties, to confer rights, and to sanction certain behavior: "Now all of this, clearly, could not exist in man if, as his own supreme legislator, he gave himself the rule of his own actions." And he concluded: "It follows that the natural law is itself the eternal law, implanted in beings endowed with reason, and inclining them toward their right action and end; it is none other than the eternal reason of the Creator and Ruler of the universe."

Pope John Paul II went on to point out the consequences of denying the natural law in the realm of government and politics:

Only God, the Supreme Good, constitutes the unshakable foundation and essential condition of morality, and thus of the commandments, particularly those negative commandments which always and in every case prohibit behavior and actions incompatible with the personal dignity of every man. The Supreme Good and the moral good meet in truth: the truth of God, the Creator and Redeemer, and the truth of man, created and redeemed by Him. Only upon this truth is it possible to construct a renewed society and to solve the complex and weighty problems affecting it, above all the problem of overcoming the various forms of totalitarianism, so as to make way for the authentic freedom of the person. "Totalitarianism arises out of a denial of truth in the objective sense. If there is no transcendent truth, in obedience to which man achieves his full identity, then there is no sure principle for guaranteeing just relations between people. Their self-interest as a class, group, or nation would inevitably set them in opposition to one another. If one does not *acknowledge transcendent truth*, then the force of power takes over, and *each person tends to make full use of the means at his disposal in order to impose his own interests or his own opinion*, with no regard for the rights of others. . . . Thus, the root of modern totalitarianism is to be found in the denial of the transcendent dignity of the human person who, as the visible image of the invisible God, is therefore by his very nature the subject of rights which no one may violate—no individual, group, class, nation, or State. *Not even the majority of a social body* may violate these rights, by going against the minority, by isolating, oppressing, or exploiting it, or by attempting to annihilate it."

The Pope went on to write:

Today, when many countries have seen the fall of ideologies which bound politics to a totalitarian conception of the world—Marxism being the foremost of these—there is no less grave a danger that the fundamental rights of the human person will be denied and that the religious yearnings which arise in the heart of every human being will be absorbed once again into politics. This is "the risk of an alliance between democracy and ethical relativism," which would *remove any sure moral reference point from political and social life, and on a deeper level make the acknowledgment of truth impossible.* Indeed, "if there is no ultimate truth to guide and direct political activity, then ideas and convictions can easily be manipulated for reasons of power. As history demonstrates, a democracy without values easily turns into open or thinly disguised totalitarianism."

Thus, in *every* sphere of personal, family, *social, and political* life, morality—founded upon truth and open in truth to authentic freedom—renders a primordial, indispensable, and immensely valuable service not only for the individual person and his growth in the good, but also for society and its genuine development.

There is no wiggle room here. The United States Constitution must be read in the framework of the natural law. Justice Scalia is wrong.

THE CHURCH AS THE TRUE GOVERNOR OF MEN

The problem with the American Constitution is that the Founding Fathers expected succeeding generations of Americans, including jurists, to be people of "civic virtue," men who would understand and respect the limits imposed by the natural law. But civic virtue proved to be a slender thread upon which to sew together a well-ordered society. For men cannot resist the wiles of the world, the flesh, and the Devil without sanctifying and actual grace. A government founded on the principle that men can order their affairs without explicitly recognizing the authority of the Vicar of Christ to be the true governor of men on matters of faith and morals was bound to fall to the forces of the French Revolution, egalitarianism, Masonry, naturalism, collectivism, statism, relativism, legal positivism, feminism, environmentalism, redistributionism, and all the rest of the ideologies that have attacked us in the past 200 years.

It is not possible for a secular republic to provide social order over a long period of time. This nation, founded as it was upon the tragically false principle of Masonic indifferentism, was doomed to its current social and moral malaise precisely because the chief defect in the Constitution—that it did not recognize the Sovereignty of Christ the King—was so overwhelming that men began to worship a document instead of the Triune God.

Catholics have always been able to adapt themselves to different political arrangements. Many of the first Catholics were good and loyal citizens of the Roman Empire. But they refused to worship the Emperor as God, and many of them paid with their very lives doing so. A disciple of our Lord can never make an idol out of a government or of the organic documents that create the specific institutional arrangements of a particular government. Governments and their organic documents are only useful if they serve the cause of building the just society, with justice having its ultimate frame of reference on matters of faith and morals in the person of Jesus Christ as He is taught by His Holy Church. Governments are means to an end, not ends in and of themselves.

EVANGELIZATION

Our Lord and Savior expects us to work for the extension of His social reign to every land and nation, including the United States of America. A lot of practicing Catholics, infected by the ethos of Americanism, believe that our country is an exception to the Lord's clear command that all nations and peoples be subordinated to His governance. But it is clearly our baptismal obligation to remake everything in Christ, to so convert our land that our law, our politics, our education, and our culture all reflect the transcendent glory of Christ the King.

Just as the barbaric peoples of both the Old and New Worlds were converted to the Cross of Christ (with what was good in those cultures being "baptized" by missionaries—and what was bad, such as human sacrifice, excised), so do we have the duty to convert the United States of America to the true faith. It is no exercise of prudence to remain silent about this task.

For reasons that will be discussed shortly, we are not likely to be successful in our political efforts at the given moment. The rot is too deep; too many young people today have known only sensuality and materialism as their *modus vivendi*. But we have the sacred responsibility of planting the seeds that may, please God, result in the flowering of a new Christendom. We have to be as bold and as courageous in proclaiming the Cross of Christ as the Apostles themselves were during the height of the Roman Empire's power. Were *they* imprudent in taking seriously their divinely-appointed mission to convert the world? If not, then how is it any act of imprudence for a Catholic to seek the conversion of this land, no less merely to use the simple reality of the natural law as the basis for legitimate interpretation of a nation's Constitution?

FREEMASONRY

Pope Leo XIII wrote extensively on all the matters of the State throughout his long and glorious pontificate. He wrote on the topic of Freemasonry in *Humanum Genus* early in his reign, elaborating on their (Freemasons) doctrine of the State which arrogates unto men that which belongs to God alone (as I noted in an earlier chapter).

It is clear that the course of legal positivism espoused by Justice Scalia has resulted in exactly what was observed and prophesied by Pope Leo XIII in 1883. A society reduced to the mere consideration of a written document—and one in which the true religion has no right to direct the application of the Divine positive and natural law—sooner or later degenerates into chaos, into a rule of the law of man over the Sovereignty of God. The fact that a number of Masons have served on the Court (Hugo Black, Earl Warren, William O. Douglas, in particular) in the past sixty years largely explains its open hostility to expressions of religious faith in public, for example.

While the Church and state do have separate spheres of activity and interest, the state has no power to dispense with that which belongs to God, namely, matters of fundamental justice which exist in the nature of things. As Leo wrote in *Sapientiae Christianae* in 1890:

> Moreover, if we judge aright, the supernatural love for the Church and the natural love of our own country proceed from the same eternal principle, since God Himself is the Author and originating Cause. Consequently it follows that between the duties they respectively enjoin, *neither can come into collision with the other*. We can, certainly, and should love ourselves, bear ourselves kindly towards our fellow-men, nourish affection for the State and the governing powers; but at the same time we can and must cherish towards *the Church a feeling of filial piety, and love for God with the deepest love of which we are capable*. The order of precedence of these duties is, however, at times, either under stress of public calamities, or through the perverse will of men, inverted. For *instances occur where the State seems to require from men as subjects one thing, and religion, from men as Christians, quite another*; and this in reality without any other ground, than that of the rulers of the State either hold the sacred power of the Church of no account, or endeavor to subject it to their own will. Hence arises a conflict, and an occasion, through such conflict, of virtue being put to the proof. The two powers are confronted and urge their behests in a contrary sense; to obey both is wholly impossible. *No man can serve two masters*, for to please the one amounts to contemning the other. As to which should be preferred no one ought to balance for an instant. It is a high crime *indeed to withdraw allegiance from God in order to please men*; an act of consummate wickedness to break the laws of Jesus Christ, in order to yield obedience to earthly rulers, or, under pretext of keeping the civil law, to ignore the rights of the Church; *we ought to obey God rather than men*. This answer, which of old Peter and the other apostles were used to give the civil authorities who enjoined unrighteous things, we must, in like circumstances, give always and without hesitation. No better citizen is there, whether in time of peace or war, than the Christian who is mindful of his duty; but such a one should be ready to suffer all things, even death

itself, rather than abandon the cause of God or of the Church.

Hence they who blame, and call by the name of sedition, this steadfastness of attitude in the choice of duty, have not rightly apprehended the force and nature of true law. We are speaking of matters widely known, and which We have before now more than once fully explained. Law is of its very essence a mandate of *right reason, proclaimed by a properly constituted authority*, for the common good. But *true and legitimate authority is void of sanction, unless it proceed from God* the supreme Ruler and Lord of all. The Almighty alone can commit power to a man over his fellow-men; nor may that be accounted as right reason which is in *disaccord with truth and with divine reason*; nor that held to be true good which is repugnant to the supreme and unchangeable good, or that wrests aside and draws away the wills of men from the charity of God.

Hallowed therefore in the minds of Christians is the very idea of public authority, in which they recognize some likeness and symbol as it were of the divine Majesty, even when it is exercised by one unworthy. A just and due reverence to the laws abides in them, not from force and threats, but from a consciousness of duty; *for God hath not given us the spirit of fear*.

But if the laws of the State are *manifestly at variance with the divine law, containing enactments hurtful to the Church, or conveying injunctions adverse to the duties imposed by religion*, or if they violate in the person of the supreme Pontiff the authority of Jesus Christ, then truly, *to resist becomes a positive duty, to obey a crime*; a crime, moreover, combined with misdemeanor against the State itself, inasmuch as every offense levelled against religion is also a sin against the State. Here anew it becomes evident how unjust is the reproach of sedition: for the obedience due to rulers *and legislators is not refused; but there is a deviation from their will in those precepts only which they have no power to enjoin*. Commands that are issued adversely to the honor of God, and hence are *beyond the scope of justice*, must be looked upon as *anything* rather than laws. . . . That this is the very contention of Apostle St. Paul, who, in writing to Titus, after reminding Christians that they are to be *subject to princes and powers, and to obey at a word*, at once adds, *And to be ready to every good work*. Thereby he openly declares that if laws of men contain injunctions contrary to the eternal law of God, it is right not to obey them. In like manner the prince of the apostles gave this courageous and sublime

151

answer to those who would have deprived him of liberty of preaching the Gospel: *If it be just in the sight of God to hear you rather than God, judge ye, for one cannot but speak the things which we have seen and heard.*

These are not words for the faint of heart. Pope Leo firmly reminds Catholics of their obligations to be counter-cultural signs of contradiction, regardless of their state in life:

Amid such reckless and widespread folly of opinion, it is, as we have said, the office of the Church to undertake the defense of truth and uproot errors from the mind, and this charge has to be at all times sacredly observed by her, seeing that the honor of God and the salvation of men are confided to her keeping. But when necessity compels, not those only who are invested with the power of rule are bound to safeguard the integrity of the faith, but, as St. Thomas maintains, "Each one is under obligation to show forth his faith, either to instruct and encourage others of the faithful, or to repel the attacks of unbelievers." *To recoil before an enemy, or to keep silence when from all sides such clamors are raised against truth, is the part of a man either devoid of character or who entertains doubt as to the truth of what he professes to believe.* In both cases such mode of behaving is base and is insulting to God, and both are incompatible with the salvation of mankind. This kind of conduct is profitable only to the enemies of the faith, for *nothing emboldens the wicked so greatly as the lack of courage on the part of the good.* Moreover, want of vigor on the part of Christians is so much the more blameworthy, as not seldom little would be needed on their part to bring to naught false charges and refute erroneous opinions; and by always exerting themselves more strenuously they might reckon upon being successful. After all, no one can be prevented from putting forth that strength of soul which is the characteristic of true Christians; and very frequently by such display of courage our enemies lose heart and their designs are thwarted. Christians are, moreover, born for combat, whereof the greater the vehemence, the more assured, God aiding, the triumph. *Have confidence; I have overcome the world.* Nor is there any ground for alleging that Jesus Christ, the Guardian and the Champion of the Church, needs not in any manner the help of men. Power certainly is not wanting to Him, but in His loving kindness He would assign to us a share in obtaining and applying the fruits of salvation procured through His grace.

The chief elements of this duty consist in professing *openly and unflinchingly the Catholic doctrine*, and in propagating it to the utmost of our power. For, as is often said, with the greatest truth, there is nothing so hurtful to Christian wisdom as that it should not be known, since it possesses, when loyally received, inherent power to drive away error.

As Pope John Paul II has done constituently throughout *his* pontificate, Leo XIII defended the right and the duty of the Church to oppose unjust laws, thus vitiating Scalia's argument that the Church has no business in public policy:

The Church alike and the State, doubtless, both possess individual sovereignty; hence, in the carrying out of public affairs, neither obeys the other within the limits to which each is restrained by its constitution. It does not hence follow, however that Church and State are in any manner severed, and still less antagonistic. Nature, in fact, has given us not only physical existence, but moral life likewise. Hence, from the tranquility of public order, whose immediate purpose is civil society, man expects that this may be able to secure all his needful well-being, and still more supply the sheltering care which perfects his moral life, which consists mainly in the knowledge and the practice of virtue. He wishes moreover at the same time, as in duty bound, to find in the Church the aids necessary to his religious perfection, which consists in the knowledge and practice of the true religion; of that religion which is the queen of virtues, because in binding these to God it completes them all and perfects them. Therefore they who are engaged in framing constitutions and in enacting laws should bear in mind the moral and religious nature of man, and take care to help him, but in a right and orderly way, to gain perfection, neither enjoining nor forbidding anything save what is reasonably consistent with civil as well as with religious requirements. On this very account the Church cannot stand by, indifferent as to the import and significance of laws enacted by the State; not in so far indeed as they refer to the State, but in so far as, passing beyond their due limits, they trench upon the rights of the Church. From God has the duty been assigned to the Church not only to interpose resistance, if at any time the State should run counter to religion, but, further, to make a strong endeavor that the power of the Gospel may pervade the law and institutions of the nations. And inasmuch as the destiny of the State depends mainly on the dispositions of those who are at the head of affairs, it follows that the Church cannot give countenance or favor to those whom she knows to be imbued with a spirit of hostility to her; who refuse openly to respect her rights; who make it their aim and purpose to tear asunder the alliance that should, by the very nature of things, connect the interests of religion with those of the State. On the contrary, she is (as she is bound to be) the upholder of those who are themselves imbued with the right way of thinking as to the relations between Church and State, and who strive to make them work in perfect accord for the common good. *These precepts contain the abiding principle by which every Catholic should shape his conduct in regard to public life."*

End of argument. "These precepts contain the abiding principle by which every Catholic should shape his conduct in regard to public life." Translation: a Catholic in public life has the obligation to see to it that transcendent truth is respected as the basis of civil law.

Pope Leo XIII, for example, was very concerned in the Nineteenth Century about positive laws emanating from parliaments and American state legislatures permitting divorce. He wrote over and over again of how the Freemasons and the Socialists were attempting to undermine the sanctity and the indissolubility of marriage. And he called upon Catholics in public life, including those who served in the judiciary, to respect the divine law, not the positive law made by man in contravention of the divine law.

The stand taken by Justice Scalia with respect to his constitutional duties is eerily similar to that taken by Mario Cuomo in the 1980s. The latter contended that he was bound by the Constitution to support abortion, that we could not "impose" a vague concept such as the natural law upon the majority of the country. The former, citing his duties as a judge, believes that he is similarly refrained by using transcendent truths as the basis of his judgments and rulings. Both are wrong. A Catholic has an obligation to defend the applicability and relevance of the Divine positive law and the natural law in matters of fundamental justice.

Positive law must be subordinated to the divine positive and natural law. This is right reason. It is the heritage of Western civilization. And certainly every Catholic who serves in public life ought to recognize what even the pagan philosophers of Greek and Roman antiquity taught: disorder within the soul, especially when sanctioned by the force of civil law, breeds disorder and injustice in society.

ARE WE BEYOND REDEMPTION?

The American republic may be beyond redemption, humanly speaking. Two generations of young people have been educated in the milieu of relativism and positivism. A lot of these people have been misled by the dissident and malformed Catholics who teach in supposedly "Catholic" educational institutions. And the net result of this crop of miseducated youth has been—and will continue to be—felt in our electoral process for years to come.

That is why it is, in my estimation, no act of "prudence" to trim one's sails in order to appear "respectable" in the eyes of the world. The world is opposed to us. The Apostles preached the full truth of Jesus Christ when the Roman Empire was at its zenith of power. We can do no less. That might mean that we will be considered fools. However, it might also mean that our humiliation and defeat at this point in salvation history will be the seedground for the flowering of a new Christendom.

THE CHURCH AND PUBLIC POLICY

Justice Scalia said that the Church should have no role to play in public policy, specifically citing the debate over welfare reform to make his point. Not making any distinctions between transcendent truths and matters of prudential judgment, however, Scalia's remarks do little more than to convince poorly catechized Catholics into thinking that the Church should stay out of all public policy debates.

As has been demonstrated at great length above, the Church does have a divinely-appointed mission to safeguard the integrity of transcendent truths as the basis of social order. She has the obligation to speak out prophetically in defense of the sanctity of innocent human life—and in defense of her own right to raise her voice in the course of civil debate over such an issue. Similarly, she has the duty to seek to protect the indissolubility of marriage, to end the manufacture and sale of contraceptives, to make sure that legislatures do not confer special recognition upon sodomites and lesbians for engaging in acts repugnant to the Divine positive law and the natural law, and to protect the rights of parents to be the principal educators of their children. These are matters of objective truth from which no one can legitimately dissent.

REVISITING OUR LEFTIST BISHOPS

What has happened in this country, however, is that the American bishops, who have had a long affiliation with the left-wing of the Democratic Party, have largely ignored their responsibility to proclaim and defend doctrinal truths in order to concentrate on their own policy pronouncements on matters of prudential judgment. Indeed, many bishops would like the average Catholic to be convinced that their pastoral letters on public policy issues (most of which find their origin in the policy wonks who work in the United States Catholic Conference) are binding upon the consciences of the faithful.

We have seen the spectacle in the past twenty years of one silly pastoral letter after another making dogma out of the collective prudential judgment of the bishops. There is no infallible Catholic approach to welfare reform or American foreign policy or to economic policy. Even orthodox, believing Catholics can in good conscience disagree with each other about how to *apply* the treasury of the Church's social teaching in concrete circumstances. What the bishops have done is to abdicate their own responsibility to teach the doctrine of the faith in all of its integrity while at the same time arrogating from laymen *their* duty to apply the Church's social teaching in the real world.

PRO-DEATH CATHOLIC DEMOCRATS

The result of this inversion of the roles proper to bishops and the laity has been the immunization of pro-abortion Catholics in public life. They now believe that, after all, abortion is merely one issue in the spectrum of the "consistent ethic of life." There *are* more important issues. This is why there has been next to no criticism of pro-death Catholic Democrats from the hierarchy; the bishops and their apparatchiks are wedded to the failed policies of statism and collectivism that date back to the administration of President Woodrow Wilson over eighty years ago now. And now these apparatchiks are going so far as to use illegal immigrants to vote in elections as a means of defeating *pro-life* candidates, as happened with Representative Robert K. Dornan in 1996.

The fact that the bishops and their minions in this country have inverted reality does not, however, negate the fact that the Church *does* have a role to play in public-policy. Yes, Justice Scalia is correct when he says that the Church's principal role is to shape souls. Absolutely. But she does, as noted before, have the solemn obligation to do what she can to speak out on matters of fundamental justice. She has a mandate from Christ to do so. And it does not make any difference what those infected with the spirit of Americanism believe about the matter.

Pope Leo XIII knew that many bishops and priests in this country were seeking to accommodate themselves to the American experience. It was "prudent," men like the late Archbishop John Ireland of St. Paul and Minneapolis wrote, not to appear "too Catholic" in a Protestant world. Catholics might not become successful in the world. They might not get elected to office. They might never advance economically out of the ghetto if they were too outspoken in defense of their faith, no less attempt to articulate the principle that this country must be converted to the social reign of Christ the King.

Writing in *Testem Benevolentiae*, Pope Leo noted:

> But in the matter of which we are now speaking, Beloved Son, the project [Americanism] involves a greater danger and is more hostile to Catholic doctrine and discipline, inasmuch as the followers of these novelties judge that a certain liberty ought to be introduced into the Church, so that, limiting the exercise and vigilance of its powers, each one of the faithful may act more freely in pursuance of his own natural bent and capacity. They affirm, namely, that this is called for in order to imitate that liberty which, though quite recently introduced, is now the law and the foundation of almost every civil community. . . . To this we may add that those who argue in that wise quite set aside the wisdom and providence of God; who when He desired in that very solemn decision [the solemn proclamation of Papal infallibility by the first Vatican Council] to affirm the authority and teaching office of the Apostolic See, desired it especially in order the more efficaciously to guard the minds of Catholics from the dangers of the present times. The license which is commonly confounded with liberty; the passion for saying and reviling everything; the habit of thinking and of

expressing everything in print, have cast such deep shadows on men's minds, that there is now greater utility and necessity for this office of teaching than ever before, lest men should be drawn away from conscience and duty.

Pope John Paul II used this very same teaching office to remind Catholics in *Evangelium Vitae* of their duty to defend the sanctity of innocent human life, and to remind us that no human institution has the authority to abrogate the divine positive and the natural law.

This is what is happening also at the level of politics and government: the original and inalienable right to life is questioned or denied on the basis of a parliamentary vote or the will of one part of the people—even if it is the majority. This is the sinister result of a relativism which reigns unopposed: the "right" ceases to be such, because it is no longer firmly founded on the inviolable dignity of the person, but is made subject to the will of the stronger part. In this way democracy, contradicting its own principles, effectively moves towards a form of totalitarianism. The State is no longer the "common home" where all can live together on the basis of principles of fundamental equality, but is transformed into a *tyrant State*, which arrogates to itself the right to dispose of the life of the weakest and most defenseless members, from the unborn child to the elderly, in the name of a public interest which is really nothing but the interest of one part. The appearance of the strictest respect for legality is maintained, at least when the laws permitting abortion and euthanasia are the result of a ballot in accordance with what are generally seen as the rules of democracy. Really, what we have here is only the tragic caricature of legality; the democratic ideal, which is only truly such when it acknowledges and safeguards the dignity of every human person, *is betrayed in its very foundations*: "How is it still possible to speak of the dignity of every human person when the killing of the weakest and most innocent is permitted? In the name of what justice is the most unjust of discriminations practiced: some individuals are held to be deserving of defense and others are denied that dignity?" When this happens, the process leading to the breakdown of a genuinely human co-existence and the disintegration of the State itself has already begun.

To claim the right to abortion, infanticide and euthanasia, and to recognize that right in law, means to attribute to human freedom a *perverse and evil significance*: that of *an absolute power* over *others and against others.* This is the death of true freedom: "Truly, truly, I say to you, every one who commits sin is a slave to sin" (Jn. 8:34) (*Evangelium Vitae*, No. 20).

No circumstance, no purpose, no law whatsoever can ever make licit an act which is intrinsically illicit, since it is contrary to the Law of God which is written in every human heart, knowable by reason itself, and proclaimed by the Church (*Evangelium Vitae*, No. 62).

In other words, American state legislatures do *not* have the authority to permit abortion. And, yes, the Church does have a role to play in public policy, especially when matters of fundamental justice are at stake. It is not possible that contingent beings, whose bodies are destined for the corruption of the grave, have the authority to determine moral right and law by acts of a legislature or a judiciary.

RECOGNIZING CHRIST AS KING

The Constitution of the Republic of Italy is no friendlier to the Catholic faith than is our own. This has not stopped Irene Pivetti from speaking out fearlessly in defense of the social rights of Christ the King. And the fact that most Catholics in this country have long been intimidated by the prevailing ethos of Constitutional government and relativism and indifferentism into refraining from such a discussion does not relieve us of our obligation to work for the establishment of a Catholic nation in law and in fact. Even though it has not been fashionable to speak in terms of recognizing the social reign of Christ the King (and even though many apologists for the American order use *Dignitatis Humanae* to say that such talk is no longer the mind of the Church), there is a desperate need for Catholics in all walks of life to awaken from their slumber. It is time to recall the words of Pope Pius XI in *Quas Primas*:

Thus the empire of our Redeemer embraces all men. To use the words of Our immortal predecessor, Pope Leo XIII: "His empire includes not only Catholic nations, not only baptized persons who, though of right belonging to the Church, have been led astray by error, or have been cut off from her by schism, but also all those who are outside the Christian faith; so that truly the whole of mankind is subject to the power of Jesus Christ." Nor is there any difference in this matter between the individual and the family or the State; for all men, whether individually or collectively, are under the dominion of Christ. In Him is the salvation of the individual, in Him is the salvation of society. "Neither is there salvation in any other, for there is no other name under heaven given to men whereby we must be saved." He is the author of happiness and true prosperity for every man and for every nation. "For a nation is happy when its citizens are happy. What else is a nation but a number of men living in concord?" If, therefore, the rulers of nations wish to preserve their people, they will not neglect the public duty of reverence and obedience to the rule of Christ. What We said at the beginning of our Pontificate concerning the decline of public authority, or lack of respect for the same, is equally true at the present day. "With God and Jesus Christ," We said, "excluded from political life, with authority derived not from God but from man, the very basis of that authority has been taken away, because the chief reason of the distinction between ruler and subject has been eliminated. The result is that human society is tottering to its fall, because it has no longer a secure and solid foundation. . . ."

If princes and magistrates duly elected are filled with the persuasion that they rule, not by their own right, but by the mandate and in the place of the Divine King, they will exercise their authority piously and wisely, they will make laws and administer them having in view the common good and also the human dignity of their subjects. The result will be order, peace, and tranquility, for there will be no longer any cause of discontent. Men will see in their king or in their rulers men like themselves perhaps unworthy or open to criticism, but they will not on that account refuse obedience if they see reflected in them the authority of Christ, God and Man. Peace and harmony, too, will result; for with the spread and the universal extension of the kingdom of Christ, men will become more and more conscious of the link that binds them together, and thus many conflicts will either be prevented entirely or at least their bitterness be diminished.

With God and Jesus Christ excluded from political life, with authority derived not from God but from man . . . the result is that human society is tottering to its fall, because it has no longer a secure and solid foundation. When once men recognize, both in private and in public life, that Christ is King, society will at last receive the great blessings of real liberty, well-ordered discipline, peace, and harmony.

It is not an imposition of anything upon anyone merely to insist the order of things created by God be recognized as the only legitimate basis of the just society. Baptized Catholics have the obligation to stand up in defense of Christ's holy truths, and to use those truths as the basis by which to judge the actions of those in public life. It is no work of "peace" to remain silent for the sake of not wanting to hurt the feelings of others; authentic Christian discipleship involves the willingness to run the risk of rejection as a means to disturb the consciences of those who are in error about right and wrong, who do not understand the proper role of government in the economy of God's creation.

MISDIRECTED AUTHORITY

Justice Scalia reaffirmed the Americanist leanings of a lot of people who have never had an exposure to Papal encyclical letters on the State. His appearance at the ChristiFidelis communion breakfast permitted him to speak authoritatively in contravention of the Church's clear social teaching. He should not be permitted such a forum again unless there is an opportunity for him to be challenged by a scholar who can dissect his errors—and quite possibly bring him to an understanding of his role as a jurist which is consistent with being a disciple of Jesus Christ.

As committed as Justice Scalia might be to the observance of the faith, and as much as he is to be commended for bringing Clarence Thomas back to the Church, he is advancing a view of law at odds with the whole patrimony of the Church *and* that of Western civilization. And he has voted to uphold legislation which penalizes good people who have sought to rescue innocent human lives. There must be an opportunity for the Justice to listen to those who will remind him that no human document or institution is above the Triune God.

By upholding FACE, for example, Scalia has committed the same crime as the Nazi judges who sentenced innocent people to prison or death simply because they dared to violate unjust laws. This calls to mind the closing scene of *Judgment at Nuremburg*, which starred Spencer Tracy and Burt Lancaster.

Called to the cell of Ernst Joning, a German judge who violated his conscience to uphold Hitler's decrees, the American judge played by Spencer Tracy listened as the man he had just convicted pleaded to be understood. "I never knew it would come to this," Joning, played by Lancaster, told the judge. Tracy looked at Lancaster straight in the eyes. "Herr Joning, you knew it would come to this the first time you sentenced a man to die you knew to be innocent."

Our duty in this country, living as we are during the *American* holocaust, is to uphold the natural law, not to posit a phony distinction between personal belief and public duty. We do not need Antonin Scalia to make such a "prudent" decision. We have a bevy of Catholics in law and in politics and in education who have been doing that for years. We need Antonin Scalia to *use* that which he says he believes in, the natural law.

Nothing less than the survival of this country depends upon recognizing and using the divine positive law and the natural law as the basis of all social order. For "You write it, I'll enforce it" is a motto that is at odds with our duty to see to it that what Christ the King has written in the hearts of all men is enforced by civil government. Without exception. And without delay.

CHAPTER NINE

Educating the Faithful to *Be* Catholic

We received a *mandate* at the time of our baptism and confirmation to be the light of the world and the salt of the earth. *That* mandate comes before any public opinion poll. The mandate we have received from Heaven is eternal; it is meant to transform our lives on a daily basis—and hence the life of our society. Christ wants each one of us to remake the world in His own Divine Image. No public opinion poll is the equal of the Redeemer of Man.

As Pope Pius XII noted in 1944:

To secure effective action, to win esteem and trust, every legislative body should—as experience shows beyond doubt—gather within it a group of select men, spiritually eminent and of strong character, who shall look upon themselves as the representatives of the entire people and not the mandatories of the mob, whose interests are often unfortunately made to prevail over the true needs of the common good—a select group of men not restricted to any profession or social standing but reflecting every phase of the people's life; men chosen for their solid Christian convictions, straight and steady judgment, with a sense of the practical and equitable, true to themselves in all circumstances; men of clear and sound principles, with sound and clear-cut proposals to make; men above all capable, in virtue of the authority that emanates from their untarnished consciences and radiates widely from them, to be leaders and heads especially in times when the pressing needs of the moment excite the people's impressionability unduly, and render it more liable to be led astray and get lost: men who—in periods of transition, generally stormy and disturbed by passion, by divergent opinions and opposing programs—feel themselves doubly under the obligation to send circulating through the veins of the people and of the state, burning with a thousand fevers, the spiritual antidote of clear views, kindly interest, a justice equally sympathetic to all, and a bias towards national unity and concord in a sincere spirit of brotherhood.

Peoples whose spiritual and moral temperaments sufficiently sound and fecund, find in themselves and can produce the heralds and implements of democracy, who live in such dispositions and know how effectively to put them into practice. But where such men are lacking, others come to take their places in order to make politics serve their ambition, and be a quick road to profit for themselves, their caste, and their class, while the race after private interests makes them lose sight of completely and jeopardize the common good (Christmas message, 1944).

Our Divine election as adopted sons and daughters of the Living God is what gives us our very identity, our very dignity as human beings. This Divine election has been won at the cost of the shedding of the Most Precious Blood of the Son of God made Man, Jesus Christ. How can we do anything which is unfaithful to Him Who has elected us to a crown of unfading Easter glory in Eternity?

CONFUSION

Much of what we face in the United States at present is the result of the confusion which has existed with the Catholic Church since the end of the Second Vatican Council. Catholic education has undergone quite a metamorphosis in the past three decades; the truths of the faith have been undermined by many teachers (at all levels of Catholic education) whose faith is based not in the Cross of Christ but in the ideologies reviewed in Chapter Four herein. And it is because of this confusion that many Catholics have never learned their faith—and have become easy prey for evangelical and fundamentalist proselytizers.

There is yet another result of the confusion which exists in Catholic education. Some of the students who are miseducated (either out of malice or ignorance) wind up embracing the ideologies pushed upon them (feminism, socialism, radical environmentalism, moral relativism, legal positivism, the contraceptive mentality). This makes it exceedingly difficult for the Church to be an effective voice in our society; many of her nominal members have absolutely no idea what she is and how they must permit themselves to be governed by her visible head, the Vicar of Christ, on matters of faith and morals.

As is no secret to anyone with a modicum of intelligence, the state of Catholic education is not good. Indeed, it is very bad. Nearly two generations of young people have been educated from Kindergarten through college (and beyond) in Catholic educational institutions without having been taught the faith in all of its integrity. Worse yet, Catholic educational institutions have actually undermined the faith, embracing all of the false slogans and false ideologies of our paganistic age. That is why so many of our co-religionists have been catechized by the prevailing culture, not by the splendor of Truth Incarnate as He has revealed Himself through Holy Mother Church.

The state of Catholic education is so bad that most of the currently existing institutions are beyond repair. Administrators and teachers in Catholic educational institutions either do not have the faith—or consciously make war against it—as is the case when active pro-aborts and open homosexualists are hired to teach. Additionally, a regular diet of heterodox speakers is fed to students in Catholic schools and universities, with almost no attention given to the living patrimony of the revelation the Church has received from her Divine Master. The Prince of Darkness and the Master of Lies has a firm grip on Catholic education, especially here in the United States of America.

CREEPING ROT

It would appear at first blush that the problems facing Catholic education in this country at present stem from the abandonment of the *Baltimore Catechism* in elementary schools following the end of the Second Vatican Council in 1965. This is true as far as it goes. However, the wholesale collapse of the integrity of Catholic education did not happen overnight. Modernism and Americanism had been undermining the moorings of doctrinal integrity for many years prior to 1965. Although masking themselves under differ disguises, these twin, related heresies helped to produce a situation in Catholic universities and professional schools which produce bitter, bitter fruit in the wake of the chaos which followed the close of Vatican II.

Modernism, the synthesis of all heresies, had been suppressed by Pope Saint Pius X earlier this century. But it did not disappear; it went underground. And even though Catholic educators had to sign an oath against modernism, its adherents subtly applied its tenets in the classroom. Process philosophy and theology, a modernist adaptation of the Hegelian dialectical process (which was co-opted by Karl Marx for his own purposes), was cleverly woven into the fabric of some courses. Oh, yes, there was lip service to scholastic thought, to be sure. A way was found, however, to subtly convince undergraduate and graduate students that absolutes might not be so absolute after all. It is this subtle undermining of absolute truths which made it possible for there to be such a warm welcome to "situation ethics" when it burst onto the scene in Catholic higher education in the 1950s.

Modernism, therefore, produced a small elite of intellectuals who would eventually control the Catholic educational apparatus in this country. Just as the student revolutionaries of the 1960s are now in control of most of the levers of our civil government, so is it the case that the rebels of the past—and those they have trained—are in charge of Catholic schools and universities. Everything is open to speculation. Nothing is certain. And the Church has no corner on the truth, you see. We must be open to "dialogue" with differing ideas; we must be open to "dialogue" with the world.

MODERNISTIC AMERICANISM

Americanism is really an expression of a form of modernism. Based as it is in Masonic indifferentism, Americanism helped to convince succeeding waves of immigrants to these shores that they had to be careful not to threaten the Protestant majority here. It was acceptable to go to Mass and practice the faith privately; it was unacceptable to appear to be too overtly Catholic, certainly very un–American to try to work for the inauguration of the social reign of Christ the King. Immigrants had to learn the "American way," which consisted of slogans such as "tolerance," "freedom of conscience," "academic freedom," and the belief that material success is a sign of one's very self-worth and identity.

Over the course of time, therefore, many Catholic immigrants and their descendants believed that it was important to "prove"

166

that they would be just as good Americans as the Protestants. To this end, Catholic education was seen as the means to advance socially and economically. A Catholic could "prove" his worth in American society by making money and gaining political power and social status. Catholic colleges and universities strove to produce successful and influential graduates who took their place in the professional life of the nation.

While it is true that Catholic colleges and universities in the Nineteenth Century and early Twentieth Century did provide students with integrity of doctrinal instruction, there was nevertheless an undercurrent of a preoccupation with material success as the penultimate goal of human existence. The keen observer of the American Catholic scene in the 1950s, Edwin O'Connor, recognized this in his epic novel, *The Last Hurrah*. A character bearing a strong resemblance to Richard Cardinal Cushing, then the Archbishop of Boston, bemoaned the feebleness of a Catholic running for public office. "Is this an example of the educated Catholic laity you keep telling me about?" he asked his monsignor-secretary. The monsignor replied, apologetically, that the candidate was typical of many then graduating from Catholic colleges.

The situation is far worse today, naturally. But it was never as good as people once believed. Catholic education in the United States has always been characterized by an element of materialism and indifferentism. Catholics were never mobilized to try to convert this nation to the true faith. Now, however, it has become an agent to reaffirm people in cultural trends which are inimical to the faith. It has helped to foster a synthetic faith which has no relationship whatsoever to what our Lord revealed to the Apostles—and has handed down to us through them and their successors under the protection of the Holy Spirit.

FAITH UNDERMINED

The immediate aftermath of the Second Vatican Council saw a total undermining of Catholic education in most dioceses. The very purpose of human existence—to know, to love, and to serve God here on earth so as to be happy with Him for all eternity in Heaven—was never mentioned. Christocentricity was replaced by anthropocentricity. Leftist ideologies and propaganda abounded. Slogans replaced thought. Outcome-based education was instituted to mire students in an ignorance which necessitated them to be led by the enlightened elites. The inspired character of Sacred Scripture was denied. Our Lord's bodily resurrection was said never to have taken place. The very nature of the Church as the Mystical Body of Christ was supplanted with a notion of the Church as the community of believers struggling to know how to live (process thought). Belief in—and reverence for—the Real Presence of Christ in the Blessed Sacrament was denigrated almost entirely. All that mattered was a sentimentalist concept of "love"; people just have to be reaffirmed in anything they do, even if they do that which is sinful. After all, who is anyone to conclude that any behavior is sinful?

It is no wonder, therefore, that Catholics miseducated in the midst of theological relativism and leftist political ideology (including statism, collectivism, redistributionism, feminism, environmentalism, population control) and the New Age movement have become willing participants in our pagan society. Catholics vote for pro-abortion candidates for public office. They patronize the smut on television and in the movies. They live for ephemeral pleasures without giving a thought to First and Last Things. They have not been trained to know, to love, and to serve the Triune God. They do not understand the purpose of human existence, which is why so many of them accept "doctor-assisted" suicide and other forms of euthanasia. They have no concept of bearing the Cross in order to make reparation for their sins and to help our Lord redeem the world. They believe they are educated when the truth is that they are utterly uneducated about anything that matters.

BACK TO THE BASICS

We have been given an intellect to know. We have been given a will to love. The object of knowledge is truth, the object of the will is love. Our Lord professed Himself—and Himself alone—to be the Way, the Truth, and the Life; He alone is to be our love. Catholic education, therefore, must first of all be about the business of teaching students to know who they are in light of Who has created them, redeemed them, and sanctifies them. Pope Leo XIII, concerned about the trends he saw in the late–Nineteenth Century, reminded all Catholics of the basic facts of social life since the Incarnation, Nativity, Life, Passion, Death, Resurrection, and Ascension of our Lord:

> Christ our Lord must be reinstated as the Ruler of human society. It belongs to Him, as do all its members. All the elements of the commonwealth; legal commands and prohibitions, popular institutions, schools, marriage, home-life, the workshop, and the palace, all must be made to come to that fountain and imbibe the life that comes from him. No one should fail to see that on this largely depends the civilization of nations, which is so eagerly sought, but which is nourished and augmented not so much by bodily comforts and conveniences, as by what belongs to the soul, viz., commendable lives and the cultivation of virtue.
>
> Many are estranged from Jesus Christ rather through ignorance than perversity; many study man and the universe around him with all earnestness, but very few study the Son of God. Let it be the first endeavor, then, to dispel ignorance by knowledge, so that He may not be despised or rejected as unknown. We call upon Christians everywhere to labor diligently to the utmost of their power to know their Redeemer. Any one who regards Him with a sincere and candid mind, will clearly perceive that nothing can be more salutary than His law, or more divine than His doctrine.

Warning his bishops as to what was happening in the world and in the Church, Leo went on to write, "Think it the chief part of your duty to engrave in the hearts of your people the true knowledge, and, We might almost say the image, of Jesus Christ, and to illustrate in your letters, your discourses, your schools and colleges, your public assemblies, whenever occasion serves, His charity, His benefits and institutions. About the 'rights of man,' as they are called, the multitude has heard enough; it is time they should hear the rights of God" (Pope Leo XIII, *Tamesti*, 1900).

Unfortunately, the lion's share of the bishops at the time were institutionalists. This remained the case well into the Twentieth Century. These men simply assumed that everything was fine within their schools and universities. Most of them did not understand, or did not want to know, the extent to which Catholicism was being undermined by political ideologies in Europe and by Americanism in the United States. As a consequence, therefore, an entire educational bureaucracy (in dioceses, in the National

Conference of Catholic Bishops/United States Catholic Conference, in the National Catholic Educational Association—NCEA, sometimes referred to as the Non–Catholic Educational Association) arose which eventually usurped the authority of bishops to direct Catholic education. And when confronted with that reality, most bishops either ceded their authority to the educrats or gave overt approval to what was being done.

LOSS OF CONTROL

As Catholic colleges and universities helped to train many of the teachers who were employed at the elementary and secondary school levels, it is important to understand how Catholic institutions began to lose control of the hiring process of their professors, either being forced to surrender that process to semi-autonomous academic departments or voluntarily seeking to hire non–Catholics as a means of demonstrating their commitment to diversity and pluralism. Several events in the 1960s helped to expedite the de–Catholicization of Catholic education at all levels.

Chief among these events was a faculty strike at St. John's University in New York in 1965. The strike revolved around a number of issues. But the striking faculty sought greater control in the hiring and firing of personnel, believing that the Congregation of the Mission (the Vincentian Fathers) which founded and ran the university placed too much emphasis on the Catholic faith.

Although the administration tried to hold the line, the strikers eventually won most of their main points, including the ceding of more autonomy to the individual academic departments concerning personnel decisions. Coupled with the Father Charles Curran crisis three years later, the devolution of hiring to the individual departments was what helped to destroy the theology department at St. John's in short order. And this happened even though St. John's was then—and remains now—still a university under the official control of the Church. If non–Catholics or dissenting Catholics are hired, then students will be exposed to people as instructors who do not understand the simple fact that all truth revolves around Christ and His Holy Church. The way is left wide open for confusion and error, as we see so plainly.

LAND O' LAKES CONFERENCE

Just a year after the St. John's strike was resolved, a number of leading Catholic college and university administrators met at the now-infamous Land O' Lakes Conference in Wisconsin. This conference took place to determine how Catholic institutions of higher learning, including professional schools, could accept Federal and state money in order to "compete" with non-sectarian and public institutions. It was the goal of the Land O' Lakes participants to make Catholic schools "respectable" in the eyes of non–Catholic institutions by making them appear to be more open to "academic freedom" and religious pluralism. Fordham University, with campuses in the Boroughs of the Bronx and Manhattan in the City of New York, was the first to "secularize" itself, divesting itself of its official ties to the Church as a Jesuit institution. Crucifixes, which hung in every classroom, were taken down. Money and human respect began to replace the faith in one Catholic institution of higher learning after another.

A major dividing line was drawn in 1968 when Father Charles Curran, a priest of the Diocese of Rochester, New York (where the ordinary at that time was Archbishop Fulton J. Sheen), teaching at the Catholic University of America in Washington, D.C., openly opposed Pope Paul VI's *Humanae Vitae*. Although the courageous Joseph Cardinal O'Boyle, the Archbishop of Washington, tried to sanction Curran, he was undermined by other American bishops. He was undermined by "theologians" across the nation, who used the crisis as the means by which they could champion the false slogan of "academic freedom" in Catholic higher education. The Vatican's surrender to Curran and his friends signaled a retreat which prompted the educational revolutionaries to become bolder and bolder. They knew that nothing was going to get in the way of their efforts to remake the faith in their own perverted image.

ERROR SPREAD

The result of the destruction of Catholic higher education was felt in a short amount of time at the elementary and secondary school levels. Sex-instruction programs were introduced there as the means to promote theological dissent, contraception, active homosexual and lesbian behavior, and abject immodesty in speech and behavior. Sex-instruction agents, such as Planned Parenthood and the Sex, Information and Education Committee of the United States (SIECUS), were welcomed as conquering heroes in Catholic schools. Graduates of Catholic colleges and universities, having been trained in theological relativism and secular political ideologies, were hired to teach the innocent how not to be innocent. Every element of the faith was undermined over the course of time, all the while with bishops and pastors and women religious assuring themselves that their charges knew the faith.

Conflict resolution, outcome-based education, self-esteem programs (such as D.A.R.E.), values clarification programs, school-to-work programs (which determines who has the "right" to go to college, a determination based largely on the basis of a student's ability to "relate" to others, i.e., accept aberrant behavior as normal and part of a pluralistic society), ideologically-based spelling programs, feminism, and New Age prayer sessions all became commonplace. God was referred to as "she." Liturgical abuses proliferated. Leftist revisionist history, both ecclesiastical and temporal, was adopted in text books and in curricula. All of the order and certainty that the faith provides was destroyed in what appeared to be a flash. And hardly anyone cared.

Students in Catholic elementary and secondary schools participate actively in our culture of death. They know almost nothing about the nature of God, original sin, the Redemptive Act, the nature of the Church, the necessity of relying upon the sacraments, the communion of saints, or the patrimony of the Church. They have no real appreciation of the interior life, are not exhorted to spend time before the Lord's Real Presence, and are discouraged from being devoted to our Lady. What they know of the faith, if they know anything at all, is distorted and incomplete.

DEPRIVED STUDENTS

Indeed, in 1995 one of my own students at the C. W. Post Campus of Long Island University two years ago was incredulous when I gave a brief synopsis of the faith in an introduction to political science course. He had never heard of original sin! And he asked me in all sincerity, "Why haven't I been taught this?"

"Because," I told him, "you have been the victim of Catholic educational fraud." He is far from alone. He is in the vast majority of graduates of Catholic high schools and religious education programs today.

The situation is tragically worse at the professional school level. With one or two exceptions, most Catholic law schools train their students in legal positivism, the belief that whatever is legal is right. Few courses are offered that provide a sound review of natural law jurisprudence. Those who are active enemies of the Church are hired to push abortion or homosexuality, as happened in 1995, when St. John's University School of Law hired Tanya Hernandez who worked for the Center for Reproductive Law and Public Policy immediately beforehand. The faith is the thing least on the minds of professors and students in most Catholic law schools, where students are even permitted to intern in pro-abortion organizations. And the same can be said about Catholic medical schools, where all manner of compromises are made with the application of Catholic doctrine in concrete medical circumstances.

Yes, it is true that there are a number of graduates from Christendom College and Franciscan University of Steubenville who are taking their places in several diocesan education offices. But the work that needs to be done will take time. Students need to be protected now against the horrors of sex-instruction and theological relativism and outright heresy.

They need to be protected against the Catholic educational establishment which has undermined the faith so very effectively. And that protection has a name: home-schooling. The state of Catholic education will not improve, therefore, until and unless bishops start to cooperate with home-schooling parents, not browbeat them into submitting their children to the same programs that have destroyed the faith so utterly in this country.

A blueprint to rebuild Christendom

Education must be founded in a fundamental respect for the splendor of Truth Incarnate, our Lord and Savior Jesus Christ. Every discipline, including the secular sciences, revolve around Him. He is the Word through Whom all things were made. It is not possible to understand anything about the world if teachers and students do not view Him as the center and the sum of the entirety of human existence. Knowledge is useless unless we understand that it is the Triune God Himself, Father, Son, and Holy Ghost, Who is the author of all knowledge. Only He is omniscient. And it is only when human beings recognize His omniscience that they can come to appreciate the fact that there is nothing in the universe that He did not design for His greater glory.

At the center, therefore, of all Catholic education is a knowledge of God. The very purpose of human existence is to know, to love, and to serve Him. To know God as a living and a loving God, a personal God, a God Who reveals Himself to His rational creatures is the first end of all educational activity. For human beings need to have a knowledge of the truth Who God is in order to understand who *they* are. If human beings do not have such a knowledge, you see, they will come in time to worship the false gods of the world, the flesh, and the Devil.

THE PURPOSE OF KNOWING

Knowing God involves understanding that He is a community of three distinct persons. The Father is the uncreated good. The Son is the exact representation of the Father's being. And the Holy Ghost is the "breath" of the mutual love which exists between Father and Son. That is, the perfect love between Father and Son eternally begets the Spirit, Who is the Person Who instructs us rational creatures in all things revealed by the Father in the Person of the Son made flesh in our Lady's virginal and immaculate womb. As Saint Paul wrote, it is only in the Holy Spirit, Who protects the Church from all teaching error on matters of faith and morals, it is only in the Holy Spirit that any of us can know the Father through the Son.

A knowledge of God's very inner life enables a person to understand who he is. Each of us is His creature, made in His image and likeness in that we have a rational, immortal soul. A soul which has been purchased by the shedding of the Most Precious Blood of our Blessed Lord and Savior, the Second Person of the Blessed Trinity made Man. A soul which is freed of original sin and born again into the very inner life of the Trinity in the baptismal font. A soul which is meant to be fed by the Body,

Blood, Soul, and Divinity of Jesus Christ in the Eucharist. A soul which is meant to enjoy the vision of the Blessed Trinity for all eternity in Heaven.

Knowing our identity as children made in God's image and redeemed on the wood of the Holy Cross equips us to see the world properly, that is, through the eyes of faith. Knowing who we are enables us to understand that there is nothing that we have to fear in this world except mortal sin. There is no cross that we will be asked to bear (physical suffering, terminal illness, unemployment, romantic rejection, misunderstanding, ingratitude, loneliness, poverty, injustice) which is beyond our capacity to endure by means of the graces won for us on Calvary. There is nothing that we, who are so frequently the beneficiaries of God's mercy in the Sacrament of Penance, can refuse to forgive others. And a knowledge of our identity helps us to realize that we must sanctify the world as befits our state in life, doing ordinary things extraordinarily well for love of the Father through the Son in Spirit and in Truth.

Catholic education *used* to be founded in providing students with this knowledge. For a knowledge of God is paramount to *loving* Him. One needs to know someone before coming to love him. We need to get to know everything that the Church teaches us about God, everything, that is, that He has revealed through the Church, in order to love Him and to appreciate Him. A love for God founded on a firm understanding of Who He is leads a person to love His Holy Church as His Mystical Body. And just as a knowledge of God leads us to understand our lowliness in relation to Him, so does a love of Him and His Church lead us into humbly submitting ourselves to the Church's magisterial authority on matters of faith and morals. Yes, a love for the Triune God leads us to becoming humble sheep of the flock who want to serve Him through His Church, which is meant to be the true governor of all men everywhere.

FOUNDATION OF LIFE

All personal and social order is premised, therefore, upon understanding and accepting these basic truths. Individual lives are meant to be lived in an awareness of the Divine Presence. Each person is called to realize that he might be asked to make an accounting of his life at any time, being prepared always for a sudden death. Each person is called to cultivate a knowledge for and love of God by spending time before the Blessed Sacrament and tender devotion to His Most Holy Mother. Each person is called to be dedicated to building up the inner life of the Blessed Trinity his soul, and to be dedicated to building up a society which seeks God's greater glory in all of its various aspects.

Pope Pius XI noted this in his marvelous encyclical letter, *Divini Illius Magistri*, issued on December 31, 1929:

> The reason is that men, created by God to His image and likeness and destined for Him Who is infinite perfection realize today more than ever amid the most exuberant material progress, the insufficiency of earthly goods to produce true happiness either for the individual or for the nations. And hence they feel more keenly in themselves the impulse towards a perfection that is higher, which impulse is implanted in their rational nature by the Creator Himself. This perfection they seek to acquire by means of education. But many of them with, it would seem, too great insistence on the etymological meaning of the word, pretend to draw education out of human nature itself and evolve it by its own unaided powers. Such easily fall into error, because, instead of fixing their gaze on God, first principle and last end of the whole universe, they fall back upon themselves, becoming attached exclusively to passing things of earth; and thus their restlessness will never cease till they direct their attention and their efforts to God, the goal of all perfection, according to the profound saying of Saint Augustine: "Thou didst create us, o Lord, for Thyself, and our heart is restless until it rests in Thee."

Pope Pius XI went on to stress:

> Whatever a Christian does even in the order of things of earth, he may not overlook the supernatural; indeed, he must, according to the teaching of Christian wisdom, direct all things towards the supreme good as to his last end; all his actions, besides, in so far as good or evil in the order of morality, that is, in keeping or not with the natural and divine law, fall under the judgment and the jurisdiction of the Church.

In other words, our own experience today is an aberration in the history of the Church. The belief that education does not revolve around Christ and His Church, something that is at the heart of the problem in Catholic education today, is responsible for why Catholics behave in ways that are indistinguishable from pagans. We have to recover the spirit of the Middle Ages, that is, the Age of Christendom. For it is Christendom which offers us the best way to form young people in the faith from the earliest years of life; it is Christendom which shows us the fruit of such a formation: a society which refers all things to Christ and His infallible Church.

EARLIER HOME-SCHOOLING IN EUROPE

The nature of life in the Middle Ages was such that most people educated their children at home. Indeed, most people worked on property in the feudal age which was adjacent to where they lived. While it is true that certain children who demonstrated a particular aptitude were sent to a craftsman to learn a trade at a relatively early age, the lion's share of children learned what they knew from their parents. And parents recognized that it was their God-given responsibility to pass on the truths of the holy faith to their children, as well as to develop within them a deep interior life of prayer. Parents understood that they would be judged by the Triune God partly on the basis of how well they had discharged their responsibilities to provide for the spiritual formation of their children.

Local parishes did play a role in sacramental preparation. The parish priest frequently gave instruction himself. And he questioned all those who would present themselves for the sacraments. But he knew that his role was subsidiary to that of the parents. There was no educational bureaucracy intent on using force and intimidation to coerce parents to bend to their own iron will. Bishops and priests understood the hierarchy that existed both in the order of creation and the order of redemption—and how the Church was supposed to foster, not undermine, parental responsibility within the family unit.

It is true that boarding schools began to arise in the late Middle Ages. And young men and women left home at an early age to enter monasteries and convents, centers of learning during the era of Christendom. The average person, however, learned at home. Plain and simple.

The rise of the industrial revolution in Europe began to

change things somewhat. The close of the feudal era meant that a lot of people no longer worked the land on which they lived. Many fathers worked long, hard hours under unspeakably horrible conditions (for little pay). Catholic schools began to proliferate in those countries which were confessionally Catholic. Indeed, Catholic schools were the only state-sanctioned schools permitted in some countries, as it was believed that everyone had to be exposed to the fullness of truth, believer and non-believer alike. Such schools, however, were authentically Catholic. And parents still had the responsibility to discharge their own responsibilities at home.

IN THE STATES

The situation in the United States was somewhat different. Although the industrial revolution hit here a bit later than in Europe, the phenomenon of the public school, which first appeared in the Eighteenth century, began to proliferate around 1840 both in rural and in urban areas. The public school had a very distinctive mission: evangelize the "gospel" of American pluralism and indifferentism. Pope Leo XIII noted in *Humanum Genus* that Freemasonry erected such systems of education to convince people that it did not make any difference what religion a person professed. What mattered was a sense of "civic responsibility" to the principles of the American regime. Overt anti-Catholicism was a hallmark of early American public education; some would argue that overt anti-Catholicism is still alive and well, manifesting itself in particularly vicious ways throughout public education.

The large number of Catholic immigrants to this country in the 1840s (and from the 1870s through 1900) made support for public education even more urgent for the WASPS and Masons. Attendance in public schools was considered an absolute prerequisite for good citizenship. Indeed, even some of the Americanist bishops of the last century, such as Archbishop John Ireland of St. Paul-Minneapolis, actually promoted the concept of public schools so as to convince the Protestant majority that Catholics desired to take their place in American social, economic, and political life. Catholics did not mean to convert this nation to Catholicism.

Other bishops, however, took their direction from the Vicar of Christ. Popes Pius IX and Leo XIII were steadfast in their insistence that Catholic schools be established in those instances where parents could not educate children at home. It was essential, they noted, that education be conducted in the framework of the truths of the faith. There was too much possibility for children to lose their faith in an atmosphere of indifferentism to entrust their education to the public schools. In the cases of those who could not attend a Catholic school, however, these popes (along with Popes Pius XI and XII) insisted that a solid program of instruction be established, once again emphasizing the principal role of parents.

INFECTED CATHOLIC SCHOOLS

As we know, however, Catholic schools eventually became infected by Americanism. The rapid decline of the state of catechesis following the immediate aftermath of the Second Vatican Council has been well documented. Adding to the problems caused by the American ethos of indifferentism and materialism was what appeared to the average Catholic to be the endorsement of theological relativism and situation ethics in the framework of Catholic schools and religious education programs. After the rapid implementation of the liturgical changes in 1969–70, the average Catholic got the impression that everything was up for grabs, including the doctrinal and moral teaching Christ entrusted to His Church through the Apostles.

A wholesale disintegration of Catholic education occurred as a result. Religious illiteracy blossomed. Ideology replaced the faith. Irreverence replaced reverence. Belief in the Real Presence was actually denied. A nebulous concept of love, based in human respect and sentimentality, was preached. The content provided by the *Baltimore Catechism*, which had provided a solid formation in the faith to three generations of Catholics, was replaced by discussion groups. Chaos reigned supreme. Church attendance declined. The practice of contraception among Catholics skyrocketed. The rate of Catholic women having abortions as a percentage of the population is actually higher than any other religious profession in this nation. Original Sin? Actual sin (both mortal and venial)? The fundamentals of the faith were hidden.

179

And they remain hidden.

An entire educational bureaucracy was created within the Church to perpetuate this abortion of souls. Although many within its ranks profess a concern about the state of Catholic religious education, the plain fact of the matter is that most Catholic educational bureaucrats believe that they are taking the faith into the Twenty-first Century. They have the right to educate children as they see fit. Parents have no role in this process other than to submit to diocesan and parish directives. After all, the bureaucrats are the professionals, right? The Catholic educational bureaucracy is a carbon copy of that which is found in public education. And the end result of their programs insofar as morality goes is indistinguishable. The lion's share of graduates of public and parochial schools are merry partakers of this culture of death.

CATHOLIC HOME-SCHOOLING

Catholic home-schooling began to emerge in the 1970s in the immediate aftermath of the confusion engendered by the Catholic educational bureaucrats after Vatican II. And it exploded in the 1980s. Evangelical and fundamentalist Protestants have discovered it, too, along with a few 1960s-type hippies who don't think that the public schools are "green" enough for their children. But the phenomenon of Catholic home-schooling is just as much a threat to the educational bureaucrats in the Church as the revival of the Tridentine Mass is to the liturgical bureaucrats.

Sadly, the revolutionaries within the Church refuse to quit. They are people consumed with hatred of what they deem to be the "pre-conciliar" Church. Anything and anyone who gets in their way must be crushed, either by the use of slogans or by the exercise of raw power over those who insist on adhering to a "faith vision" that they believe is outdated. No wonder there is such a kinship between the revolutionaries within the Church and the left-wing of the pro-abort Democratic Party: they all share a common vision of life and of how to deal with adversaries. All opposition to their enlightened positions is illegitimate and must be eradicated.

As one who has taught in a home-school religious education program for the past four years, I can attest to the fact that the students who are home-schooled know their faith well. They are in love with the Triune God. They are young people full of energy and zeal for the faith. They are committed to the pursuit of excellence as befits redeemed creatures living for the glory of God. They are unfailingly well-mannered and self-disciplined. And they have demonstrated a competency in written and verbal communication that is almost impossible to find at the university level today, yes, even in graduate programs.

Home-schooling has become the first line of defense for parents against the onslaught of modernism and theological relativism in Catholic religious education programs and schools. This is to say nothing of the vicious manner in which the innocence of purity of Catholic youth continues to be robbed by so-called "sex education" programs taught on the premises of Catholic educational institutions. Home-schooling has become the seedbed for vocations to the priesthood and consecrated religious life. And it has produced young people who are more prepared for college and university education than those who graduate from public or parochial high schools.

GUARDING THE FAITH

Protecting the integrity of Catholic education is an indispensable means to assure the evangelization of Protestants and non-Christians. Catholics will not seek to convert others if they do not understand the faith, if they do not view the world through the eyes of faith. Catholics have the responsibility to lead every society in which they find themselves into the one sheepfold of Peter. As Pope Pius XI explained in *Divini Illius Magistri*:

> All this the Church has been able to do because her mission to educate extends equally to those outside the Fold, seeing that all men are called to enter the kingdom of God and reach eternal salvation. Just as today when her missions scatter schools by the thousands in districts and countries not yet Christian, from the banks of the Ganges to the Yellow River and the great island and archipelagos of the Pacific Ocean, so in every age the Church by her missionaries has educated to Christian life and to civilization the various peoples which now constitute the Christian nations of the civilized world.
>
> Hence it is evident that both by right and in fact the mission to educate belongs preeminently to the Church, and that no

one free from prejudice can have a reasonable motive for opposing or impeding the Church in this her work, of which the world today enjoys the precious advantages.

This right of the Church to educate all men everywhere is founded on a respect for her domestic cell, the family, to serve as her bedrock for the continuation of her influence in society. Pius XI wrote:

> The family therefore holds directly from the Creator the mission and hence the right to educate the offspring, a right inalienable because inseparably joined to the strict obligation, a right anterior to any right whatever of civil society and of the State, and therefore inviolable on the part of any part on earth.

Even the Church herself has to recognize, as Pius XI, noted that parents have the right to protect their children from the evils of a secular society, especially the evils of what we call today sex-instruction. Neither the Church nor the State has the right to rob parents of their right to protect the innocence and the purity of their children.

> Another very grave danger is that naturalism which nowadays invades the field of education in that most delicate matter of purity of morals. Far too common is the error of those who with dangerous assurance and under an ugly term propagate a so-called sex-education, falsely imagining they can forearm youths against the dangers of sensuality by means purely natural, such as a foolhardy initiation and precautionary instruction for all indiscriminately, even in public; and, worse still, by exposing them at an early age to the occasions, in order to accustom them, so it is argued, and as it were to harden them against such dangers.
>
> Such persons grievously err in refusing to recognize the inborn weakness of human nature, and the law of which the Apostle speaks, fighting against the law of the mind; and also in ignoring the experience of facts, from which it is clear that, particularly in young people, evil practices are the effect not so much of ignorance or intellect as of weakness of a will exposed to dangerous occasions, and unsupported by means of grace.

The bishops of the United States have failed the cause of Catholic education. Catholic education here, having been corrupted by Americanist indifferentism almost from its outset, has been undermined in the past thirty years by theological relativists and liturgical revolutionaries. If bishops were really serious about assisting parents in their duty to educate their children, the following steps would be taken in each diocese:

1. Every form of sex-instruction, including so-called chastity education, must be eliminated.

2. Every attempt to deny the sacraments to home-schooled children unless their parents used the failed catechetical texts mandated by local dioceses must cease.

3. Private, independent Catholic schools and academies should be encouraged as a means of circumventing the morass of so-called Catholic education at the parish and diocesan level. Similarly, bishops must instruct priests to recognize that home-schooling was the norm in Catholic education prior to the Masonic-inspired effort to mandate public education out of the home 150 years ago. Bishops and priests and ecclesiastical bureaucrats must not thwart the efforts of parents to provide their children with the fullness of the splendor of Truth Incarnate, Truth Crucified and Resurrected.

4. Only those people who are faithful Catholics, those who accept everything the Church teaches on matters of faith and morals without any degree of dissent, must be hired to teach in all Catholic educational institutions. This includes seminaries, colleges, universities, and professional schools. Anyone not of one mind and one heart with the Church must be dismissed posthaste if they are unwilling to admit the errors of their ways.

5. Bishops should be in the vanguard of organizing Eucharistic and Marian processions for the young.

6. Devotion to the saints should be among the first priority of bishops. Bishops should go to parishes and give seminars to young people about the lives of the saints.

7. The bloated Catholic educational bureaucracy, which exists at the national and diocesan levels, must be eliminated. Entirely. *Bishops*, not bureaucrats, are the principal

teachers of their dioceses. This is especially so regarding those bureaucrats who are intent on destroying the faith. Good-bye, United States Catholic Conference Office of Education and the Non-Catholic Education Association, er, that is, the National Catholic Education Association (NCEA).

8. Vocations to the priesthood and consecrated religious life must be fostered by bishops and by faithful, orthodox priests and religious assigned by bishops for this purpose. Families must be encouraged to foster vocations by their own dedication to the faith.

9. Bishops must be in the vanguard of urging families to avoid the near occasions of sin, namely, to avoid any form of entertainment which promotes and/or glorifies evil.

10. No catechetical text can be used in any Catholic educational institution which contains any degree of doctrinal impurity or theological infidelity.

11. Interdicts must be placed on Catholic universities and colleges which countenance, in the name of "academic freedom," theological perspectives and political ideologies alien to the faith.

12. Bishops must issue pastoral letters which reaffirm the right of parents to home-school their children—and they must oppose any effort on the part of state authorities to browbeat parents who choose to exercise this precious right.

13. Alternative methods of learning, such as distance learning, must be embraced, not opposed, by the bishops.

The state of Catholic education is absolutely critical to the survival of the faith in this nation. The bishops have it within their power to set Catholic education on the right path by embracing home-schooling, the means by which educated and well-formed Catholics are beginning to take their place in the Church.

If the bishops do not do so, however, those parents who do home-school—and who send their children to orthodox privately run Catholic schools—are going to be the leaders in Catholic education in this country, not the bishops. As the late Archbishop Fulton J. Sheen noted years ago, the laity has always saved the Church in times of crisis. The fact that faithful parents are homeschooling their children in the face of severe opposition from Church and State is a telling contemporary example of how the laity are indeed saving the bishops from their own wanton destruction of the faith.

THE FAILURE OF PUBLIC EDUCATION

Any educational system which does not teach a student that he is a child of the Triune God, that he has been redeemed by the shedding of our Lord's Most Precious Blood, that he has a responsibility to pursue excellence at all times as befits one who is made in the image and likeness of God, is bound to fail. This is true even in the natural and applied sciences (biology, chemistry, physics, medicine, engineering, mathematics), as one untrained in light of the Cross of Christ will be incapable of seeing how the truths of the true faith are meant to penetrate and enlighten all knowledge at all times.

The two-party system has helped to perpetuate and to exalt the fraud of American public education, principally as the means by which graduates will know a "better" life. Translation? More money and more material goods, the means to "happiness," it is alleged. Politicians of both major parties believe in the myth that secular education is the way to social "progress." As Paul Johnson noted in *Modern Times*, however:

> Even more tragic and painful was the loss of illusions over education. This was, indeed, the central mirage of the decade of illusion [the 1960s]. It was an old liberal belief, popularly by Macaulay, that universal education alone could make democracy tolerable. That accomplished manufacturer of progressive clichés, H. G. Wells, had defined modern history as a "race between education and catastrophe." This belief survived the melancholy fact that the nation which took Hitler to its heart and waged his fearful war with passionate industry was easily the best-educated on earth. In the 1950s the myth that education was the miracle cure for society emerged stronger than ever. No one believed in it more devotedly than [Lyndon] John-

son. As President he said: "The answer for all our national problems comes in a single word. That single word is education."

THE REVIVAL OF THE CATHOLIC FAMILY

In addition to education, another element for changing the culture in which we live is the revival of the Catholic family. Civilizations rise and fall on the basis of family stability. The family has been under attack for sixty years by the quasi-socialists in the federal government; it is only a Catholic family, with a faith life centered around the Eucharist and the Mother of God, which is going to provide the seedbed for a Catholic nation.

Pope John Paul II emphasized this theme in his homily at Aqueduct Racetrack on October 6, 1995:

In practical terms, this truth tells us that there can be no life worthy of the human person without a culture—and a legal system—that *honors and defends marriage and the family*. The well-being of individuals and communities depends on the healthy state of the family. A few years ago, your National Commission on America's Urban Families concluded, and I quote: "The family trend of our time is the de-institutionalization of marriage and the steady disintegration of the mother-father child raising unit. . . . No domestic trend is more threatening to the well-being of our children and to our long-term national security." I quote these words to show that it is not just the Pope and the Church who speak with concern about these important issues.

Society must strongly re-affirm the right of the child to grow up in a family in which, as far as possible, both parents are present. Fathers of families must accept their full share of responsibility for the lives and upbringing of their children. Both parents must spend time with their children, and be personally interested in their moral and religious education. Children need not only material support from their parents, but more importantly a secure, affectionate and morally correct environment.

Catholic parents must learn to form their family as a "domestic church," *a church in the home* as it were, where God is honored, his law is respected, prayer is a normal event, virtue is transmitted by word and example, and everyone shares the hopes, the problems and the sufferings of everyone else. All this is not to advocate a return to some outdated style of living: it is to return to *the roots of human development and human happiness!*

He elaborated on this theme the very next day at St. Patrick's Cathedral on October 7, 1995:

When a man and a woman bind themselves to each other without reservation in their decision to be faithful "in sickness and in health, in good times and in bad," to be the exclusion of every other physical love, they become cooperators with the Creator in bringing new life into the world. You parents can look with love at your children and say: this is "flesh of my flesh." Your life is defined by your fatherly and motherly desire and duty to give your children the best: a loving home, an upbringing, an eternity. Above all, *through Baptism you make it possible for your children to become God's beloved sons and daughters, mystically united with Christ, incorporated into his Church!* Beneath the high altar at this Cathedral, together with the former Cardinals and Archbishops of New York, there is buried the *Servant of God Pierre Toussaint*, a married man, a one-time slave from Haiti. What is so extraordinary about this man? He radiated a most serene and joyful faith, nourished daily by the Eucharist and visits to the Blessed Sacrament. In the face of constant, painful discrimination he understood, as few have understood, the meaning of the words: "Father, forgiven them; they do not know what they are doing." No treasure is as uplifting and transforming as the light of faith.

From many points of view, these are difficult times for parents who wish to pass on to their children the treasure of the Catholic faith. Sometimes you yourselves are not sure what the Church stands for. There are false teachers and dissenting voices. Bad examples cause great harm. Furthermore, a self-indulgent culture undermines many of the values which are at the basis of sound family life.

There are two immediate things which the Catholic families of America can do to strengthen home-life. *The first is prayer*: both personal and family prayer. Prayer raises our minds and hearts to God to thank him for his blessings, to ask him for his help. It brings the saving power of Jesus Christ into the decisions and actions of everyday life.

One prayer in particular I recommend to families: the one we have just been praying, *the Rosary.* And especially the

Joyful Mysteries, which help us to meditate on the Holy Family of Nazareth. Uniting her will with the will of God, Mary conceived the Christ Child, and became the model of every mother carrying her unborn child. By visiting her cousin Elizabeth, Mary took to another family the healing presence of Jesus. Mary gave birth to the Infant Jesus in the humblest of circumstances and presented him to Simeon in the Temple, as every baby may be presented to God in Baptism. Mary and Joseph worried over the lost Child before they found him in the Temple, so that parents of all generations would know that the trials and sorrows of family life are the road to closer union with Jesus. To use a phrase made famous by the late Father Patrick Peyton: *The family that prays together, stays together*!

The second suggestion I make to families is to use the *Catechism of the Catholic Church* to learn about the faith and to answer the questions that come up, especially the moral questions which confront everyone today. Dear Parents, you are *educators because you are parents. I exhort and encourage* the Bishops and the whole Church in the United States to help parents fulfill their vocation to be the first and most important teachers to their children.

Families produce children who get married and pass on the faith. They also provide the foundation for vocations to the priesthood and consecrated religious life. We need to pray fervently for priestly vocations. We need men to devote their lives to incarnating Christ anew under the appearance of bread and wine, to medicating souls with the salve of Christ's healing love in the Sacrament of Penance. We need men who are fearless in their loving proclamation of the Truth Who is Jesus Christ. We need shepherds of souls, fishers of men, apostles for the Third Millennium of Christianity.

SANCTITY

All of this requires holiness. It will be holiness which sees us through the current storms that beset us. God is permitting this scourge for a reason. He is permitting His *Mystical* Body to be racked and tortured just as He submitted His own *Physical* Body to be nailed to the wood of the Holy Cross. Now is the time for a fundamental metanoia of spirit which will blaze a path of authentic spiritual renewal in ourselves—and hence in our nation.

To be a person of holiness is to live a life in concert with the Beatitudes. We must be poor in spirit, detached from the things, people, and places of this world. We must detest sin, be humble in bearing—and single-hearted in our efforts to do the will of God. For it is in doing the will of God that we can become the peacemakers called blessed, people who make peace between themselves and God.

An important aspect of growing in the faith—and of understanding social problems from the perspective of Divine Truth—is the assiduous study of the Church's social teaching. There is a vast treasury of writings to guide us as we consider how to respond, in practical terms, to the challenges that face us today.

We must become agents of authentic spiritual renewal during these quincentennial years. Columbus planted the faith on these shores. We must re-plant those seeds by intensifying our life of prayer, receiving the Eucharist with fervor, spending time before the Blessed Sacrament to beg the Lord for guidance in our society, and to place ourselves ever more fully under the maternal patronage of the Mother of God, the Mother of us all.

The Catholic Church has stood four-square in opposition to all types of tyrants (from Nero to Henry VIII to the French Revolutionaries to Napoleon to Lenin to Stalin to Hitler to Mao—and to the tyranny of public opinion). We, as members of the Mystical Body of Christ, must stand up for life against the tyranny of the crowd at present.

The democratic fascism which characterizes the Clinton Administration must be combated both spiritually and politically. It is important that the hierarchy and the laity work together fearlessly in defense of the Truth for which our spiritual ancestors willingly shed their blood. True love is willing to suffer for the object of its affection; the object of our affection is none other than Christ and His Holy Church. Our Lord died for each member of His Mystical Body. Which one of us can do any less?

CHAPTER TEN

Beyond 1996

The 1996 elections provided what turned out to be a *missed* opportunity for faithful Catholics to stand up and make a real difference in how this country is governed.

What actually happened, however, was very sad. A lot of well-meaning people told us that we had to accept the "lesser" of two evils; others, motivated by crass careerism wanted the life issue to go away altogether. There were a lot of those careerists who told pro-lifers to "go along" with whomever the Republican Party nominated for President and Vice President. This resulted in the nomination of Robert Joseph Dole, a man who was a pro-life fraud.

Dole voted to confirm *every* single pro-abortion judge Bill Clinton nominated for the Federal bench, going on at great length to *praise* Ruth Bader Ginsburg and Stephen Breyer for their "qualifications" to serve on the U.S. Supreme Court. What this man never realized was that no person who supports abortion is qualified to serve in *any* position of government, including dog-catcher, as such a person does not understand the origin of law, God, and its end, the protection of the sanctity of all innocent human life.

Dole also proudly voted in support of funding for fetal-experimentation, the Freedom of Access to Clinic Entrances Bill, funding for Planned Parenthood, and outcome-based education. He also supported the so-called "hard cases" exceptions as a matter of principle; he is in favor of the killing of children, towing the line of the National Right to Life Committee, which was the recipient of a healthy $650,000 from the Republican National Committee. And he tried to get rid of the life issue once the primary season was over, floating the idea of a "declaration of tolerance" to unite Republicans of "good will" on the life issue.

As mentioned before, however, there is salvation in no political party. Political parties only are useful if they serve as instruments of the promotion of objective standards of justice. If a political party is committed to careerism, to winning for the sake of winning, then it is unworthy of our support. As much as we would have liked to rid ourselves of William Jefferson Blyth Clinton and his band of social engineers, what good would have been done for the nation if the Republican Party simply acquiesced to focus groups and polling data, relegating the life issue to the back burner? Electoral politics is not about winning; it is about the advancement of the objective moral order.

PRO-LIFE PLANK

The Republican Party in recent years has been attempting to distance itself from the pro-life plank in its platform. A number of its prominent political consultants have reveled in the fact that pro-abortion Catholic Republicans have won major office (Rudolph Giuliani, George Pataki, Susan Molinari, Richard Riordan), believing that being pro-life is an electoral liability. This conclusion is self-serving, particularly in light of the fact that many pro-life candidates were elected to national, state, and local offices in 1994. Republican Party professionals want to find an excuse to abandon the pro-life plank in the party's platform because *they* are uncomfortable with it, because they do not want to offend the lifestyle of "young, upwardly mobile professionals" (yuppies).

The Republican Party was born out of the shards of the Whig Party, which had been formed in the 1830s for the "high-minded" purpose of serving as the opposition to the Democratic Party. The Whigs more or less had a "big tent" approach of its own on the issue of slavery; those of its leaders who believed that the Party should oppose slavery vigorously formed the Republican Party in the 1850s when it became apparent that the mainstream Whigs were interested only in electoral survival. The Whig Party was moribund within a few years. The same thing can happen with the Republican Party. That is why many committed Catholics have abandoned the Republican Party for the fledgling U.S. Taxpayers Party; they are fed up with rhetoric and lip service that do nothing to help reverse the culture of death.

DEMOCRATIC PARTY

Not much mention has been made in this chapter of the Democratic Party as it has become so institutionally wedded to the promotion of moral evils as civil rights. Its social programs have failed; its economic positions are based upon a recycled Marxism, which thrives on class warfare, seeks to penalize those who have become financially successful by the fruit of their own labor. (Catholic social teaching, of course, confirms the right of individuals to own property, to realize the fruit of their own labors. However, wealth implies a social responsibility, recognizing that all of the talents we have come from God. Although leaving the development of concrete socio-economic models to those who have the specific competency to do so, the Church offers the principles to guide economic development. And authentic development is based upon a rejection of both collectivism *and* unbridled individualism, which reduces national life to the acquisition of private wealth as an end in and of itself, with no eternal dimension.) While Bill Clinton won handily over the incompetent and vacuous Dole, his political party is an irrelevancy. All it can do is to appeal for votes on the basis of fear-mongering. Democrats especially like to fan the flames of fear in the direction of those who believe in our Lord and use that belief for the basis of how they view the world and their role in it (a fear that Colin Powell himself has expressed, to the delight of many Republican Party professionals).

INVOLVEMENT

Faithful Catholics need to involve themselves in the support of specific candidates who are unreservedly pro-life. They need to encourage others to run for office, should they themselves be unable or unwilling to do so. But Catholics who involve themselves directly in politics have to fortify their spiritual lives in a very special way, for the temptations offered by electoral politics are many.

Once a person starts to compromise on matters of fundamental principles in order to achieve a short-term goal, it is easy to justify further compromises. A taste of the excitement and energy produced by a political campaign can become so intoxicating that a person who is well-formed intellectually may find his spiritual life shriveling away, his time being consumed with the "activity" of politics. Any Catholic involved in electoral politics has to put Christ first, to think with His mind, to do the Father's will, to understand first and foremost that he has been elected in the baptismal font to serve in the world as an Apostle of the world which has no end.

Naturally, there is nothing divinely revealed about particular electoral strategies. None of these are received from the hand of God. A clear sign that a Catholic involved in politics is heading for trouble, however, is when he starts to think that circumstances necessitate silence on abortion. So many people accept it, he might reason, that it is pointless to discuss it in the context of a political campaign. But this temptation betrays the responsibility a statesman has to stand up in defense of objective truth, to serve as a political educator, even if that means the loss of popularity and/or electoral office. It is then that a person begins to think with the mind of the world to such an extent that the things of God are never mentioned.

A MISSED OPPORTUNITY

This is what happened during the first years of President Ronald Reagan's administration. Although rhetorically committed to the restoration of legal protection for innocent human life in the womb, Reagan did little in terms of policy to achieve that goal. His first emphasis was on the economy. Indeed, a friend of mine told me in 1981, "If Reagan gets the economy going, they'll give him anything he wants." But they, the Democratically-controlled House of Representatives, did not. Reagan did not use the bully pulpit of the Presidency to try to change minds on the pro-life issue. And practically everything the Reagan and George Bush administrations did by executive orders to limit abortion and/or fetal experimentation was reversed by several strokes of a pen by William Jefferson Blyth Clinton on January 22, 1993. We have had enough of promises, enough of politics as usual.

Therefore, a Catholic must resist the temptations to "go along" with some grand Republican Party strategy to win elections. The winning of elections means nothing if evil is permitted to go unchecked as a constitutionally guaranteed "right," if the

Federal government can use the full weight of its law enforcement apparatus to harass and persecute the defenders of innocent human life. The winning of elections means nothing if judicial appointees are recycled positivists, justifying everything from abortion to euthanasia to sodomy to "same-sex marriages." Parties must stand for things, and Catholics who involve themselves in a political party's activity must run the risk of ostracism and expulsion from its ranks to serve as a conscience to guide the careerists as they seek to pursue electoral expediency at the cost of true principles of justice.

VOTE FOR AUTHENTICALLY CATHOLIC CANDIDATES

One of the principal reasons this discourse is being written is to remind my co-religionists that we have to avoid being in the situation of voting for the lesser of two evils. We have to support candidates who are faithful to everything the Church teaches that is binding on our consciences on matters of fundamental justice. The only thing that will stop such people from winning nominations and elections is not voting for them and our not encouraging others to do so.

Pope Leo XIII addressed this matter in his encyclical letter *Sapientiae Christianae* (1890):

> As to those who mean to take part in public affairs they should avoid with the very utmost care two criminal excesses: so-called prudence and false courage. Some there are, indeed, who maintain that it is not opportune boldly to attack evil-doing in its might and when in the ascendant, lest, as they say, opposition should exasperate minds already hostile. These make it a matter of guesswork as to whether they are for the Church or against her; since on the one hand they give themselves out as professing the Catholic faith, and yet wish that the Church should allow certain opinions, at variance with her teaching, to be spread abroad with impunity. They moan over the loss of faith and the perversion of morals, yet trouble themselves not to bring any remedy; nay, not seldom, even add to the intensity of the mischief through too much forbearance or harmful dissembling. These same individuals would not have any one entertain a doubt as to their good-will towards the Holy See; yet they have always a something by way of reproach against the supreme Pontiff. The prudence of men of this cast is of that

kind which is termed by the Apostle Paul *wisdom of the flesh and death* of the soul, *because it is not subject to the law of God, neither can it be.* Nothing is less calculated to amend such ills than prudence of this kind. For the enemies of the Church have for their object—and they hesitate not to proclaim it, and many among them boast of it—to destroy outright, if possible, the Catholic religion, which is alone the true religion. With such a purpose in hand they shrink from nothing; for they are fully conscious that the more faint-hearted those who withstand them become, the more easy will it be to work out their wicked will. Therefore they who cherish the *prudence of the flesh* and who pretend to be unaware that every Christian ought to be a valiant solider of Christ; they who would fain obtain the rewards owing to conquerors, while they are leading lives of cowards, untouched in the fight, are so far from thwarting the onward march of the evil-disposed that, on the contrary, they even help it forward. . . .

The like disposition and the same order should prevail in every Christian State by so much the more that the political prudence of the Pontiff embraces diverse and multiform things; for it is his charge not only to rule the Church, but generally so to regulate the actions of Christian citizens that these may be in apt conformity to their hope of gaining eternal salvation.

For example, a lot of pro-life voters in 1996 were deceived by the Christian Coalition and the National Right to Life Committee into thinking that Senators Bob Dole and Phil Gramm were acceptable choices. But they represented politics as usual. Gramm joined Dole in the support of Breyer and Ginsburg, as well as FACE, effectively ending attempts to rescue children peacefully from the hands of the baby-killers. (Would they have voted for a bill to protect the Nazi death campus?) Both men have voted for fetal experimentation. They do not understand what an abortion is and how it is connected to most of the social and economic problems we are facing at present. And both men vied for the support of the Fortune 500 crowd, the financiers whose companies are in the vanguard of promoting contraception and abortion around the world. And they are far from alone in the Republican Party.

Indeed, we have reached a situation today where many in the Republican Party believe that the only measure of being pro-life is a conditional opposition to partial-birth abortion. Almost everyone who counts himself as "pro-life" in the Republican Party today supports a "little bit" of abortion, that is, the killing of children in the alleged "hard cases" of rape, incest, and threats to the physical life of the mother. But that is *not* a pro-life position. Not at all.

There is nothing in *Evangelium Vitae* to assert that Pope John Paul II believes that the direct, intentional killing of an innocent human life to save the life of another, even a mother, is morally permissible. Indeed, it is our obligation as Catholics to catechize our fellow citizens about the sanctity of each human life.

The Holy Father wrote the following about the conditions necessary for accepting legislation which fails to stop all abortions:

> A particular problem of conscience can arise in cases where a legislative vote would be decisive for the passage of a more restrictive law, aimed at limiting the number of authorized abortions, in place of a more permissive law already passed or ready to be voted on. Such cases are not infrequent. It is a fact that while in some parts of the world there continue to be campaigns to introduce laws favoring abortion, often supported by powerful international organizations, in other nations—particularly those which have already experienced the bitter fruits of such permissive legislation—there are growing signs of a re-thinking in this matter. In a case like the one just mentioned, when it is not possible to overturn or completely abrogate a pro-abortion law, an elected official, *whose absolute personal opposition to procured abortion was well known*, could licitly support proposals aimed at *limiting the harm* done by such a law and at lessening its negative consequences at the level of general opinion and public morality. This does not in fact represent an illicit cooperation with an unjust law, but rather a legitimate and proper attempt to limit its evil aspects (*Evangelium Vitae*, No. 73).

NO EXCEPTIONS

Note the condition the Pope attaches to this paragraph: "Whose *absolute* personal opposition to procured abortion was well known." Absolute means no exceptions. As Dr. Bernard Nathanson said recently, medical science has advanced to such an extent that no pregnancy can be considered a threat to a mother's life. Even forgetting about the clear law of God on this matter for a moment, medical science has made it clear that there is no need for civil law to provide for a "life of the mother" exception when it comes to defending innocent life in the womb.

It is necessary for authentically Catholic candidates to realize that it is possible to win public support by being 100% Catholic. People are hungering for truth. They need to be challenged with *all* of the truth, not 98% or 99.9% of the truth. They need to be reminded that each human life is precious to the Triune God and deserving of our respect and love, as the Holy Father notes so eloquently in *Evangelium Vitae*. It is time for us in my view, therefore, to take a firm "no exceptions" stand when voting for every office in every election.

A resolute "no exceptions" policy when voting for candidates in primaries will make it less likely that Catholics, and all other Americans who support the sanctity of all innocent human life, will be faced with the odious prospect of voting for a person in the general election who believes that he has to support exceptions as a matter of principle. We must remember that most of the states which restricted abortion prior to the 1960s had the exceptions provision in their statutory books, giving the wealthy and the famous the loophole they needed to kill their children. All cooperating physicians had to do was to certify some kind of problem, usually mental distress, and the child could be killed. Do we really think that those who have made quite a handsome living from killing children this past quarter of a century are going to deny themselves an income by complying with laws that permit abortion only in the hard cases? No, such killers will simply certify each case to fall into the "exceptions" category, rendering such a law meaningless. To be pro-life is to try to work as hard as possible to nominate and elect only those individuals who are absolutely opposed to abortion.

PRESERVING THE *STATUS QUO*

Indeed, mainstream Republican leaders were determined to stop Patrick Buchanan precisely because of his no-exceptions pro-life position. He had to be caricatured and demonized as a means of preserving the *status quo*. While no man is a secular savior, and while I had my own disagreements with Buchanan on matters of substance and strategy, Bill Clinton would not have gotten a free ride back to the White House had the articulate and principled Buchanan been the Republican nominee instead of Dole (or if Buchanan had accepted the nomination of the Taxpayers Party).

Suffice to say here and now that it is time for faithful Catholics to take their civic responsibilities seriously, and to believe that our Lord wants us to be involved in the process as a means of advancing His sacred truths as the only legitimate basis of the just society. The only thing that will stop us from having an impact, if not being successful, is our lack of belief in the power of His grace to effect what, in the human order of things, would appear to be a miracle: the conversion of individual hearts and souls to the social kingship of Jesus Christ.

CHANGE OF HEART

We must pray for those who do not understand us. We must make reparation for our sins—and for the sins of our fellow Americans. We must fast and make sacrifices to win the conversion of those who support, approve, condone—or are indifferent to the crimes against God being committed in our land. We must persevere in prayer—particularly, as noted, prayer before the Blessed Sacrament and to the Mother of God. Prayer does indeed work miracles.

Miracles are possible, are they not? We must make a real effort in the years ahead to elect candidates who are committed to the restoration of First and Last Things as the guiding principles of the just society. This involves not only the presidency and vice presidency, but every single elected office (local officials, state legislators, governors, mayors, school board officials). The social engineers who control our education, for example, must lose their present power of accreditation to force a "multi-cultural" agenda which is meant to brainwash students into an acceptance of such evils as abortion, contraception, and sodomy, to name a few. And it must be our goal to remove the coercive power of the state over any aspects of education whatsoever.

UNITED HEARTS

We need the help of others to protect life, to restore sanity to our laws and our culture. We need to pray and to work to bring our evangelical Christian and Orthodox Jewish friends (who agree with us on many moral issues) into the one Sheepfold of Peter. This unity, which Satan fears mightily, is something achievable if we spend time before the Blessed Sacrament, and try to fulfill our Lady's Fatima requests. True ecumenism, as Pope Pius XI noted, involves speaking the truth in charity. And true charity wills what God does, that each person be a member of the one, true Church.

We must remember that the final victory belongs to Christ and His Holy Church. We should never lose heart or be discouraged by the things of this passing world. Concerned, yes. But not discouraged. Our Lord is permitting His Mystical Body, the Church, to be racked and tortured just as He permitted His own physical Body to be racked and tortured on the Holy Cross. He wants us to do what the Blessed Mother, Saint John, and Mary Magdalene did: to stand by the foot of the Cross, understanding that His grace is sufficient for us to endure any cross that we are asked to bear.

We must never doubt the Father's wisdom. He wants us alive in this troubling time to be Christ's leaven in the midst of the world. We are neither optimists nor pessimists (which G. K. Chesterton has described as happy idiots and sad idiots, respectively). We are Catholics. We trust totally in the graces won for us on Calvary to do the work that is required of us to save our immortal souls, and to proclaim the Gospel in the midst of an unbelieving world. We should arise each day with gratitude, thanking the Triune God that He has brought us to another day to do His will, to be His disciples, to be counter-cultural signs of contradiction in a world looking for salvation in all of the wrong places.

FAITH

As Mother Teresa reminded us so frequently, God is concerned not with success, but with fidelity. To keep us humble, God may not permit us to see in this life the fruit of the seeds we plant for the restoration of Christendom. The Apostles themselves did not see its establishment; all of them were long dead before the Roman Empire collapsed. Barring a miracle, which we pray and work for, we may be long dead before there is an America built on Catholic principles, one that is subordinate to the social reign of Christ the King. We need not worry about concrete, tangible results. We need to do what God expects of us. We need to see all things with the eyes of faith.

Pope John Paul eloquently addressed the need for faith in these troubling times during his homily in Oriole Park at Camden Yards on October 8, 1995:

> Today though, some Catholics are tempted to discouragement or disillusionment, like the Prophet Habakkuk in the First Reading. They are tempted to cry out to the Lord in a different way: why does not God intervene when violence threatens his people; why does God let us see ruin and misery; why does God permit evil? Like the Prophet Habakkuk, and like the thirsty Israelites in the desert at Meribah and Massah, our trust can falter; we can lose patience with God. In the drama of history, we can find our dependence upon God burdensome rather than liberating. We too can "harden our hearts."
>
> And yet the Prophet gives us an answer to our impatience: "If God delays, wait for him; he will surely come, he will not be late." A Polish proverb expresses the same conviction in another way: "*God takes his time, but he is just.*" Our waiting for God is never in vain. Every moment is our opportunity to model ourselves on Jesus Christ—to allow the power of the Gospel to transform our personal lives and our service to others, according to the spirit of the Beatitudes. "Bear your share of the hardship which the gospel entails," writes Paul to Timothy in today's Second Reading. This is no idle exhortation to endurance. No, it is an invitation to enter more deeply into the *Christian vocation* which belongs to us all by Baptism. There is no evil to be faced that Christ does not face with us. There is no enemy that Christ has not already conquered. There is no cross to bear that Christ has not already borne for us, and does not now bear with us. And on the far side of every cross we find the newness of life in the Holy Spirit, that new life which will reach its fulfillment in the resurrection. This is our *faith*. This is our *witness* before the world.

Pope Pius XI had written in a similar manner seventy years before in *Quas Primas*:

> We may well admire in this wonderful wisdom of the Providence of God, Who, ever bringing good out of evil, has from time to time suffered the faith and piety of men to grow weak,

and allowed Catholic truth to be attacked by false doctrines, but always with the result that truth has afterwards shone out with greater splendor, and that men's faith, aroused from its lethargy, has shown itself more vigorous than before.

God uses all things to effect His Holy Will. He uses our successes and our failures for His greater glory. He uses all of our prayers, all of our sacrifices, all of our tears, all of our joys. He uses everything. It is our responsibility to keep our hands on the plow, to continue to plant the seeds, to attend to our interior life of prayer, to become the best formed and the best *in*-formed Catholics we can by the grace won for us on Calvary.

As Our Lord told us:

Behold, I am sending you like sheep in the midst of wolves; so be shrewd as serpents and simple as doves. But beware of people, for they will hand you over to courts and scourge you in their synagogues, and you will be led before governors and kings for my sake as a witness before them and the pagans. When they hand you over, do not worry about how you are to speak or what you are to say. You will be given at that moment what you are to say. For it will not be you but the Spirit of your Father speaking through you. Brother will hand over brother to death, and the father his child; children will rise up against parents and have them put to death. You will be hated by all because of my name, but whoever endures to the end will be saved. . . . No disciple is above his teacher, no slave above his master. It is enough for the disciple that he become like his teacher, for the slave that he become like his master. If they have called the master of the house Beelzebul, how much more those of his household.

Therefore, do not be afraid of them. Nothing is concealed that will not be revealed, nor secret that will not be known. What I say to you in darkness, speak in the light; what you hear whispered, proclaim on the housetops. And do not be afraid of those who kill the body but cannot kill the soul; rather, be afraid of the one who can destroy both soul and body in Gehenna. . . . Everyone who acknowledges me before others, I will acknowledge before my heavenly Father. But whoever denies me before others, I will deny before my heavenly Father (Mt. 10:16–22, 24–28, 32–33).

Are *we* ashamed of Christ and His doctrine before men? Are *we* willing to take our Lord into the voting booth? Are *we* willing

CHRIST IN THE VOTING BOOTH

to pray and to work for the glorious restoration of the Traditional Latin Mass? Are *we* willing to work for the social reign of Christ the King and Mary our Queen.

Our answers to those questions will determine what kind of people we are, and whether this experiment in self-government known as the United States of America will experience true freedom in Christ and Holy Church or continued slavery under the iron will of political careerists and social engineers.

As Pope Pius XI noted in *Quas Primas*:

> We firmly hope, however, that the Feast of the Kingship of Christ, which in the future will be yearly observed, may hasten the return of society to our loving Savior. It would be the duty of Catholics to do all they can to bring about this happy result. Many of these, however, have neither the station in society nor the authority which should belong to those who bear the torch of truth. This state of things may perhaps be attributed to a *certain slowness and timidity in good people, who are reluctant to engage in conflict or oppose but a weak resistance; thus the enemies of the Church become bolder in their attacks. But if the faithful were generally to understand that it behooves them ever to fight courageously under the banner of Christ their King, then, fired with apostolic zeal, they would strive to win over to their Lord those hearts that are bitter and estranged from Him, and would valiantly defend His rights.*

Viva Cristo Rey!

BIBLIOGRAPHY

Agonito, Joseph. *The Building of an American Catholic Church: The Episcopacy of John Carroll*, New York: Garland Publishing, Inc., 1988.

Dolan, Jay P. *The American Catholic Experience*, Garden City, Doubleday, 1985.

Gibbons, James Cardinal. *A Retrospective of Fifty Years*, Baltimore: John Murphy Company, 1955.

Johnson, Paul. *Modern Times*, New York: HarperCollins, 1992.

Kirk, Russell. *The Roots of American Order*, Washington, D.C.: Regnery Gateway, 1992.

Leckie, Robert. *American and Catholic*, Garden City: Doubleday, 1970.

Melville, Annabelle. *John Carroll of Baltimore*, New York: Charles Scribner's Sons, 1955.

Solzhenitsyn, Aleksandr I. *A World Split Apart*, New York: Harper Torch Books, 1978.

The Great Encyclical Letters of Pope Leo XIII, Rockford, Illinois: TAN Books and Publishers, Inc., 1995 (Original publication: New York: Benzinger Brothers, 1903).

Catechism of the Catholic Church, 1994.

Encyclical Letters of Pope Leo XIII
Humanum Genus, 1883.

Immortale Dei, 1885.

Libertas Praestantissimum, 1888.

Sapientiae Christianae, 1890.

Testem Benevolentiae, 1899 (Apostolic Letter).

Tamesti, 1900.

Encyclical Letters of Pope Pius XI

Ad Urbi Arcano, 1922.

Quas Primas, 1925.

Quadregesimo Anno, 1931.

Divini Redemptoris, 1937.

Casti Connubii, 1931.

Divini Illius Magistri, 1929.

Encyclical Letters of Pope Pius XII
Ad Summi Pontificatus, 1939.

Mediator Dei, 1947.

Encyclical Letter of Pope Paul VI
Humanae Vitae, 1968.

Encyclical Letters of Pope John Paul II
Centesimus Annus, 1991.

Evangelium Vitae, 1995.

Veritatis Splendor, 1993.

Apostolic Exhortations of Pope John Paul II
Familiaris Consortio, 1981.

Catechesi Tradendae, 1979.

Reconciliatio et Paenitentiae, 1984.

Homilies and Addresses of Pope John Paul II
Address to Univ '81 Students, April 19, 1981.

Address to Bishops of the United States, Monterey, California, September 15, 1987.

Homily, Mass at Giants Stadium, East Rutherford, New Jersey, October 4, 1995.

Homily, Mass at Aqueduct Race Track, Ozone Park, New York, October 5, 1995.

Homily, Mass at Central Park, New York, New York, October 6, 1995.

Address to Families, St. Patrick's Cathedral, New York, New York, October 6, 1995.

Homily, Mass at Oriole Park at Camden Yards, Baltimore, Maryland, October 7, 1995.

ABOUT THE AUTHOR

Thomas A. Droleskey, Ph.D., is the publisher and editor of *Christ or Chaos*, a monthly newsletter, and is a contributing editor of *The Wanderer*, the oldest weekly national Catholic newspaper.

Dr. Droleskey received his B.A. in political science from St. John's University (New York) in 1973, his M.A. from the University of Notre Dame in 1974, and his Ph.D. from the State University of New York at Albany in 1977. He has taught in numerous colleges and universities around the nation since January of 1974, receiving awards for excellence in teaching. His years of service at the C. W. Post Campus of Long Island University, where he has served as an adjunct professor of political science since January of 1991, were recognized in 1996 by the Department of Political Science.

He was the co-winner of the 1995 Chesterbelloc Award, presented by the Chesterton Society of Toledo, Ohio, and he was the recipient of the 1996 Christ the King Award, presented by the Christian Law Institute in November of 1997 in El Paso, Texas. He was the candidate for Lieutenant Governor of the New York State Right to Life Party in 1986, and he ran for Supervisor of the Town of Oyster Bay, New York, on the Right to Life Party line in 1997.

Dr. Droleskey has spoken before hundreds of groups around the nation in the past fifteen years, principally on the life issue. He campaigned actively for pro-life candidates in 1995–96, emphasizing the importance of our praying and working for the Social Reign of Christ the King. He was one of three keynote speakers at the annual meeting of the Michigan Christian Coalition in

1997, using that opportunity to urge separated brethren to seek full communion with the one, Holy Roman Catholic Church founded by our Lord upon the Rock of Peter, the Pope.

In addition to other written works under development and consideration, a sixteen-hour video-series, *Catholicizing America*, is also being marketed at the time of this book's publication.

Droleskey is the Second Vice President of the Society of Catholic Social Scientists.

As of the printing of this book, Dr. Droleskey is running against incumbent Sen. Alfonse D'Amato in a primary election for the New York State Right to Life Party's nomination for U.S. Senator. He is running to advance the social reign of Christ the King and Mary our Queen.